GRAMMAR AND BEYOND 2B

Second Edition

with Academic Writing

Randi Reppen

CAMBRIDGE
UNIVERSITY PRESS

CAMBRIDGE
UNIVERSITY PRESS

University Printing House, Cambridge CB2 8BS, United Kingdom

One Liberty Plaza, 20th Floor, New York, NY 10006, USA

477 Williamstown Road, Port Melbourne, VIC 3207, Australia

314–321, 3rd Floor, Plot 3, Splendor Forum, Jasola District Centre, New Delhi – 110025, India

79 Anson Road, #06–04/06, Singapore 079906

Cambridge University Press is part of the University of Cambridge.

It furthers the University's mission by disseminating knowledge in the pursuit of
education, learning and research at the highest international levels of excellence.

cambridge.org
Information on this title: cambridge.org/9781108779814

© Cambridge University Press 2021

First published 2013
Second edition 2021

20 19 18 17 16 15 14 13 12 11 10 9 8 7 6 5 4 3 2 1

Printed in Dubai by Oriental Press

A catalogue record for this publication is available from the British Library

ISBN Student's Book 2B with Online Practice 978-1-108-77981-4

Additional resources for this publication at www.cambridge.org/grammarandbeyond

About the Author

Randi Reppen is Professor of Applied Linguistics and TESL at Northern Arizona University (NAU) in Flagstaff, Arizona. She has over 20 years' experience teaching ESL students and training ESL teachers, including 11 years as the Director of NAU's Program in Intensive English. Randi's research interests focus on the use of corpora for language teaching and materials development. In addition to numerous academic articles and books, she is the author of *Using Corpora in the Language Classroom* and a co-author of *Basic Vocabulary in Use*, 2nd edition, both published by Cambridge University Press.

Corpus Consultants

Michael McCarthy is Emeritus Professor of Applied Linguistics at the University of Nottingham, UK, and Adjunct Professor of Applied Linguistics at Pennsylvania State University. He is a co-author of the corpus-informed *Touchstone* series and the award-winning *Cambridge Grammar of English*, both published by Cambridge University Press, among many other titles, and is known throughout the world as an expert on grammar, vocabulary, and corpus linguistics.

Jeanne McCarten has over 30 years of experience in ELT/ESL as a teacher, publisher, and author. She has been closely involved in the development of the spoken English sections of the *Cambridge International Corpus*. Now a freelance writer, she is co-author of the corpus-informed *Touchstone* series and *Grammar for Business*, both published by Cambridge University Press.

Advisory Panel

The ESL advisory panel has helped to guide the development of this series and provided invaluable information about the needs of ESL students and teachers in high schools, colleges, universities, and private language schools throughout North America.

Neta Simpkins Cahill, Skagit Valley College, Mount Vernon, WA

Shelly Hedstrom, Palm Beach State College, Lake Worth, FL

Richard Morasci, Foothill College, Los Altos Hills, CA

Stacey Russo, East Hampton High School, East Hampton, NY

Alice Savage, Lone Star College-North Harris, Houston, TX

Scope and Sequence

Unit	Theme	Grammar	Topics
PART 1 The Present			
UNIT 1 page 2	Are You Often Online?	Simple Present	Simple Present (p. 4) Time Clauses and Factual Conditionals (p. 9)
UNIT 2 page 16	Brainpower	Present Progressive and Simple Present	Present Progressive (p. 18) Simple Present and Present Progressive Compared (p. 21)
UNIT 3 page 30	What's Appropriate?	Imperatives	Imperatives (p. 32) *Let's . . .* (p. 36)
PART 2 The Past			
UNIT 4 page 42	Entrepreneurs	Simple Past	Simple Past (p. 44) Simple Past of *Be* and *There Was / There Were* (p. 50)
UNIT 5 page 56	Science and Society	Simple Past, Time Clauses, *Used To,* and *Would*	Time Clauses and the Order of Past Events (p. 58) Past with *Used To* and *Would* (p. 61)
UNIT 6 page 70	Memorable Events	Past Progressive	Past Progressive (p. 72) Using *When* and *While* with Past Progressive (p. 76)
PART 3 Nouns, Determiners, and Pronouns			
UNIT 7 page 82	Privacy Matters	Count and Noncount Nouns	Count Nouns and Noncount Nouns (p. 84) Noncount Nouns: Determiners and Measurement Words (p. 89)

Avoid Common Mistakes	Academic Writing
Avoiding *amn't*; remembering a comma after a time clause at the beginning of a sentence	**Doing Research Online** • Find a reliable source • Evaluate an Internet source
Remembering a form of *be* with the present progressive; remembering *-ing* for the present progressive	**Opinion Writing** Writing prompt: *Should governments spend more money on space exploration?* • Identify purpose • Supporting details • Brainstorm
Avoiding *No* in imperatives; remembering an apostrophe in *Don't* and *Let's*	• Evaluate evidence • The imperative in academic writing
Avoiding the past form after *did not* and *didn't*; avoiding putting a time expression between the subject and the verb	• Organize an essay • Thesis statements • The simple past in academic writing
Remembering a subject in time clauses; remembering the *-d* in *used to* for affirmative statements	• Plan the essay • Write the first draft
Avoiding a time clause as a complete sentence; remembering a comma when the time clause comes first in a sentence	• Revise and edit
Remembering a determiner with a singular count noun; avoiding *a/an* with a noncount noun; avoiding plural noncount nouns	**Expository Writing** Writing prompt: *Choose a new area of technology or invention to analyze. Write a report about its advantages and disadvantages, and include a prediction in the conclusion.* • Use a T-chart to identify advantages and disadvantages • Brainstorm

Avoid Common Mistakes	Academic Writing
Remembering *a/an* the first time you mention a new idea; avoiding *the* with generalizations	• Plan and write an introductory paragraph
Remembering *to* or *for* with certain verbs; avoiding double pronouns	• Introduce advantages and disadvantages • Complete the first draft • Revise and edit
Remembering when to use the simple past; remembering when to use the present perfect	**Comparison-and-Contrast Writing** Writing prompt: *Compare and contrast the whale shark and the tiger shark.* • Use Venn diagrams • Combine sentences
Avoiding *never* in negative statements; avoiding *ever* in affirmative statements	• Write topic sentences • Plan body paragraphs
Remembering *have* with the present perfect progressive; avoiding the present progressive with *for* and *since*	• Write the first draft • Revise and edit
Avoiding misspelling adjectives ending in *-ful*; remembering to put opinion adjectives first	**Argumentative Writing** Writing prompt: *Do you agree or disagree with the following statement? "The fashion industry is harmful to society and the environment." Use reasons and examples to support your answer.* • Identify strong arguments • Brainstorm and organize • Use descriptive adjectives
Remembering to use adverbs to describe how something happened; avoiding putting an adverb between the verb and the object; remembering that some adverbs have the same form as adjectives	• Introductory paragraphs in argumentative essays • Body paragraphs in argumentative essays • Use adverbs of degree
Using prepositions correctly	• Write with cohesion • Write the first draft • Revise and edit

Unit	Theme	Grammar	Topics
PART 6 The Future			
UNIT 16 page 204	Life Lists	Future (1)	*Be Going To*, Present Progressive, and Simple Present for Future Events (p. 206)
UNIT 17 page 216	Getting Older	Future (2)	Future with *Will* (p. 218) Future with *Will*, *Be Going To*, and Present Progressive (p. 222)
UNIT 18 page 230	Learning to Communicate	Future Time Clauses and Future Conditionals	Future Time Clauses (p. 232) Future Conditionals; Questions with Time Clauses and Conditional Clauses (p. 236)
PART 7 Modal Verbs and Modal-like Expressions			
UNIT 19 page 244	Amazing Science	Ability	Ability with *Can* and *Could* (p. 246) *Be Able To* (p. 250)
UNIT 20 page 260	Good Causes	Requests and Offers	Permission (p. 262) Requests and Offers (p. 266)
UNIT 21 page 274	The Right Job	Advice and Suggestions	Advice (p. 276) Suggestions (p. 280)
UNIT 22 page 286	How to Sell It	Necessity, Prohibition, and Preference	Necessity and Prohibition (p. 288) Preference (p. 292)
UNIT 23 page 298	Life Today, Life Tomorrow	Present and Future Probability	Present Probability (p. 300) Modals of Future Probability (p. 303)

Avoid Common Mistakes	Academic Writing
Remembering *be* with *going to*; remembering *be* before the subject in *Wh-* questions with *be going to*	**Opinion Writing** Writing prompt: *Should colleges and universities require students to take physical education classes?* • Brainstorm reasons and evaluate evidence • Plan an opinion essay
Remembering *will* before the main verb with the future; remembering the base form of the verb after *will*	• State opinions • Structure opinion essays
Avoiding *will* in the conditional clause; avoiding *will* in the time clause	• Use future conditionals • Write the first draft • Revise and edit
Remembering to spell *cannot* as one word; remembering the *be* and *to* in *be able to*	**Cause-and-Effect Writing** Writing prompt: *Describe the human causes of climate change and the effects climate change can have on the planet.* • Organize a cause-and-effect essay • Describe causes and effects • Brainstorm
Avoiding *could* in short answers to requests for permission; avoiding *could* or *would* in responses to requests to do things	• Describe causes and effects • Use causes and effects to express solutions or predictions • Make requests in academic writing
Remembering *had* in *had better*; avoiding *could not* in negative suggestions	• Maintain paragraph coherence • Choose strong supporting details • Use formal modals for advice and suggestions
Avoiding an infinitive with *would rather*; remembering *would* before *rather*	• Write an effective hook • Use modals of necessity and prohibition • Write the first draft
Avoiding *can* for present or future probability; avoiding *couldn't* for uncertainty	• Use modals to express future possibility • Revise and edit

Unit	Theme	Grammar	Topics
PART 8 Verbs + Prepositions and Phrasal Verbs			
UNIT 24 page 310	Getting Along at Work	Transitive and Intransitive Verbs Verbs and Prepositions	Transitive and Intransitive Verbs (p. 312) Verb + Object + Preposition Combinations (p. 314) Verb + Preposition Combinations (p. 316)
UNIT 25 page 324	Money, Money, Money	Phrasal Verbs	Intransitive Phrasal Verbs (p. 326) Transitive Phrasal Verbs (p. 329)
PART 9 Comparatives and Superlatives			
UNIT 26 page 336	We Are All Different	Comparatives	Comparative Adjectives and Adverbs (p. 338) Comparisons with *As . . . As* (p. 343)
UNIT 27 page 350	The Best and the Worst	Superlative Adjectives and Adverbs	Superlative Adjectives and Adverbs (p. 352)
PART 10 Gerunds and Infinitives			
UNIT 28 page 360	Managing Time	Gerunds and Infinitives (1)	Verbs Followed by Gerunds or Infinitives (p. 362) Verbs Followed by Gerunds and Infinitives (p. 365)
UNIT 29 page 374	Civil Rights	Gerunds and Infinitives (2)	More About Gerunds (p. 376) More About Infinitives (p. 379)
PART 11 Clauses and Conjunctions			
UNIT 30 page 386	Sleep	Subject Relative Clauses (Adjective Clauses with Subject Relative Pronouns)	Subject Relative Clauses (p. 388) More About Subject Relative Clauses (p. 392)
UNIT 31 page 400	Viruses	Object Relative Clauses (Adjective Clauses with Object Relative Pronouns)	Object Relative Clauses (p. 402) More About Object Relative Clauses (p. 406)
UNIT 32 page 414	Special Days	Conjunctions and Adverb Clauses	Conjunctions (p. 416) Adverb Clauses (p. 420)

Avoid Common Mistakes	Academic Writing
Remembering the object with a transitive verb; using prepositions with verbs	**Description and Analysis** Writing prompt: *Describe the trends in a multiple line graph, and analyze the data. Do some additional research to discuss the trends you identify.* • Understand and interpret line graphs • Use noun and verb phrases to describe graphs
Remembering a particle in phrasal verbs; avoiding putting an object pronoun after a particle	• Choose the important details from a graph • Write the concluding paragraph
Avoiding using *more* and *-er* together; remembering the second as in *as . . . as* comparisons	• Use comparatives to describe and analyze graphs • Write the first draft
Remembering irregular superlative forms; avoiding an object pronoun before a superlative	• Use superlatives in academic writing • Revise and edit
Using infinitives and gerunds after verbs; remembering *to* in infinitives	**Summary and Response** Writing prompt: *Write a summary paragraph of "Nontraditional Weddings." Then write a response paragraph giving your opinion about the changes in wedding traditions described in the article.* • Analyze a text • Summarize a text
Avoiding plural verbs with gerund subjects; avoiding infinitives after prepositions; remembering *It* and *to* in *It* sentences	• Paraphrase • Respond to a writer's ideas • Use gerunds and infinitives in academic writing
Avoiding a subject pronoun after a subject relative pronoun; remembering the relative pronoun in a subject relative clause	• Write a personal response • Use subject relative clauses in summary writing
Avoiding *who* in possessives; avoiding *whom* in subject relative clauses; avoiding an object pronoun at the end of an object relative clause	• Use object relative clauses in a personal response • Write the first draft
Remembering a comma after the adverb clause when it is first	• Revise and edit • Use adverb clauses to connect contrasting ideas

Introduction to *Grammar and Beyond*, 2nd edition

Grammar and Beyond is a research-based and content-rich grammar and academic writing series for beginning to advanced-level students. The series focuses on the most commonly used English grammar structures and practices all four skills in a variety of authentic and communicative contexts.

Grammar and Beyond is Research-Based

The grammar presented in this series is informed by years of research on the grammar of written and spoken English as it is used in college lectures, textbooks, academic essays, high school classrooms, and conversations between instructors and students. This research, and the analysis of over one billion words of authentic written and spoken language data known as the *Cambridge International Corpus*, has enabled the authors to:

- Present grammar rules that accurately represent how English is actually spoken and written

- Identify and teach differences between the grammar of written and spoken English

- Focus more attention on the structures that are commonly used, and less on those that are rarely used, in writing and speaking

- Help students avoid the most common mistakes that English language learners make

- Choose reading topics that will naturally elicit examples of the target grammar structure

- Introduce important vocabulary from the Academic Word List

Special Features of *Grammar and Beyond*

Realistic Grammar Presentations

Grammar is presented in clear and simple charts. The grammar points presented in these charts have been tested against real-world data from the *Cambridge International Corpus* to ensure that they are authentic representations of actual use of English.

Data from the Real World

Many of the grammar presentations and application sections include a feature called Data from the Real World. Concrete and useful points discovered through analysis of corpus data are presented and practiced in exercises that follow.

Avoid Common Mistakes

Every unit features an Avoid Common Mistakes section that develops students' awareness of the most common mistakes made by English language learners and gives them an opportunity to practice detecting and correcting these errors. This section helps students avoid these mistakes in their own work. The mistakes highlighted in this section are drawn from a body of authentic data on learner English known as the *Cambridge Learner Corpus*, a database of over 35 million words from student essays written by non-native speakers of English and information from experienced classroom teachers.

Academic Vocabulary

Every unit in *Grammar and Beyond* includes words from the Academic Word List (AWL), a research-based list of words and word families that appear with high frequency in English-language academic texts. These words are introduced in the opening text of the unit, recycled in the charts and exercises, and used to support the theme throughout the unit. By the time students finish each level, they will have been exposed several times to a carefully selected set of level-appropriate AWL words, as well as content words from a variety of academic disciplines.

Academic Writing

Every unit ends with an Academic Writing section. In Levels 1 through 3, this edition of *Grammar and Beyond* teaches students to write academically using writing cycles that span several units. Each writing cycle is organized around a writing prompt and focuses on a specific type of academic writing, such as descriptive, narrative, and process. Students move through the steps of the writing process - Brainstorm, Organize, Write, Edit - while learning and practicing new writing skills and ways to incorporate the unit grammar into their writing. In Level 4, the entire scope and sequence is organized around the types of essays students write in college, and focuses on the grammar rules, conventions, and structures needed to master them.

Series Levels

The following table provides a general idea of the difficulty of the material at each level of *Grammar and Beyond*. These are not meant to be interpreted as precise correlations.

	Description	TOEFL IBT	CEFR Levels
Level 1	Beginning	20 – 34	A1 – A2
Level 2	Low Intermediate to Intermediate	35 – 54	A2 – B1
Level 3	High Intermediate	55 – 74	B1 – B2
Level 4	Advanced	75 – 95	B2 – C1

Student Components

Student's Book with Online Practice

Each unit, based on a high-interest topic, teaches grammar points appropriate for each level in short, manageable cycles of presentation and practice. Academic Writing focuses on the structure of the academic essay in addition to the grammar rules, conventions, and structures that students need to master in order to be successful college writers. Students can access both the Digital Workbook and Writing Skills Interactive using their smartphones, tablets, or computers with single log-in. See pages xviii–xxiii for a Tour of a Unit.

Digital Workbook

The Digital Workbook provides additional online exercises to help master each grammar point. Automatically-graded exercises give immediate feedback for activities such as correcting errors highlighted in the Avoid Common Mistakes section in the Student's Book. Self-Assessment sections at the end of each unit allow students to test their mastery of what they learned. Look for 🖥 in the Student's Book to see when to use the Digital Workbook.

Writing Skills Interactive

Writing Skills Interactive is a self-grading course to practice discrete writing skills, reinforce vocabulary, and give students an opportunity with additional writing practice. Each unit has:

- Vocabulary review
- Short text to check understanding of the context
- Animated presentation of target unit writing skill
- Practice activities
- Unit Quiz to assess progress

Teacher Resources

A variety of downloadable resources are available on Cambridge One (cambridgeone.org) to assist instructors, including the following:

Teacher's Manual

- Suggestions for applying the target grammar to all four major skill areas, helping instructors facilitate dynamic and comprehensive grammar classes
- An answer key and audio script for the Student's Book
- Teaching tips, to help instructors plan their lessons
- Communicative activity worksheets to add more in-class speaking practice

Assessment

- Placement Test
- Ready-made, easy-to-score Unit Tests, Midterm, and Final in .pdf and .doc formats
- Answer Key

Presentation Plus

Presentation Plus allows teachers to digitally project the contents of the Student's Books in front of the class for a livelier, interactive classroom. It is a complete solution for teachers because it includes easy-to-access answer keys and audio at point of use.

Acknowledgements

The publisher and author would like to thank these reviewers and consultants for their insights and participation:

Marty Attiyeh, The College of DuPage, Glen Ellyn, IL

Shannon Bailey, Austin Community College, Austin, TX

Jamila Barton, North Seattle Community College, Seattle, WA

Kim Bayer, Hunter College IELI, New York, NY

Linda Berendsen, Oakton Community College, Skokie, IL

Anita Biber, Tarrant County College Northwest, Fort Worth, TX

Jane Breaux, Community College of Aurora, Aurora, CO

Anna Budzinski, San Antonio College, San Antonio, TX

Britta Burton, Mission College, Santa Clara, CA

Jean Carroll, Fresno City College, Fresno, CA

Chris Cashman, Oak Park High School and Elmwood Park High School, Chicago, IL

Annette M. Charron, Bakersfield College, Bakersfield, CA

Patrick Colabucci, ALI at San Diego State University, San Diego, CA

Lin Cui, Harper College, Palatine, IL

Jennifer Duclos, Boston University CELOP, Boston, MA

Joy Durighello, San Francisco City College, San Francisco, CA

Kathleen Flynn, Glendale Community College, Glendale, CA

Raquel Fundora, Miami Dade College, Miami, FL

Patricia Gillie, New Trier Township High School District, Winnetka, IL

Laurie Gluck, LaGuardia Community College, Long Island City, NY

Kathleen Golata, Galileo Academy of Science & Technology, San Francisco, CA

Ellen Goldman, Mission College, Santa Clara, CA

Ekaterina Goussakova, Seminole Community College, Sanford, FL

Marianne Grayston, Prince George's Community College, Largo, MD

Mary Greiss Shipley, Georgia Gwinnett College, Lawrenceville, GA

Sudeepa Gulati, Long Beach City College, Long Beach, CA

Nicole Hammond Carrasquel, University of Central Florida, Orlando, FL

Vicki Hendricks, Broward College, Fort Lauderdale, FL

Kelly Hernandez, Miami Dade College, Miami, FL

Ann Johnston, Tidewater Community College, Virginia Beach, VA

Julia Karet, Chaffey College, Claremont, CA

Jeanne Lachowski, English Language Institute, University of Utah, Salt Lake City, UT

Noga Laor, Rennert, New York, NY

Min Lu, Central Florida Community College, Ocala, FL

Michael Luchuk, Kaplan International Centers, New York, NY

Craig Machado, Norwalk Community College, Norwalk, CT

Denise Maduli-Williams, City College of San Francisco, San Francisco, CA

Diane Mahin, University of Miami, Coral Gables, FL

Melanie Majeski, Naugatuck Valley Community College, Waterbury, CT

Jeanne Malcolm, University of North Carolina at Charlotte, Charlotte, NC

Lourdes Marx, Palm Beach State College, Boca Raton, FL

Susan G. McFalls, Maryville College, Maryville, TN

Nancy McKay, Cuyahoga Community College, Cleveland, OH

Dominika McPartland, Long Island Business Institute, Flushing, NY

Amy Metcalf, UNR/Intensive English Language Center, University of Nevada, Reno, NV

Robert Miller, EF International Language School San Francisco – Mills, San Francisco, CA

Marcie Pachino, Jordan High School, Durham, NC

Myshie Pagel, El Paso Community College, El Paso, TX

Bernadette Pedagno, University of San Francisco, San Francisco, CA

Tam Q Pham, Dallas Theological Seminary, Fort Smith, AR

Mary Beth Pickett, GlobalLT, Rochester, MI

Maria Reamore, Baltimore City Public Schools, Baltimore, MD

Alison M. Rice, Hunter College IELI, New York, NY

Sydney Rice, Imperial Valley College, Imperial, CA

Kathleen Romstedt, Ohio State University, Columbus, OH

Alexandra Rowe, University of South Carolina, Columbia, SC

Irma Sanders, Baldwin Park Adult and Community Education, Baldwin Park, CA

Caren Shoup, Lone Star College – CyFair, Cypress, TX

Karen Sid, Mission College, Foothill College, De Anza College, Santa Clara, CA

Michelle Thomas, Miami Dade College, Miami, FL

Sharon Van Houte, Lorain County Community College, Elyria, OH

Margi Wald, UC Berkeley, Berkeley, CA

Walli Weitz, Riverside County Office of Ed., Indio, CA

Bart Weyand, University of Southern Maine, Portland, ME

Donna Weyrich, Columbus State Community College, Columbus, OH

Marilyn Whitehorse, Santa Barbara City College, Ojai, CA

Jessica Wilson, Rutgers University – Newark, Newark, NJ

Sue Wilson, San Jose City College, San Jose, CA

Margaret Wilster, Mid-Florida Tech, Orlando, FL

Anne York-Herjeczki, Santa Monica College, Santa Monica, CA

Hoda Zaki, Camden County College, Camden, NJ

We would also like to thank these teachers and programs for allowing us to visit:

Richard Appelbaum, Broward College, Fort Lauderdale, FL

Carmela Arnoldt, Glendale Community College, Glendale, AZ

JaNae Barrow, Desert Vista High School, Phoenix, AZ

Ted Christensen, Mesa Community College, Mesa, AZ

Richard Ciriello, Lower East Side Preparatory High School, New York, NY

Virginia Edwards, Chandler-Gilbert Community College, Chandler, AZ

Nusia Frankel, Miami Dade College, Miami, FL

Raquel Fundora, Miami Dade College, Miami, FL

Vicki Hendricks, Broward College, Fort Lauderdale, FL

Kelly Hernandez, Miami Dade College, Miami, FL

Stephen Johnson, Miami Dade College, Miami, FL

Barbara Jordan, Mesa Community College, Mesa, AZ

Nancy Kersten, GateWay Community College, Phoenix, AZ

Lewis Levine, Hostos Community College, Bronx, NY

John Liffiton, Scottsdale Community College, Scottsdale, AZ

Cheryl Lira-Layne, Gilbert Public School District, Gilbert, AZ

Mary Livingston, Arizona State University, Tempe, AZ

Elizabeth Macdonald, Thunderbird School of Global Management, Glendale, AZ

Terri Martinez, Mesa Community College, Mesa, AZ

Lourdes Marx, Palm Beach State College, Boca Raton, FL

Paul Kei Matsuda, Arizona State University, Tempe, AZ

David Miller, Glendale Community College, Glendale, AZ

Martha Polin, Lower East Side Preparatory High School, New York, NY

Patricia Pullenza, Mesa Community College, Mesa, AZ

Victoria Rasinskaya, Lower East Side Preparatory High School, New York, NY

Vanda Salls, Tempe Union High School District, Tempe, AZ

Kim Sanabria, Hostos Community College, Bronx, NY

Cynthia Schuemann, Miami Dade College, Miami, FL

Michelle Thomas, Miami Dade College, Miami, FL

Dongmei Zeng, Borough of Manhattan Community College, New York, NY

Tour of a Unit

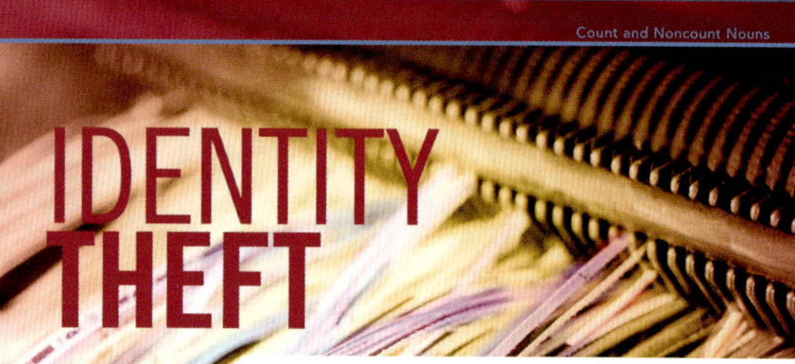

begins with an overview that describes the grammar in an easy-to-understand summary.

boost fluency by providing grammar practice in a variety of different contexts.

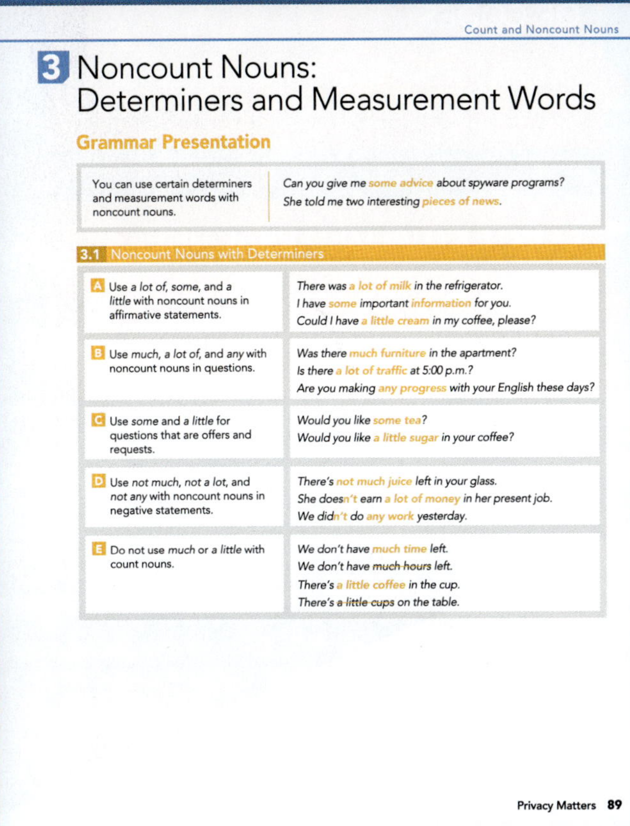

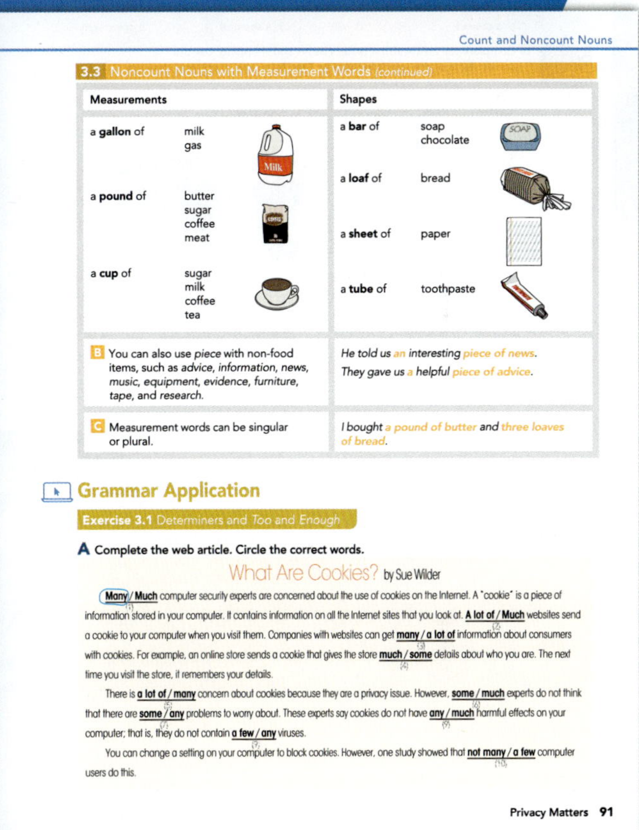

provide clear guidance on the form, meaning, and use of the target grammar for ease of instruction and reference.

keeps students engaged with a wide variety of exercises that introduce new and stimulating content.

Tour of a Unit **xix**

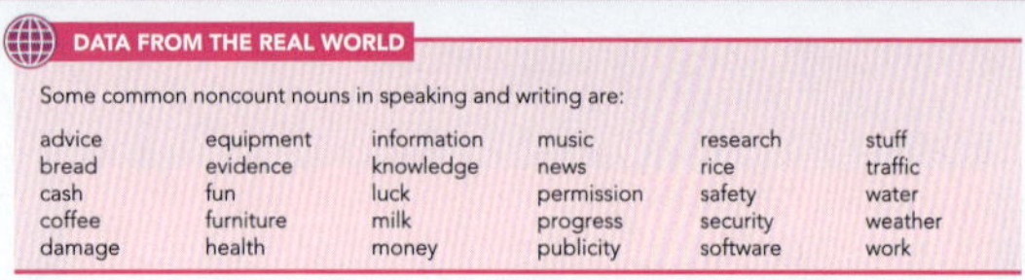

DATA FROM THE REAL WORLD

takes students beyond traditional information and teaches them how the unit's grammar is used in authentic situations, including differences between spoken and written use.

QR CODES

give easy access to audio at point of use.

CONTEXTUALIZED PRACTICE

moves from controlled to open-ended, teaching meaningful language for real communicative purposes.

HOW TO USE A QR CODE

1 Open the camera on your smartphone.

2 Point it at the QR code.

3 The camera will automatically scan the code.
   If not, press the button to take a picture.

* Not all cameras automatically scan QR codes.
  You may need to download a QR code reader.
  Search "QR free" and download an app.

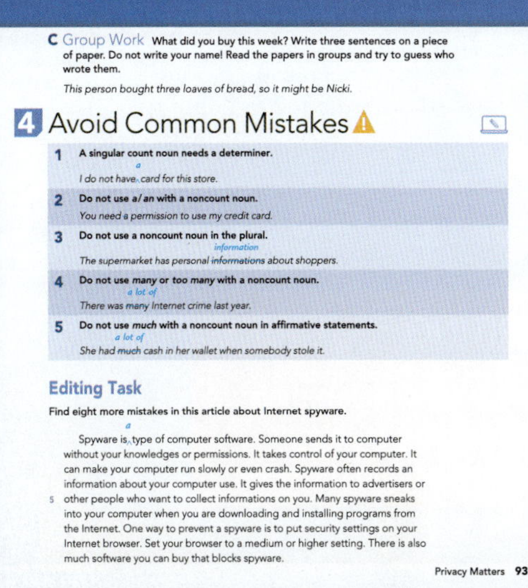

AVOID COMMON MISTAKES

is based on a database of over 135,000 essays. Students learn to avoid the most common mistakes English language learners make and develop self-editing skills to improve their speaking and writing.

EDITING TASK

gives learners an opportunity to identify and correct commonly made errors and develop self-editing skills needed in their university studies.

ACADEMIC WRITING

concentrates on specific stages of the writing process: Brainstorm, Organize, Write, Edit.

REAL WORLD MODEL

incorporates the unit grammar into common types of writing for students to understand and analyze.

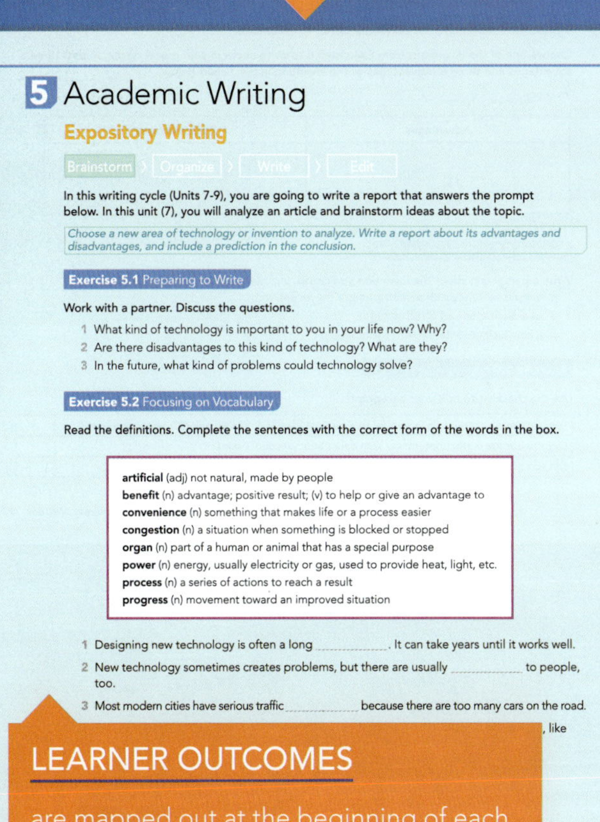

LEARNER OUTCOMES

are mapped out at the beginning of each writing cycle and section.

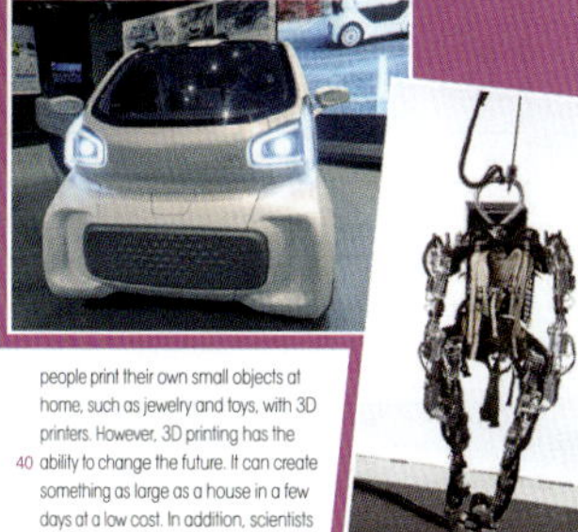

SKILL BOXES
provide clear explanations of carefully selected writing skills.

MY WRITING
helps students develop their academic writing at various stages of the writing process.

Count and Noncount Nouns

Exercise 5.3 Comprehension Check

Read the text on page 95. Work with a partner. Ask and answer the questions.

1 Will flying cars solve traffic problems? Why or why not?
2 How can 3D printers be used by medical doctors?
3 To which two groups of people could the robot exoskeleton be useful?
4 Does the author believe that technology is always a benefit to people?

Exercise 5.4 Noticing the Grammar and Structure

Complete the tasks. Compare your answers with a partner.

1 Underline the thesis statement. Circle all the non-count nouns in it.
2 Match each invention in the body paragraphs to a non-count noun in the thesis statement.
  a robot suit b flying car c 3D printer
3 Circle one advantage and put a box around one disadvantage of each invention.
4 How does the writer organize the information in paragraphs 2-4?
5 Find and highlight two uses of the determiner *a lot of* in paragraphs 4-5. What kind of noun follows it?

Using A T-Chart

A T-chart is a kind of graphic organizer. It is useful for examining two sides or aspects of a topic, such as advantages and disadvantages or pros and cons.

Exercise 5.5 Applying the Skill

Choose one invention in the text, and complete the T-chart. Add at least one advantage and one disadvantage to the T-chart.

Invention: ___________________________

Advantages	Disadvantages

96 Unit 7 Count and Noncount Nouns

My Writing

Exercise 5.6 Brainstorming Ideas

Work with a partner. Write down one modern invention in each area of technology in the chart. Do research online if necessary.

medicine	
home	
space	
transportation	
entertainment	
computers	

Exercise 5.7 Identifying Advantages and Disadvantages

Choose one of the inventions from Exercise 5.6 to write about in your report. Write at least three advantages and three disadvantages of the invention in the T-chart below.

Invention: ___________________________

Advantages	Disadvantages

Exercise 5.8 Writing a Paragraph

Write a paragraph about the invention you chose. Include:
- a topic sentence with a description of the invention
- its advantages and disadvantages
- a concluding sentence with a prediction

Exercise 5.9 Editing Your Writing

Use the checklist to edit your paragraph.

Did you use a noncount noun to refer to a general idea and then give details about that idea?	
Did you use the correct determiner with count and noncount nouns?	
Did you avoid the common mistakes in the chart on page 93?	

Privacy Matters 97

APPLICATION EXERCISES
give students scaffolded practice of the writing skills.

Kahoot!

for Grammar and Beyond
cambridge.org/kahoot/grammarandbeyond

What is Kahoot!?

Kahoot! is a game-based learning platform that makes it easy to create, share and play fun learning games and trivia quizzes in minutes. You can play Kahoot! on any mobile device or laptop with an internet connection.

What can you use kahoots for?

Kahoots can be used for review, formative assessment or homework.

When should you play Kahoot?

You can play kahoot quizzes before starting the unit as a diagnostic, during the unit as formative assessment, or at the end of a unit to test student knowledge.

To launch a live game in the classroom, find the kahoot for the level and unit and simply click on "play".

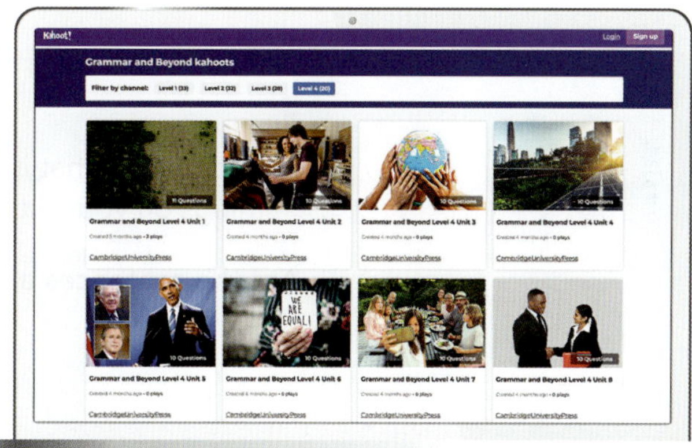

Quiz Your English app

Quiz Your English is a fun new way to practice, improve, and test your English by competing against learners from all around the world. Learn English grammar with friends, discover new English words, and test yourself in a truly global environment.

- Learn to avoid common mistakes with a special section just for *Grammar and Beyond* users
- Challenge your friends and players wherever they are
- Watch where you are on the leaderboards

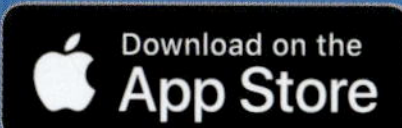

Life Lists

1 Grammar in the Real World

ACADEMIC WRITING

Opinion writing

A **What exciting things do you want to do someday? Read the blog about a "life list." What does the writer hope to do someday?**

B Comprehension Check **Answer the questions.**

1 What is a life list?

2 What is one reason to create a life list?

3 What are two tips to help you create a life list?

C Notice **Find the sentences in the article and complete them.**

1 I _________________ ride in a hot-air balloon.

2 I _________________ travel to all 50 states in the United States.

3 _________________ you _________________ create a life list, too?

4 Understand that it _________________ take time to accomplish the things on your list.

Are the sentences about the present or the future?

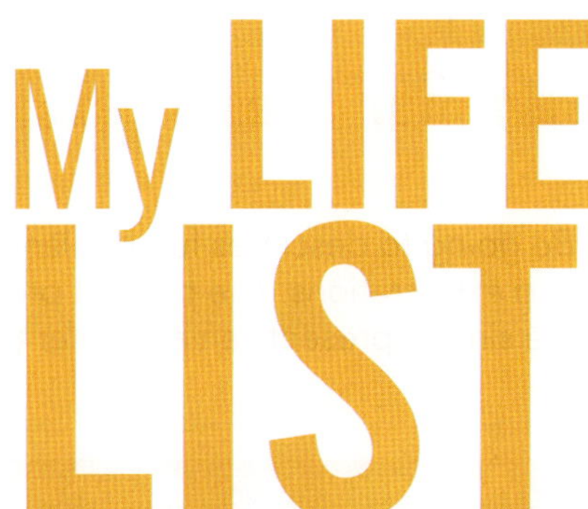

September 23

posted by: Lisa Sanchez

Welcome to a new feature of my blog – my life list. What is a life list? It's a list of things that you **are going to do** before you die, if you can. Here are some things on my life list:

- I'**m going to ride** in a hot-air balloon.

- I'**m going to live** in Spain.

- I'**m going to write** a poem.

- I'**m going to travel** to all 50 states in the United States.

Psychologists[1] agree that life lists are motivating. They encourage people to try new things. However, to achieve the goals on your list, you need to be realistic[2] and have a plan. For example, I'**m not visiting** all 50 states this year. I don't have the money! First, I'**m going to make** a plan to save money for each trip, and I'**m going to do** research on the places I want to visit. That is the point of a life list. It motivates you to work toward your goals. I'**m going to have to** work to accomplish my life list!

Are you **going to create** a life list, too? Here are some tips:

1   Make a list that reflects the direction you want for your life. For example, I want to understand more about the world, so travel is a big part of my life list.

2   Understand that it **is going to take** time to accomplish the things on your list – maybe a lifetime!

If you follow these simple steps, you **aren't going to be** disappointed. Your life **is going to be** full of new adventures and new accomplishments.

---

[1]**psychologist:** someone who studies the mind and emotions and their relationship to behavior

[2]**realistic:** showing an understanding of how things really are

Be Going To, Present Progressive, and Simple Present for Future Events

Grammar Presentation

Be going to describes future plans, predictions, and expectations. The present progressive and the simple present can also refer to the future.

*I'm **going to ride*** in a hot-air balloon.

*I'm **moving*** to Spain next month.

*My flight **leaves*** at 7:00 tomorrow morning.

2.1 Be Going To: Statements

STATEMENTS

Subject	Be	(Not) going to	Base Form of Verb	
I	am			
You We They	are	(not) going to	live	in Spain.
He She It	is			

CONTRACTIONS

Affirmative	Negative	
I'm	I'm not	
You're We're They're	You're not We're not They're not	You aren't We aren't They aren't
He's She's It's	He's not She's not It's not	He isn't She isn't It isn't

2.2 Be Going To: Yes/No Questions and Short Answers

Be	Subject	Going to	Base Form of Verb
Am	I		
Are	you we they	going to	visit Spain?
Is	he/she/it		

Short Answers

Yes, I **am**.	No, I'm **not**.
Yes, you **are**. Yes, we **are**. Yes, they **are**.	No, you **aren't**. No, we **aren't**. No, they **aren't**.
Yes, he/she/it **is**.	No, he/she/it **isn't**.

2.3 *Be Going To*: Information Questions

Wh- Word	Be	Subject	Going to	Base Form of Verb
What	**am**	I		see?
Where **When**	**are**	you we they	**going to**	go?
	is	he / she / it		

Wh- Word	Be	Going to	Base Form of Verb
Who **What**	**is**	**going to**	visit Spain? happen?

2.4 Using *Be Going To*, Present Progressive, and Simple Present

A Use *be going to* when future plans are *not* specific or definite.	*I'm going to visit* Spain someday. (I don't know when exactly.) *I'm going to have* a baby before I'm 35. (This is my plan, but I'm not pregnant yet.)
B Use the present progressive when future plans are specific or definite.	*I'm visiting* Spain next week. (I have plane tickets and my plan is definite.) *I'm having* a baby in June. (I'm pregnant and I know when the baby will be born.)
C Use *be going to* to talk about predictions, expectations, or guesses.	*You're going to have* fun in Miami next week.
D Use *be going to* when a future event is certain to happen because there is evidence for it. Do not use the present progressive.	*Look at those clouds. It's going to rain soon.* *Look at those clouds. It is raining soon.*
E Use the simple present, not *be going to*, for scheduled events in the future, such as class schedules, timetables, and itineraries. Some common verbs for this meaning are *arrive, be, begin, finish,* and *leave*.	*My flight is tomorrow.* *I leave at 7:00 a.m.*

Grammar Application

Complete the sentences with the correct form of *be going to* and the verbs in parentheses.

1 Lisa's blog *is going to motivate* (motivate) people to create life lists.
2 Jessica _______________________ (create) a life list on her blog. Here are two of the goals she wants to put on her list.
3 She _______________________ (not miss) the family reunion this year.
4 Jessica and her twin sister Kelly _______________________ (attend) a twins convention someday.
5 Sam _______________________ (not achieve) any of his goals this year, but someday he will.
6 Here are some things that I _______________________ (do) someday.
7 I _______________________ (take) a trip to New York.
8 I _______________________ (learn) martial arts someday.
9 My mother and I _______________________ (ride) in a hot-air balloon for her birthday.
10 Remember, you _______________________ (not do) everything in one year!

A Complete the conversation with the correct form of *be going to* and the verbs in parentheses.

Marco Hey, Julio. What _are_ you _going to do_ (do) now?
                        (1)   (1)
Julio I'm going to start a new job.
Marco Where _____________ you _____________________ (work)?
                    (2)   (2)
Julio At the Central Café.
Marco Nice! What _____________ you _____________________ (do) there?
                        (3)   (3)
Julio I'm going to cook! I always wanted to be a chef – it's number 10 on my life list.
Marco That's great! _____________ you _____________________ (get) some training?
                            (4)   (4)
Julio Yes. I'm going to learn a lot on the job! And I'm also going to take a class at Briteway Community College.
Marco What _____________ you _____________________ (take)?
                    (5)   (5)
Julio I'm going to take a class on food safety.
Marco That's great. _____________ it _____________________ (be) hard?
                            (6)   (6)
Julio No, I don't think so.
Marco What _______________________ (happen) with the rest of your life list?
                                (7)
Julio Oh, the trip to China?
Marco Yes. When _____________ that _____________________ (happen)?
                        (8)   (8)
Julio Well, first I'm going to earn a good salary at the Central Café. I'm going to save a lot of money, and then I'm going to go to China.
Marco That sounds like a plan!

B Write questions about Julio for the answers below. Use *be going to.*

1 _What is he going to do?_
He's going to start a new job.

2 _______________________
He's going to work at the Central Café.

3 _______________________
He's going to cook.

4 _______________________
Yes, he's going to learn a lot on the job.

5 _______________________
Yes, he's going to take a class at the community college.

6 _______________________
He's going to take a class on food safety.

7 _______________________
No, he doesn't think the class is going to be hard.

Exercise 2.3 *Be Going To*, Present Progressive, or Simple Present?

A Listen and complete the conversation with the form of the verbs that you hear: *be going to*, present progressive, or simple present.

Anne	So, Jin, what __are__ you __going to do__ (do) this weekend? (1) (1)
Jin	I'm finally _______________________ (accomplish) one of my big goals: (2) I _______________________ (ride) in a hot-air balloon. (3)
Anne	Wow! Did you already make a reservation?
Jin	Yes. I _______________________ (take) the flight that goes over the ocean. (4)
Anne	The ocean! You _______________________ (have) a great time. (5)
Jin	Yeah, and I heard the weather report. It _______________________ (be) great (6) this weekend. Do you want to come?
Anne	When _______________ you _______________ (go)? (7) (7)
Jin	We _______________________ (meet) in the park at noon on Sunday, and (8) the flight _______________________ (leave) at 1:00 p.m. (9)
Anne	I'd love to come, but I have other plans.
Jin	What _______________ you _______________ (do)? (10) (10)
Anne	I _______________________ (go) to the airport on Sunday (11) afternoon. I _______________________ (pick up) an old friend. She (12) _______________________ (stay) with me for a week, and her flight (13) _______________________ (arrive) right at noon. (14)
Jin	Well, it sounds like you _______________________ (have) a good time, too! (15)

B Listen again and check your answers.

A Complete another entry from Lisa's blog. Use *be going to*, the present progressive, or the simple present and the verb in parentheses. Use contractions where possible.

Achieving #7 on My Life List

January 15
posted by: Lisa Sanchez

Finally! I *'m going to achieve* (achieve) goal number seven on my life
(1)
list! I've bought my ticket, so it's definite now. I _______________
(2)
(move) to Spain! I _______________ (leave) on Friday, February 3.
(3)
I got a job, too! I _______________ (work) as a tour guide for a hotel
(4)
in Barcelona. I _______________ (start) on March 3, so I planned a
(5)
little trip. I _______________ (travel) around the country for three
(6)
weeks. I already bought a rail pass.

I've checked the weather, too. It _______________ (be) great.
(7)
It _______________ (be) nice the entire time. Any advice?
(8)

2 Responses   <u>leave one</u>

Robert: Lisa, you _______________ (have) a fantastic time!
(9)
But watch out – I've been to Spain many times in the winter. It _______________
(10)
(rain). You _______________ (need) an umbrella.
(11)

Amy: Hey Lisa, I _______________ (travel) in Spain at the same time!
(12)
I bought a rail pass, too! I _______________ (arrive) in Catalonia
(13)
on February 11. I _______________ (stay) at the youth hostel.
(14)
I made a reservation for three days. There's a big festival in Catalonia in February. I've heard

a lot about it. It _______________ (be) fun. Do you want to meet up?
(15)

B Pair Work   Compare your answers with a partner. For each answer, explain the reason for
the verb form you chose.

A On a separate piece of paper write six things for your life list. Begin with *I'm going to . . .*

I'm going to ride a horse on the beach.

B Pair Work Ask questions with *be going to* about your partner's list. Then write down the six things your partner wants to do.

A *What are you going to do?*

B *I'm going to ride a horse on the beach.*

A *Where are you going to do that?*

3 Avoid Common Mistakes ⚠️ 

> **1** **Use *be* with *going to* to describe future plans.**
>
>   *is*
> She⌃going to write a poem someday.
>
> **2** **Use the correct form of *be* with *going to*.**
>
>   *are*
> Jared and Jason ~~is~~ going to go to a twins convention next year.
>
> **3** **Use *be* before the subject in *Wh-* questions with *be going to*.**
>
>   *are you*
> What ~~you are~~ going to do?

Editing Task

Find and correct eight more mistakes in this web interview about life lists.

Life Lists

The following is the second in a series by Alex Wu of interviews with people about their life lists.

Alex	So, Heather, what ⌃*are* you and your husband ~~are~~ going to put on your life lists?
Heather	We going to put a lot of things on our list. We going to do some things together and some
5	things separately.
Alex	What Tom is going to do?
Heather	Well, Tom is a twin. He and his brother is going to attend the International Twins Convention.
Alex	I've heard of that. That's right here in Ohio.
Heather	Right. In fact, the convention is this weekend. They going to drive there on Saturday.
10 **Alex**	That's usually an outdoor event, right?
Heather	Yes, and unfortunately, it going to rain this Saturday.
Alex	Too bad. What they are going to do?
Heather	The event is going to be inside at a hotel now.
Alex	That's good. I bet they is going to have a great time this weekend.

4 Academic Writing

Opinion Writing

Brainstorm > Organize > Write > Edit

In this writing cycle (Units 16-18), you are going to write an opinion essay. In this unit (16), you are going to look at an essay and then brainstorm reasons and evidence for and against the prompt below.

> *Should colleges and universities require students to take physical education classes?*

Exercise 4.1 Preparing to Write

Work with a partner. Discuss the questions.

1 Are any of the activities on your life list related to food or exercise? Describe them and discuss when and where you are going to do them.

2 What are you going to eat tonight for dinner? Do you consider it healthy?

3 What kind of information is on food packages in your country? How do you use this information?

4 How should the government regulate unhealthy food and drinks like soda, chips, and candy?

Exercise 4.2 Focusing on Vocabulary

Read the definitions. Then complete the sentences with the correct form of the words in bold.

> **balanced diet** (n) a daily eating program that has a healthy mix of different kinds of foods
>
> **campaign** (n) a group of activities designed to motivate people to take action, such as giving money or changing behavior
>
> **junk food** (n) food that is unhealthy but quick and easy to eat
>
> **nutritional** (adj) relating to food and the way it affects a person's health
>
> **obesity** (n) the condition of being extremely overweight
>
> **portion** (n) an amount of food served to one person

1 This year I am going to start eating a _________________ consisting of fish, a little meat, some dairy products, and a lot of fruit, vegetables, and grains.

2 I love _________________ like potato chips and hot dogs, but I do not eat them often because they are bad for my health.

3 _________________ is a serious problem all over the world. In some countries, more than 50% of adults are overweight.

4 One way to lose weight is to eat smaller _________________ of food.

5 Next year our company is going to start a _________________ to encourage workers to eat better and work out more in order to improve their health.

6 Snacks like candy and potato chips have little _________________ value. Fruits and vegetables are a healthier choice.

Tackling Obesity

Obesity has become a major problem in many parts of the world, but it is especially common in the United States. There, the number of obese adults has more than doubled over the past 25 years. Nearly 70% of American adults are
5 overweight or obese, and this trend is only going to get worse. Experts predict that over 57% of American children will become obese adults. Obesity can cause major health problems like heart disease and diabetes problems. In the United States alone, 1 in 5 deaths is linked to obesity—that is
10 almost 300,000 deaths per year. Tackling obesity is a difficult task. In my opinion, it should be the shared responsibility of individuals, governments, and the media.

First, individuals need to live healthier lives. One way for people to fight obesity is to eat smaller **portions** and to eat
15 better food. An average man needs around 2,500 calories per day, while an average woman requires around 2,000, but most Americans eat more than that. We need to eat a **balanced diet** and maintain a healthy weight. A healthy diet includes approximately 50% fruits and vegetables; 30%
20 carbohydrates, such as bread, rice, potatoes, and pasta; 15% proteins, like meat, fish, eggs, and beans; and 5% dairy products, such as milk and cheese. It does not include much sweet food like candy or cookies. Better diets will definitely lead to fewer health problems.

25 Governments around the world must also fight obesity in their countries. In many countries, laws require food packaging to show accurate **nutritional** information. In the United States, large restaurant chains must list the number of calories for items on their menus. These restaurants must
30 also provide nutritional information about fat, sodium, and cholesterol amounts if a customer asks for it. This information helps people know the nutritional value of the food they eat when they are not cooking at home or eating packaged food. In addition, some countries tax foods
35 that are high in fat, such as pizza and potato chips, and in refined sugar, like chocolate and candy. This makes **junk food** too expensive for people to buy in large quantities and can lead to better health. Clearly, more government action is going to improve the rates of obesity in their countries.

40 Finally, the media and advertising can help with the problem of obesity. For example, Malaysia banned all junk food ads when children were watching TV in 2007. The reason was to protect children from the influence of advertising while they learn how to choose between treats and foods that are
45 good for them. In some countries, educational **campaigns** on TV encourage people to eat five portions of fruit and vegetables per day. Experts say that eating more fruit and vegetables could save up to 2.7 million lives every year. No public campaign to fight obesity is going to be completely
50 successful without the help of television and online media.

To summarize, individuals, governments, and the media all need to work together to reduce obesity. Individuals must take responsibility for their meal choices and eat healthier foods in smaller portions. At the same time, governments
55 should pass laws that encourage healthier lifestyles. Finally, the media can teach people about healthier eating habits and not advertise junk food to children. I believe that if individuals, governments, and the media do their part, then an end to obesity in the near future is possible. If not, we
60 are going to see many more health problems in the world.

Read the text on page 213. Work with a partner. Ask and answer the questions.

1 According to the writer, what three groups are responsible for fighting obesity?
2 What two predictions does the writer mention in paragraph 1?
3 According to the article, what does a balanced diet include?
4 What can the media do to help people make healthier food choices?

Exercise 4.4 Noticing the Grammar and Structure

Complete the tasks. Then compare your answers with a partner's.

1 Underline the writer's personal opinion in paragraph 1. Circle the phrase that introduces it. Put a box around the areas that the writer will discuss in the body paragraphs.
2 How many body paragraphs support the writer's opinion? Do they include mostly opinions or facts?
3 Underline the writer's personal opinion in the last paragraph. Compare it to the thesis statement in paragraph 1. How are they different? How are they the same?
4 Look at the last sentence in paragraphs 2-5. Why does the writer use future forms in these sentences?

Brainstorming Reasons and Evaluating Evidence

When planning your opinion essay, it is important to think about both sides of an issue, not just your opinion. You can use a T-chart to brainstorm a list of reasons for and against the issue. This process will help you understand the topic more clearly and choose the best reasons and evidence to support your opinion.

Next, brainstorm as many reasons for your opinion as possible. Ask yourself: "Why do I think this?" Write your answers in a list. Then choose the best two or three reasons to write about.

Finally, brainstorm as many supporting details and evidence as possible for your top two or three reasons. Evaluate your evidence and choose the strongest details to write about.

Exercise 4.5 Applying the Skill

Work with a partner. Review the text on page 213, and complete the tasks.

1 Complete the table in your own words.

Writer's opinion (thesis):	
Reason 1:	Evidence:
Reason 2:	Evidence:
Reason 3:	Evidence:

2 What prediction does the writer make at the end of each body paragraph? Do you agree with these predictions? Why or why not?

My Writing

Exercise 4.6 Planning Your Opinion Essay

Review the writing prompt on page 212. Complete the tasks, then discuss with a partner.

1 Use the T-chart. Brainstorm at least four reasons for and four reasons against the issue.

Reasons for	Reasons against

2 Use the table to brainstorm.

- Write your opinion.
- Choose the strongest reasons to support it.
- Make a list of evidence to support your reasons.
- Make a prediction or recommendation for future action.

My opinion:	
Reason 1:	Evidence: 1 2
Prediction 1:	
Reason 2:	Evidence: 1 2
Prediction 2:	
Reason 3:	Evidence: 1 2
Prediction 3:	

Exercise 4.7 Writing a Paragraph

1 Choose one of your reasons in Exercise 4.6, and write a body paragraph. Include your evidence and your prediction or recommendation for future action.

2 Share your paragraph with a partner for feedback.

Getting Older

1 Grammar in the Real World

A What do you think it's like to be 100 years old? Read the magazine article about centenarians. What are some of the effects of people living longer?

B Comprehension Check Answer the questions.

1 What will happen to the population by the end of the twenty-first century, according to the U.S. Census Bureau?
2 What are two negative effects of a large number of centenarians?
3 What is one positive effect of aging?
4 Why do older people tend to be happier?

C Notice Find the sentences in the article and complete them.

1 There ___________________ be several million centenarians in the United States by the end of the twenty-first century.

2 What changes ___________________ we see with so many people over 100?

3 For example, more people ___________________ have illnesses such as cancer and heart conditions.

4 Many older people ___________________ possibly not have enough money to support themselves for a longer period of time.

Do we use *will* to talk about the future, the present, or the past?

In 2000, there were 50,281 people over the age of 100 in the United States. In 2014, there were 72,197. This number **will** grow, and as a result, many more people **will** live to see their 100th birthday. In fact, there **will** be several million centenarians in the United States by the end of the twenty-first century. This is according to the U.S. Census Bureau. What changes **will** we see with so many people over 100?

The United States **will** see many changes because of this. For example, more people **will** have illnesses such as cancer and heart conditions. According to a study by the University of Albany in New York, we **will** probably not have enough doctors to take care of them. In addition, these changes **will** affect government services. This means that there **will** be less money for programs such as Social Security[2] and Medicare.[3] Many older people **will** possibly not have enough money to support themselves for a longer period of time. As a result, many **will** need to work in their 70s and even in their 80s.

On the other hand, there are some very positive aspects of aging. One is increased happiness. A study by Stanford University in California found that older people tend to be happier than younger people. Why? As people age, they change their goals. They know they have less time ahead of them, and as a result, they focus on the present. They spend more time on their relationships and know themselves better. This leads to increased happiness.

As people live longer, there **will** be more of us in the world. With more people who are happier, though, perhaps the world **will** be a happier place.

[1]**centenarians:** people aged 100 or older

[2]**Social Security:** a U.S. government program that gives financial help to people who are old, people whose husbands or wives have died, and people who cannot work

[3]**Medicare:** a U.S. government program that pays part of the medical expenses of people 65 or older

Centenarians[1]

2 Future with *Will*

Grammar Presentation

Will describes events that take place in the future.	There **will** be several million centenarians in the United States by the end of the twenty-first century.

2.1 Statements

Subject	Will (Not)	Base Form of Verb
I You He / She / It We They	**will** **will not** **won't**	help people.

2.2 Yes / No Questions and Short Answers

Will	Subject	Base Form of Verb
Will	I you he / she / it we they	help?

Short Answers	
Yes, I **will**.	No, I **won't**.
Yes, you **will**.	No, you **won't**.
Yes, he / she / it **will**.	No, he / she / it **won't**.
Yes, we **will**.	No, we **won't**.
Yes, they **will**.	No, they **won't**.

2.3 Information Questions

Wh- Word	Will	Subject	Base Form of Verb
How **Where** **When**	will	we they	solve the problem?

Wh- Word	Will	Base Form of Verb
What	will	happen?

2.4 Using *Will*

A Use *will* to make predictions. Predictions are things that people believe about the future.	*Many people* **will** *live to 110.* *There* **will** *be several million centenarians by the end of the twenty-first century.*
B You can use *likely, possibly, probably, certainly, definitely,* and *undoubtedly* after *will* and before the main verb to show different degrees of certainty. In negative statements, these adverbs can usually go between *will* and *not* or before *won't*.	*Humans* **will possibly** *live to 200 in the distant future.* *Technology* **will undoubtedly** *change the world.* *They* **will probably not** *do much physical work.* *They* **definitely won't** *do much physical work.*

2.4 Using *Will* (continued)

Maybe and *perhaps* start a sentence. **less certain**　　　　　　　**more certain** maybe　　　　　　　　　　certainly possibly　　likely　　　　definitely perhaps　　probably　　undoubtedly	**Maybe** older people will not have enough money. **Perhaps** the world will be a happier place.
C Use the full forms (*will, will not*) in formal writing.	Increased population **will** lead to crowding. People **will not** need to work so hard in the future.
Use the contracted forms (*'ll, won't*) in informal situations.	**I'll** live in a little house near the ocean. We **won't** have to work very hard.

DATA FROM THE REAL WORLD

Research shows that the normal position for adverbs of certainty is after *will*.	Many older people **will possibly** not have enough money to support themselves.
You can also put the adverb before *will* to add emphasis, but this is less common.	My parents didn't have to work in their 70s, but I **probably will**.

Grammar Application

Exercise 2.1 *Will*: Statements

Complete the statements with *will*. Use the verbs in parentheses.

1 People __*will live*__ (live) longer in the future.

2 In fact, many people ________________ (see) their 100th birthday.

3 This means that there ________________ (be) a lot more healthy older people.

4 These healthy older people ________________ (need) something productive to do.

5 Therefore, many people ________________ (not retire) at the age of 60 or 65.

6 They ________________ (work) in their 70s.

7 However, they ________________ (not do) as much physical work.

8 This ________________ (help) the economy, as it ________________ (not cause) problems for government programs such as Social Security and Medicare.

A Complete the questions in an online interview with an expert on aging. Use *will* and the correct form of the words in parentheses.

Chris Zurawski's **Future Blog**

I recently interviewed Dr. Sam Young. Dr. Young is an expert on aging and how it will change the government and the economy. Following is our discussion.

Q Dr. Young, ___*will people live*___ (people / live) longer in the future?
(1)

A Yes. People will live longer. Life expectancy will increase in most countries.

Q ______________________ (why / people / have) longer lives?
(2)

A Well, they'll have better medical care, and that will mean a healthier life.

Q ______________________ (people / live) longer everywhere in
(3)
the world?

A I think so. A lot of countries will have more centenarians. There will be millions in countries such as the United States and Japan.

Q So, ______________________ (everyone / be) healthy?
(4)

A Well, no, not everyone. People will live longer, but they'll have more long-term illnesses such as cancer and diabetes.

Q I'm only 24. I'm worried about Social Security. ______________________
(5)
(what / happen) to Social Security?

A Social Security will begin to have serious problems in the future. Something will need to change.

Q But let's say it doesn't change. ______________________
(6)
(what / happen)?

A In that case, Social Security payments will be very low, or they won't be available at all.

Q So, ______________________ (how / people
(7)
like me / support) ourselves?

A Even today, Social Security provides only about one-third of the average person's income. So, just like now, most people will need other sources of income as they age.

Q ______________________ (what other
(8)
sources of income / people / have)?

A A lot of people your age will work longer. You'll keep your jobs. Some will work part-time, but many will continue to work full-time for many years.

B Add adverbs to some of Dr. Young's statements. Use the cues in parentheses to choose an adverb with the appropriate degree of certainty. Sometimes more than one answer is correct.

certainly	likely	perhaps	probably
definitely	maybe	possibly	undoubtedly

probably

1 Life expectancy will increase in most countries. (in the middle)

2 Better medical care will mean a healthier life. (more certain)

3 A lot of countries will have more centenarians. (in the middle)

4 People will have more long-term illnesses such as cancer and diabetes. (less certain)

5 Social Security will begin to have serious problems in the future. (in the middle)

6 Social Security payments will be very low. (in the middle)

7 Most people will need other sources of income as they age. (more certain)

8 A lot of people your age will work longer. (less certain)

9 Many will continue to work full-time for many years. (more certain)

Exercise 2.3 *Will*: Questions, Answers, and Adverbs

A Listen to an informal conversation about the future. Complete the summary of Sara's ideas. Circle the correct words.

Sara thinks she probably <u>will / will not</u> live to be 100. She thinks
(1)

she <u>will probably / will probably not</u> have problems with money in old age.
(2)

B Listen again. Circle the correct adverb.

1 Sara will <u>probably / certainly</u> live to be about 85 or 90.

2 Sara will <u>perhaps / undoubtedly</u> work in her 80s.

3 At 80, Sara will <u>probably / definitely</u> have the same job she has now.

4 After retirement, Sara will <u>possibly / definitely</u> travel or garden.

5 Sara will <u>perhaps / very likely</u> not have enough money to travel.

6 Sara thinks she <u>possibly / certainly</u> won't get Social Security.

7 Sara thinks the government will <u>probably / undoubtedly</u> not have any money left in the future.

Listen again and check your answers.

C Group Work Use *will* and adverbs of certainty to talk about your future. Discuss these questions and give your own ideas.

- How long do you think you'll live? Why do you think that?
- How long will you work? What kind of job will you have at age _______ ?
- What will you do after you retire?

A *How long do you think you'll live?*
B *I'll probably live to be about 100.*
C *Perhaps I'll live to be 90. I hope so.*

3 Future with *Will, Be Going To,* and Present Progressive

Grammar Presentation

Will, *be going to*, and the present progressive can describe future events.	Life expectancy **will** increase. I**'m going to** look for a new job. She**'s starting** a retirement account next week.

3.1 Using *Will, Be Going To,* and Present Progressive for the Future

A Use *will* or *be going to* to talk about plans in the future. Use the present progressive for arranged events.	*I'll open a retirement account soon.* *I'm going to open a retirement account soon.* (This is my intention, what I want to do.) *I'm opening a retirement account next week.* (I have an appointment at the bank at a specific time next week. It's scheduled.)
B Use *will* or *be going to* to make predictions, expectations, or guesses about the future.	*More people will live longer in the future.* *More people are going to live longer in the future.*
C Use *be going to* when a future event is certain to happen because there is evidence for it.	*Look at those dark clouds. It's going to rain.* *We have a lot of work to do. We are not going to finish until 6:30.*
D Use *will* for immediate decisions.	*I have to go. I'll call you later.* (= I just decided to call you.) *I have to go. I'm going to call you later.* *I have to go. I'm calling you later.*

3.1 Using *Will, Be Going To,* and Present Progressive for the Future *(continued)*

E Use *be going to* for intentions: things you hope or intend to do in the future.	*I am healthy. I'm going to live to be 100 years old!* *I'm not going to retire and sit at home.*
Do not use *will* or the present progressive with intentions.	*I am healthy. I ~~will live~~ to be 100 years old!* *I am healthy. I'm ~~living~~ to be 100 years old!*
F Use *will* and *be going to* with adverbs to show different degrees of certainty about future events. You can use *likely, possibly, probably, certainly, definitely,* and *undoubtedly* after *be* and before *going to* when you want to show different degrees of certainty. For negative statements, put the adverb immediately after *be*.	*He definitely won't retire this year.* *He hasn't studied. He is probably going to fail the exam.* *People are certainly going to work longer in the future.* *They are probably not going to take any English courses next year.*
Maybe and *perhaps* can start sentences with *be going to*.	*Perhaps the government is going to fix Social Security.*

less certain ⟷ **more certain**

maybe		certainly
possibly	likely	definitely
perhaps	probably	undoubtedly

🌐 DATA FROM THE REAL WORLD

Research shows that *will* is 20 times more common in academic writing than *be going to*.

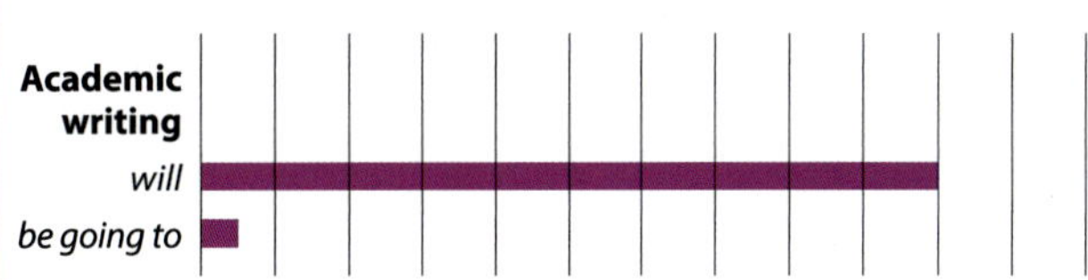

Write: *People **will be** happier in the future.*

Research shows that *be going to* is three times more common in speaking than *will*.

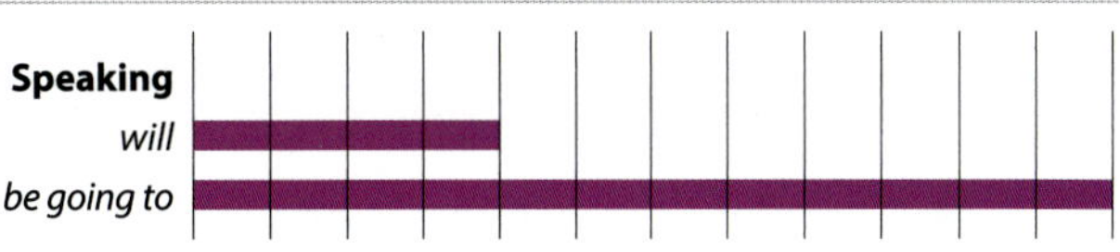

Say: *"Everyone's going to work to age 70 in the future."*

Complete this university press release. Circle *will* or the present progressive. If both are possible, circle both.

For Immediate Release

New Program at Bay City University for Senior Citizens

Bay City, September 5

Life expectancy <u>is increasing</u> / (<u>will increase</u>) in the future.
(1)
This means that the population of Bay City <u>will grow</u> / <u>is growing</u>
(2)
as well, and the number of Bay City students over the age
of 60 <u>will increase</u> / <u>is increasing</u> someday. Already, the
(3)
number of people over 60 who want to study is growing, and
it <u>is probably doubling</u> / <u>will probably double</u> in the next 20 years.
(4)
As a result, Bay University <u>is needing</u> / <u>will need</u> more programs and
(5)
more courses for older students.

Therefore, Bay City University <u>will announce</u> / <u>is announcing</u> plans
(6)
later this week for a new department for students over 60 called Lifelong
Learning. The department <u>will open</u> / <u>is opening</u> officially next year.
(7)
However, Lifelong Learning <u>is holding</u> / <u>will hold</u> an orientation event
(8)
this Friday afternoon to introduce the department. Interested students
can talk to instructors from the department about the courses they
<u>are teaching</u> / <u>will teach</u> next year.
(9)

A Complete the conversation with *will* or *be going to* and the words in parentheses. Sometimes, both are correct.

Lisa What *are you going to do* (do) in your old age?
(1)

Zack Well, I've thought about this. I ______________ (not retire) early.
(2)
Maybe I'll retire in my 70s, but not before. Anyway, after retirement, I
______________ (travel).
(3)

Lisa   That's expensive. You ________________ (not have) the money!
(4)

Zack   You know, you're right. I ________________ (start) a savings account right
(5)
away. How about you? What ________ you ________________ (do) in your old age?
(6)   (6)

Lisa   Well, I ________________ (go) back to school.
(7)

Zack   But you don't like school now. You ________________ (not like) it later.
(8)

Lisa   I ________________ (change) my attitude. In fact, I ________________
(9)   (10)
(change) it right now! Let's go to the library and study.

Zack   That's a great idea! I ________________ (drive).
(11)

B Pair Work Compare your answers with a partner. Discuss the reason for your choices.

Exercise 3.3 Adverbs

A What will life be like when you are old? Read some predictions about the future. Add an
adverb that matches the degree of certainty in parentheses.

certainly	maybe	probably
definitely	perhaps	undoubtedly
~~likely~~	possibly	

likely

1 Robots will∧do all of our housework. (in the middle)

2 Computers won't have keyboards. (in the middle)
   We are going to use our voices to communicate
   with them. (less certain)

3 There will be no ice in the Arctic. (more certain)

4 People are not going to drive their own cars. (less certain)
   Satellites or computers will control them. (less certain)

5 Space flight is going to be available to anyone. (more certain)
   People will take vacations in space. (more certain)

B Pair Work Do you agree or disagree?

> A *I agree with number 1. Robots will definitely do all of our housework.*
> B *Why do you think that?*
> A *We already have this type of robot today. People use robots to build cars . . .*

C Over to You Make predictions about your life in the future. Use *will*, *be going to*, and adverbs. Compare your predictions with a partner.

> A *What will your life be like in the future?*
> B *I'm going to make a lot of money. I'm definitely going to retire early. How about you?*

4 Avoid Common Mistakes ⚠ 

1 Use *will* before the main verb in statements about the future.

      will

In the future, people ‸ *live to 110.*

2 Use *will* for predictions, not *would*.

      will

Perhaps, a few years from now, I ~~would~~ have a job with a good salary.

3 Use *be* with *going to* for the future.

      am

I take good care of myself. I ‸ *going to live to be 100 years old!*

4 Use the base form of the verb after *will*.

      live

People will ~~to~~ live longer in the future. He will ~~lives~~ longer.

Editing Task

Find and correct eight more mistakes in this interview with an actor.

For Immediate Release

Pablo Percy A lot of women actors quit around the

age of 40 or 50. They say there

aren't good parts for older women.

What ~~would~~ *will* you do in your later years?

5 **Melanie Hinton** Well, I won't retire and sit at home. I work

until I'm 90!

Pablo Percy But there aren't many good parts for older

women. How would you find work?

Melanie Hinton The entertainment business is changing. In the future, there be

10 a lot more older people making movies *and* watching movies.

That means there would definitely be more parts for older

people, including older women, in the future.

Pablo Percy Are you sure?

Melanie Hinton Absolutely. In fact, I wouldn't wait for these parts. I will to write

15 my own scripts. I going to have a script ready next year.

Pablo Percy What is it going to be about?

Melanie Hinton I going to write a love story about two 80-year-olds.

Pablo Percy Sounds wonderful!

5 Academic Writing

Opinion Writing

Brainstorm > Organize > Write > Edit

In Unit 16, you looked at an opinion essay and brainstormed reasons and evidence for your essay to answer the prompt below. In this unit (17), you will learn language for stating opinions and how to structure your essay, and you will write an introductory paragraph.

> *Should colleges and universities require students to take physical education classes?*

Stating Opinions

It is important to state your opinion clearly in an opinion essay. You can use opinion phrases or modals to state your opinion. These words and phrases are common in the thesis statement and in the conclusion of an opinion essay.

Opinion phrases *In my opinion,* *In my view,* *I believe (that)* *I think (that)*	In my opinion, gardens, pets, and young people are a valuable part of a good senior care centers. I think that older people should live at home as long as possible for several reasons.
Modals *should / should not* *ought to* *need to / do not need to* *must / do not have to*	People of all ages **should** exercise every day to remain healthy when they are old.

Exercise 5.1 Applying the Skill

Work with a partner. Ask and answer the questions. Then write a thesis statement. Use an opinion phrase or modal to express your opinion.

1 Should governments provide free public transportation for people after they retire?

____

2 Should older workers have to retire so younger people can find jobs?

____

3 Do you agree or disagree with the following statement? It is a good idea to have older and younger people in the same college classes.

____

Stucturing Opinion Essays

The **introductory paragraph** gives the topic or issue, some background information, and the thesis statement. The background information can include a short history, interesting statistics, or other information that explains the issue and shows why it is important. The thesis statement clearly states the writer's opinion and suggests what the body paragraphs will be about.

The **body paragraphs** support the writer's opinion. Each paragraph has a topic sentence that connects to the thesis. Each body paragraph supports its topic sentence with details and evidence.

The **concluding paragraph** summarizes the writer's opinion and the most important reasons and evidence in the essay. It usually ends with a prediction or a recommendation for future action.

Exercise 5.2 Applying the Skill

Work with a partner. Read the introductory paragraphs for two opinion essays. Then complete the tasks.

(1) In many countries, people are working longer in life. For example, the average retirement age in the U.S. has been rising since 2000, and this trend will likely continue in the future. At the same time, many college graduates are having difficulty finding work in their fields of study. As a result, many believe that older workers should retire to provide more job openings. However, I believe that losing older workers will definitely weaken a company because there will be fewer mentors for new hires, experts in specific areas, and people with knowledge of the business's history and culture.

(2) Some people believe that seniors should all get free public transportation after they retire. Others don't think the government should provide that. In my opinion, seniors should be allowed to ride public transportation at no cost. Free public transportation is safer for those who are not comfortable driving and helpful to those with limited incomes after they stop working.

1 Identify the background information. What type does each writer use? How effective is it?
2 Identify the thesis statement. What is each writer's opinion? What will each writer discuss in the body paragraphs?
3 Compare the introductory paragraphs. Which one is stronger? Discuss your reasons.

My Writing

Exercise 5.3 Writing Your Introductory Paragraph

1 Review the prompt on page 228 and your My Writing work in Unit 16.
2 Make notes about your topic, background information, and thesis statement.
3 Write your introductory paragraph.
4 Share your paragraph with a partner for feedback.

Future Time Clauses and Future Conditionals

Learning to Communicate

1 Grammar in the Real World

A What do you know about learning a language? Read the passage from a textbook. How do humans learn to communicate?

B Comprehension Check Answer the questions.

1 According to the textbook excerpt, how many words does a typical two-year-old child know?
2 What do children talk about before ages four or five?
3 What happens after children learn to read?
4 Two things make it possible for humans to learn language. What are they?

C Notice Find the sentences in the textbook passage and complete them.

1 ________________ he is six, he ________________ learn to form
      (a)   (b)
correct grammatical sentences.

2 ________________ he starts school, he ________________ begin to
      (a)   (b)
read and write.

3 ________________ he starts to read, he ________________ learn to
      (a)   (b)
speak about things that are not happening right around him.

4 ________________ he is literate, Jake ________________ learn about
      (a)   (b)
a thousand words every year.

Do the words in the a blanks refer to place or time?
Do the verbs in the b blanks talk about the present or the future?

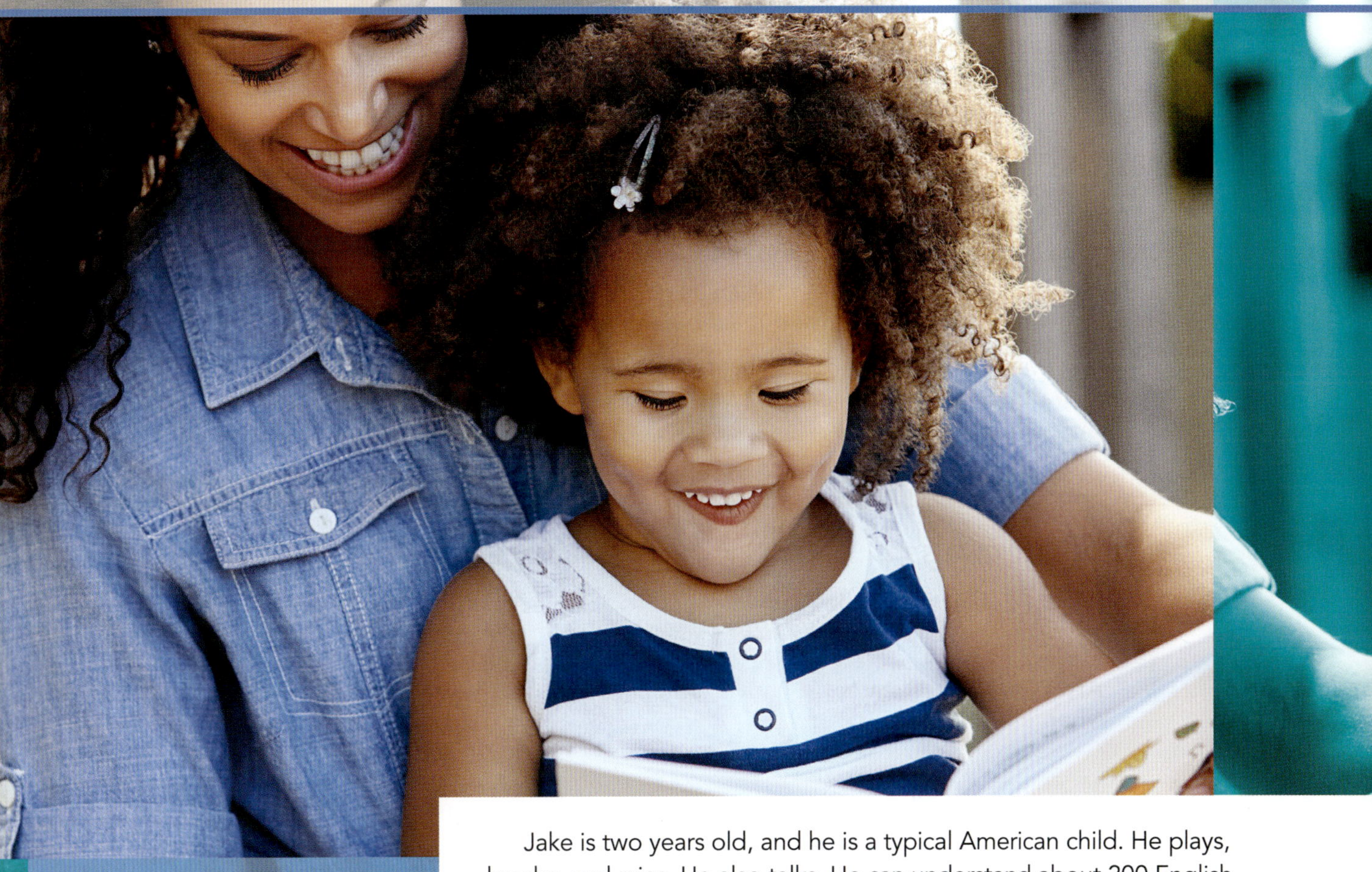

CHILDREN and LANGUAGE LEARNING

¹**literate:** able to read and write
²**genetic feature:** a characteristic of living things passed on from parents to children

Jake is two years old, and he is a typical American child. He plays, laughs, and cries. He also talks. He can understand about 200 English words. He uses fixed phrases. For example, he says "all gone" when he finishes his food. **Until he is about four or five, Jake will talk** mostly
5 about things around him — where he is and what he is doing at the moment. **When he is five years old, he will understand** thousands of words and will speak normally. **Before he is six, he will learn** to form correct grammatical sentences.

When he starts school, he will begin to read and write.
10 **After he starts to read, he will learn** to speak about things that are not happening right around him — the past, the future, and faraway people and places. **Once he is literate,¹ Jake will learn** about a thousand words every year. **When he is 18, he will be** ready for college. He will have all the language and world knowledge he needs for his classes.
15 Then, for the rest of his life, he will continue to learn.

Was Jake born with the ability to learn to speak, read, and write? Many experts say yes. Animals often live close to human beings, but they do not learn human language. Therefore, Jake must have a natural ability to learn his language. However, he speaks English only because
20 his parents and the people around him use English.

Learning how to communicate is a combination of natural, genetic features² and our social environment. We need both things to be "human."

2 Future Time Clauses

Grammar Presentation

Future time clauses show the time and order (first or second) of a future event.

FIRST EVENT   SECOND EVENT
Once he is literate, *he will learn about a thousand words every year.*

FIRST EVENT   SECOND EVENT
After he starts to read, *he will learn to speak about things that are not happening around him.*

2.1 Future Time Clauses

FUTURE TIME CLAUSE				MAIN CLAUSE			
Time Word	Subject	Simple Present		Subject	*Will*	Base Form of Verb	
Before **After** **When**	he	starts	school,	he	will	learn	to read.

MAIN CLAUSE				FUTURE TIME CLAUSE			
Subject	*Will*	Base Form of Verb		Time Word	Subject	Simple Present	
He	will	learn	to read	**before** **after** **when**	he	starts	school.

2.2 Using Future Time Clauses

A Use future time clauses to say when the event in the main clause happens.

Use *after* when the event in the time clause happens first.

learns to read

X

starts school

FIRST EVENT · SECOND EVENT

After she starts school, she will learn to read.

Use *when* when two events happen at or around the same time.

When he graduates from high school, he will go to college.

Use *as soon as* or *once* when the event in the main clause happens immediately after the event in the time clause.

X · X

leaves college · gets a job

FIRST EVENT · SECOND EVENT

As soon as he leaves college, he will get a job.

Once he is literate, he will learn thousands of new words.

Use *before* when the event in the main clause happens first.

SECOND EVENT · FIRST EVENT

Before Anne starts school, she will learn hundreds of words.

Use *until* to show when the event in the main clause will stop or change.

talks about immediate environment

X

four or five years old

Until he is about four or five, Jake will talk mostly about his immediate environment.
(Jake will stop doing this when he is four or five.)

B The time clause can come before or after the main clause. Remember to use a comma when the time clause comes first.

As soon as he leaves college, he will get a job.

He will get a job *as soon as he leaves college.*

C Even though the verb in the time clause is in the simple present, it refers to a future event.

He will learn more English *before he visits* California *next year*.

I will stay in school *until I graduate two years from now*.

Grammar Application

Exercise 2.1 Future Time Clauses

Circle the correct verb.

1 Larisa is a typical three-year-old Russian girl. Before she **will start / starts** school at age 5, she **learns / will learn** to print her name in the Cyrillic alphabet: Лариса.

2 Her parents **will teach / teach** her to read simple words like *cat* (Кот) before she **will start / starts** school, too.

3 When she **goes / will go** to kindergarten, Larisa **starts / will start** to learn to read and write more simple words.

4 She **will learn / learns** even more words as soon as she **starts / will start** primary school.

5 Once Larisa **gets / will get** to the first grade, she **learns / will learn** to use handwriting instead of printing.

6 When she **is / will be** about nine years old, she **will recognize / recognizes** thousands of words.

7 She **reads / will read** some of her textbooks in English when she **goes / will go** to college.

8 After she **will finish / finishes** college, she **knows / will know** tens of thousands of words.

А	Б	В	Г	Д	Е	Ё
Ж	З	И	Й	К	Л	М
Н	О	П	Р	С	Т	У
Ф	Х	Ц	Ч	Ш	Щ	Ъ
Ы	Ь	Э	Ю	Я		

Exercise 2.2 Time Words

Complete the description of a class in American Sign Language (ASL). Circle the correct time word.

ASL 101: Thursday, 7:00–9:00 p.m.   Room 203, Davidson Hall

Before / Until (1) the course begins, you will receive a questionnaire about why you are interested in studying American Sign Language. This information will help us plan the course.

Until / Once (2) the course begins, we will not speak in class. **As soon as / Until** (3) classes start, we will communicate only in sign language.

When / Before (4) the course begins, we will learn the basic signs for greeting new people: Hello, My name is . . . , I live in . . . , etc. This is a good place to start. We will practice these signs **as soon as / until** (5) you can use them automatically.

Until / When (6) you begin studying sign language, it will be quite difficult. But **after / until** (7) you know the basics, it will become much easier. **Until / Before** (8) the course ends, you will learn to use a lot of sign language and have a lot of fun!

Exercise 2.3 More Future Time Clauses

A Dave is going to take all four levels of Spanish at Bay City College. Read the information about how many words a typical student in the program knows at each level. Complete the statements about Dave. Use the verbs in parentheses and the numbers in the chart.

	Starting Vocabulary	**Ending Vocabulary**
Level 1 student	about 500 words	about 1,500 words
Level 2 student	about 1,500 words	about 2,500 words
Level 3 student	about 2,500 words	about 3,500 words
Level 4 student	about 3,500 words	about 5,000 words

1 When he starts Level 1, Dave _____*will know*_____ (know) about ___*500*___ words.

2 When he finishes Level 1, Dave ________________ (know) about ________________ words.

3 Dave will try to learn 1,000 more words before he ________________ (finish) Level 2.

4 Dave will not start Level 3 until he ________________ (know) about ________________ words.

5 Once he ________________ (reach) Level 4, Dave ________________ (know) more

than ________________ words.

6 Once Dave ________________ (read) and ________________ (write) Spanish fluently,

he ________________ (apply) for a job in Spain.

B Pair Work Complete each sentence in a way that is true for you. Then discuss your answers with a partner.

1 I _____*will continue*_____ (continue) to study English until I _____*speak the language well*_____ .

2 When I ________________________ (finish) this English course, I ________________________ .

3 I ________________ (get) a job as soon as I ________________________________ .

4 Before I ________________________ (complete) this course, I ________________________ .

A *I'll continue to study English until I speak it well. How about you?*
B *I'll continue to study English until I read and write it well.*

A *I'll get a job as soon as I finish all the classes in this program. How about you?*
B *I'll get a job as soon as I finish my job training course.*

C Group Work Tell a group member about your partner's answers in B. Compare your answers.

A *Mei will get a job as soon as she finishes all the courses in this program.*
B *Rob will get a job as soon as he finishes the program, too.*

3 Future Conditionals; Questions with Time Clauses and Conditional Clauses

Grammar Presentation

Future conditional sentences describe possible situations in the future.

If I pass all my exams, I will go to college.
If Dave learns to read and write Spanish well, will he get a job in Spain?

3.1 Future Conditionals: Statements

FUTURE CONDITION				MAIN CLAUSE			
If	Subject	Simple Present		Subject	*Will*	Base Form of Verb	
If	he	passes	his exams,	he	will	go	to college.

MAIN CLAUSE				FUTURE CONDITION			
Subject	*Will*	Base Form of Verb		*If*	Subject	Simple Present	
He	will	go	to college	**if**	he	passes	his exams.

3.2 *Yes / No* Questions

FUTURE CONDITION OR FUTURE TIME CLAUSE				MAIN CLAUSE			
If / Time Word	Subject	Simple Present		*Will*	Subject	Base Form of Verb	
If After When	she	learns	Spanish,	will	she	get	a job in Spain?

MAIN CLAUSE				FUTURE CONDITION OR FUTURE TIME CLAUSE			
Will	Subject	Base Form of Verb		*If / Time Word*	Subject	Simple Present	
Will	she	get	a job in Spain	**if after when**	she	learns	Spanish?

3.3 Information Questions

FUTURE CONDITION OR FUTURE TIME CLAUSE				MAIN CLAUSE			
If/Time Word	Subject	Simple Present		Wh- Word	Will	Subject	Base Form of Verb
If **After** **When**	you	finish	this class,	what	will	you	do?

MAIN CLAUSE				FUTURE CONDITION OR FUTURE TIME CLAUSE			
Wh- Word	Will	Subject	Base Form of Verb	If/Time Word	Subject	Simple Present	
What	will	you	do	**if** **after** **when**	you	finish	this class?

3.4 Using Future Conditional Clauses and Future Time Clauses

A	Use *if* to refer to a situation that is possible in the future but that we cannot be certain about.	*If he finishes the program, he will get a job.* (We don't know if he will finish the program.)
B	Use *when* to refer to a situation at a point in the future that is expected or likely to happen.	*When he finishes the program, he will get a job.* (We expect him to finish the program.)
C	Use a main verb in the simple present in the conditional clause.	*If she gets a better job, she will be very happy.* *If she will get a better job, she will be very happy.*
D	Use a comma in writing when the conditional clause or time clause comes first.	*If she arrives late, she will miss the lecture.* *When they finish their work, they will leave.*

DATA FROM THE REAL WORLD

Research shows that in conversation, people often use time clauses and conditional clauses alone in answers.

A *When will you start Level 3 of your course?*
B *As soon as I finish Level 2.*

A *Will you take another English course next year?*
B *Yes, if I have time.*

Grammar Application

Listen to an interview with a scientist about Edna the ape. After you listen, write the verbs in the correct form.

Bob Diaz Edna is a mature female ape. Researchers are going to try to find out if they can teach Edna to communicate. We asked Dr. Sheila Viss, one of the researchers, about the study. Dr. Viss, if you ___*teach*___ (teach) Edna, ___*will*___
(1)   (2)
she ___*learn*___ (learn) human language?
(2)

Dr. Viss That is what we hope to find out. First, if we ________________ (use) American
(3)
Sign Language, Edna ________________ (learn) the meaning of some signs.
(4)
For example, we think Edna ________________ (use) the sign for "more" if she
(5)
________________ (want) more food.
(6)

Bob Diaz If Edna ________________ (learn) a sign that works in one situation, ________________
(7)   (8)
she ________________ (use) the same sign in a different situation?
(8)

Dr. Viss Yes. For example, we think Edna ________________ (make) the sign for a toy
(9)
when she ________________ (want) a different toy.
(10)

Bob Diaz So, if she ________________ (want) something special, ________________ she
(11)   (12)
________________ (combine) the signs?
(12)

Dr. Viss We think she will. If she ________________ (do) this, Edna ________________
(13)   (14)
(make) simple sentences. For example, when she ________________ (want)
(15)
food quickly, she ________________ (make) the signs for "give-food-hurry."
(16)

Bob Diaz When she ________________ (learn) to communicate, ________________ she
(17)   (18)
________________ (learn) quickly?
(18)

Dr. Viss Well, probably not. Edna will learn slowly compared to a human child.

Exercise 3.2 More Future Conditionals

A Pair Work New words and expressions come into English every day. Match these new words with their definitions. They appear in most new dictionaries. Discuss with a partner how you think these expressions became popular.

1 blowback (noun) _________

2 to friend (verb) _________

3 a screenager (noun) _________

a a young person who spends a lot of time in front of a computer

b a bad result of a political action

c to add someone to your list of friends on a social networking site

e

f

g

friend[2] /ˈfrend/ **verb** to connect with someone on a social website so that you can share information, pictures, etc.: *A lot of people from my old job have friended me.*

B Read the sentences about how a new word or expression enters the language. Combine the sentences to make future conditional sentences. If the conditional clause is first, use a comma.

1 People use new words and expressions every day. The new words survive.

   If people use new words and expressions every day, the new words will survive.

2 You have a new development in technology. You get a new word that describes it.

   ____

3 New words also enter the language. There is a big world event such as a war.

   ____

4 Someone uses the new word on the Internet. People copy it.

   ____

5 For example, you use the word. Your social networking friends use it, too.

   ____

6 A new word or expression becomes popular. A lot of people use it.

   ____

7 A person on a TV news show says the new word. It sounds important.

   ____

8 A new word appears in the dictionary. A lot of people use it in speaking and in writing.

   ____

9 People stop using the new word or expression. It dies.

   ____

A Listen to a campus radio interview with Jawad, a student. Complete the sentences about his plans.

1 Jawad will be successful if he ____ .

2 Jawad will get a good job if he ____ .

3 If he does well in his English classes, Jawad ____

____ .

4 Jawad will apply for a job when ____ .

5 When he graduates and gets his certificate, Jawad ____ .

B Pair Work Discuss your plans with a partner. Ask questions like the ones in the interview. Use time clauses and future conditional clauses where appropriate.

- Why are you here at [your school]?
- What are your plans?
- After you finish the program, what will you do?
- How will you feel when . . . ?

A Why are you here at the community college?
B Well, I'm here for my career. If my English improves, I'll probably find a better job.

4 Avoid Common Mistakes ⚠

1   **Use the simple present in the conditional clause, not _will_.**

If I ~~will~~ get good grades, I will go to college next year.

2   **Use _will_ in the main clause, not the simple present.**

                 will know
If she learns 1,000 words every year, she ~~knows~~ 3,000 words in three years.

3   **Use the simple present in the time clause, not _will_.**

      finishes
When he ~~will finish~~ this course, he will take a vacation.

4   **Use _if_ for something that is possible. Use _when_ for something that you are certain will happen.**

   _If_
~~When~~ I become rich, I will help poor people.

Editing Task

Find and correct nine more mistakes in this web article about how birds can learn.

Intelligent Crows

A team of scientists is doing experiments with crows to test their intelligence. This is what the scientists think will happen:

                      are
- When the crows ~~will be~~ thirsty, they will look for water.

5

- As soon as they will fi nd water, they drink it.
- If there is no water, the crows search for it.
- If they don't get the water easily, the crows think of ways to get it.

For example, if the water will be in a narrow tube, it will be difficult to

10   reach it. However, the scientists think that the crows will learn the following:

- If they will drop a stone into the tube, the water level will rise.
- If they will drop more stones, the level will rise more.
- The crows drop stones into the tube until the crows reach the water.
- When the experiment is successful, the scientists will prove that crows

15   are intelligent birds.

5 Academic Writing

Opinion Writing

Brainstorm > Organize > **Write** > **Edit**

In Unit 17, you looked at how to structure an opinion essay, and you wrote an introductory paragraph for the prompt below. In this unit (18), you will complete, revise, and edit your essay.

> *Should colleges and universities require students to take physical education classes?*

Using Future Conditionals in Opinion Essays

Writers use future conditionals to connect ideas and evidence and to make predictions. *If* clauses can make your writing clearer and more logical.

According to experts, if schools require children to learn a foreign language, those students will communicate better in their native language.

Exercise 5.1 Applying the Skill

For each condition, write a prediction or result. Then combine the information in a future conditional sentence.

1 **Condition:** Colleges require one semester of study in another country.

   Prediction/Result: ____

   Sentence: ____

2 **Condition:** Students must do a summer internship related to their major.

   Prediction/Result: ____

   Sentence: ____

3 **Condition:** All textbooks are digital.

   Prediction/Result: ____

   Sentence: ____

My Writing

Exercise 5.2 Writing Your First Draft

Review your My Writing work in Units 16 and 17. Write your opinion essay. Include your introductory paragraph from Unit 17, at least two body paragraphs, and a concluding paragraph with a prediction or recommendation for future action. Use at least one future conditional.

Exercise 5.3 Revising Your Ideas

1 Work with a partner. Use the questions to give feedback on your partner's essay.

- Which of your partner's ideas seem strongest to you?
- Which of your partner's ideas need to be explained more clearly?
- What could your partner add or remove to make the essay stronger and easier to understand?
- Do you agree or disagree with your partner's opinion? Why?

2 Use the feedback from your partner to revise your essay.

Exercise 5.4 Editing Your Writing

Use the checklist to review and edit your essay.

Did you answer the writing prompt completely?	
Does your introductory paragraph include background information and a thesis statement?	
Does your thesis statement clearly state your opinion and suggest what the body paragraphs will be about?	
Did you use opinion phrases or modals correctly to express your opinion?	
Do your body paragraphs give reasons and evidence to support the thesis?	
Did you summarize your opinion and main points in the conclusion?	
Did you include a prediction or recommendation for future action?	

Exercise 5.5 Editing Your Grammar

Use the checklist to review and edit the grammar in your essay.

Did you use future forms correctly to make predictions or future recommendations?	
Did you use future conditionals to make your writing clearer and more logical?	
Did you avoid the common mistakes in the charts on page 211, 226, and 241?	

Exercise 5.6 Writing Your Final Draft

Apply the feedback and edits from Exercises 5.3 to 5.5 to write the final draft of your essay.

1 Grammar in the Real World

A Can you think of three recent medical inventions? Read the article from a science magazine. Which invention do you think is the most interesting?

B Comprehension Check Match the technology with what it does.

1 The "ishoe" _**b**_

2 The Rocket-Powered Arm ______

3 The Autonomous Wheelchair ______

4 The Smart Pill ______

a understands the human voice.

b tells NASA scientists if you have problems with balance.

c helps you pick things up.

d gives doctors information about their patients' health.

C Notice Look at the verbs in **bold** in the article. Underline the verbs that are about the past. Circle the verbs that are about the future.

Medical BREAKTHROUGHS

Some medical problems need engineers, not doctors. Technology **can** often solve problems when doctors alone **can't** help. Here are some examples of medical breakthroughs[1] from the world of engineering.

The "ishoe"

Often when astronauts return from space, they **are not able to** balance.[2] MIT student Erez Lieberman invented the "ishoe" to deal with
5 this problem. The ishoe is a pad that goes inside a shoe and uses sensors[3] to send information about balance to a computer or cell phone. NASA scientists use this information to help the astronauts recover their balance. Lieberman
10 **could** see that his invention had other uses, for example, diagnosing[4] balance problems in elderly people.

The Autonomous Wheelchair

In the future, people **will be able to** tell
15 their wheelchairs where they want to go. The Autonomous Wheelchair **can** learn to recognize its environment by listening to its user's instructions. In addition, it uses Wi-Fi[5] to build a map of the person's home.

20 The Smart Pill

The doctor **can't** always be sure if some people are taking their medication. Now a "smart" pill **can** tell a doctor when a patient last took his or her medication and report on the
25 state of the person's health at the time.

The Rocket-Powered Arm

Another invention from space research is the Rocket-Powered Arm. Until recently, people with artificial arms **were not able to** lift heavy
30 objects. Now there is a new kind of power for artificial arms – rocket fuel. With rocket-powered arms, people **will be able to** lift objects up to 20 pounds.

These are just some of the amazing
35 technological advances that will help improve people's lives. Who knows what other inventions they will come up with?

---

[1]breakthrough: an important discovery or development that helps to solve a problem

[2]balance: have weight equally divided so something or someone can stay in one position

[3]sensor: a device that discovers and reacts to changes in things such as movement, heat, and light

[4]diagnose: recognize the exact disease or condition a person has

[5]Wi-Fi: a method of connecting to the Internet without using wires

2 Ability with *Can* and *Could*

Grammar Presentation

Can and *could* describe ability and possibility.

Technology **can** *often solve problems when doctors alone* **can't** *help.*

Lieberman **could** *see that his invention had other uses.*

2.1 Statements

Subject	Modal Verb	Base Form of Verb
I You He / She / It We They	can can't cannot could couldn't could not	help people.

2.2 Yes / No Questions and Answers

Modal Verb	Subject	Base Form of Verb	Short Answers		
Can Could	I you he / she / it we they	help?	Yes, No,	I you he / she / it we they	can. can't. could. couldn't.

2.3 Information Questions

Wh- Word	Modal Verb	Subject	Base Form of Verb	
How Where When	can could can	we they you	solve	the problem?

Wh- Word	Modal Verb	Subject	Base Form of Verb
What Who	can could	we they you	help?

Modal Verbs and Modal-like Expressions: See page A7.

2.4 Using *Can* and *Could*

A You can use *can / can't* to talk about general ability and what people know how to do.	*My grandfather **can** swim, but he **can't** walk very well.* *Engineers **can** solve problems when doctors **can't**.*
B You can use *can / can't* to talk about people's senses and mental abilities.	***Can** you **see** that tall building on the left?* *Some patients **can't remember** if they took their medication.*
C You can use *can / can't* to talk about what is or is not possible and about known facts.	*Elderly people **can** have serious health problems after a fall.* *Technology **can't** solve every problem.*
D Use *could / couldn't* for the past.	*Lieberman **could** see other uses for his product.* *In the past, people with artificial arms **couldn't** lift heavy objects.*

Grammar Application

Exercise 2.1 *Can and Can't*: Statements

Complete the article about how a computer is helping a man. Use *can* or *can't* and the verbs in the box.

breathe	~~move~~	move	move	send	speak	talk	use

Connecting with ERICA

When he was younger, Steve Nichols was very fit. However, in 2016 he learned he had ALS, a disease that causes loss of muscle control. Now Nichols **can't move** most of his body. For example, he ________ (2) his tongue. Because of this, he ________ (3) . He also has trouble breathing. He ________ (4) without a machine.

However, Nichols ________ (5) ________ (5) his eyes. His computer, ERICA, has software that changes text to speech, so he ________ (6) to his wife and family. When Nichols looks at a letter on the keyboard on his computer screen, the computer types that letter. With ERICA, he ________ (7) e-mails. In addition, he ________ (8) the Internet. ERICA keeps Nichols connected to the rest of the world.

A Engineers in Japan have created nurse robots to help care for patients. Unscramble the words to write questions about these robots. Use *can*.

1 what / do / these robots / ?

   What can these robots do?

2 speak / they / ?

3 understand / how many languages / they / ?

4 they / patients / lift / ?

5 one robot / how much weight / lift / ?

6 a robot / recognize / people / ?

7 they / give medicine / to people / ?

8 make / what kinds of decisions / they / ?

B Listen to an expert answer the questions in A. Write the answers.
Write things the nurse robots *can* do.

1 *They can do a lot of things.*

2

3

4

5

6

7

8

C Notice Listen again. Write three things nurse robots *can't* do.

1

2

3

Exercise 2.3 *Can, Can't, Could, or Couldn't?*

A Complete the paragraph with *can, can't, could,* or *couldn't*.

Do You Use This Technology?

Before the invention of smartphones, you _____*could*_____ (1) easily contact family and friends away from their homes or offices. Now you _____________ (2) talk to them anywhere you like and however you like! You _____________ (3) send instant messages through an app or do a video call. You _____________ (4) text, talk, email, or send a picture or just an emoji. It's up to you. There's only one thing you _____________ (5) do yet and that's send yourself! Do you remember when we didn't have these devices? Back then, we _____________ (6) watch TV shows on the subway and we _____________ (7) surf the Internet on the train. It seems pretty strange now that we _____________ (8) do all these things. Many people don't even need to know where things are anymore because we have map apps on our phones. _____________ (9) you still read a paper map? If you_____________ (10), don't worry. Just tap on your app, tell it where you want to go, and follow the directions. You _____________ (11) do that 20 years ago!

B Group Work **Make your own list of four important inventions in everyday life. Then compare your lists in a group and discuss the questions. Use inventions in these areas or your own ideas.**

Inventions in . . .

- medicine   • travel   • communication   • home appliances   • entertainment

1 Can you remember (or imagine) life without these inventions? What was it like?
2 What can people do now that they couldn't do before these inventions?
3 As a group, choose the three most important inventions. What are they? Why are they the most important?

3 Be Able To

Grammar Presentation

You can use *be able to* to talk about ability and possibility.

*Some astronauts **are not able to** balance after a space flight. People **will be able to** talk to their wheelchairs.*

3.1 Statements About the Present, Past, and Future

PRESENT AND PAST

Subject	*Be*	*(Not) Able To*	Base Form of Verb	
I	am / 'm was			
You We They	are / 're were	(not) able to	use	a computer.
He / She / It	is / 's was			

FUTURE

Subject	*Will (Not)*	*Be Able To*	Base Form of Verb	
I You We They He / She / It	will / 'll will not won't	be able to	use	a computer.

3.2 Yes/No Questions and Short Answers About the Present and Past

Be	Subject	*Able To*	Base Form of Verb	
Are	you	**able to**	lift	heavy objects?
Were				

Short Answers		
Yes, I **am.**	No, **I'm not.**
Yes, I **was.**	No, **I wasn't.**

3.3 Yes/No Questions and Short Answers About the Future

Will	Subject	*Be Able To*	Base Form of Verb	
Will	you	**be able to**	lift	heavy objects?

Short Answers	
Yes, I **will.**	No, I **won't.**

3.4 Information Questions About the Present, Past, and Future

PRESENT AND PAST

Wh- Word	Be	Subject	Able To	Base Form of Verb
When How How often	are were	you	able to	go?

Wh- Word	Be	Able To	Base Form of Verb
Who	is / 's was	able to	go?

FUTURE

Wh- Word	Will	Subject	Be + Able To	Base Form of Verb
When How How often	will	you	be able to	go?

FUTURE

Wh- Word	Will	Be + Able To	Base Form of Verb
Who	will / 'll	be able to	go?

3.5 Using *Be Able To*

A You can use *be able to* to talk and write about ability in the present, past, or future.

*Sometimes astronauts **are not able to** balance after a space flight.*

*In the past, artificial arms **weren't able to** lift heavy objects.*

*In the future, people **will be able to** tell their wheelchairs where to go.*

B You can use *be able to* to talk and write about possibility.

*People **will be able to** talk to their wheelchairs in the future.*

C In affirmative statements, you can use *was / were able to* for a specific event or a specific action that someone completed successfully in the past. Do not use *could*.

Lieberman **was able to** *design a special shoe a few years ago.*

Lieberman ~~could design~~ *a special shoe a few years ago.*

Both forms are correct in negative statements.

In the past, they **weren't able to** *lift heavy objects.*

In the past, they **couldn't** *lift heavy objects.*

D You can use *be able to* after *going to, want to, would like to, need to,* and *have to.*

In the future, people **are going to be able to** *use these inventions.*

Many people **would like to be able to** *use these inventions now.*

Do not use *can (can't)* or *could (couldn't)* after these verbs.

Scientists want to **be able to** *invent new technologies.*

~~Scientists want to can invent new technologies.~~

 *Can* and *could* are more common than *be able to* in everyday conversation, especially in present time. Use *be able to* if you need to sound more formal.

Can *your phone open your front door?*

The most advanced robots **are** *now* **able to** *make facial expressions.*

DATA FROM THE REAL WORLD

People sometimes use *be unable to* instead of *be not able to*. This is more common in formal writing or speaking.

Formal: *When many astronauts return from space, they* **are unable to** *balance.*

Informal: *When many astronauts return from space, they* **are not able to** *balance.*

 Grammar Application

Exercise 3.1 Questions and Answers

A Complete the article from a magazine. Use a form of *be able to* and the verbs in parentheses. Then, on a separate piece of paper, write what numbers can use *could* instead of *was able to*.

Seeing Through You

___Are___ brain scanners ___able to see___ (see)
(1)   (1)
your thoughts? _________________________
                                 (2)
they _____________________(read) your mind?
            (2)
_____________________ they _____________________ (see) your
            (3)   (3)
memories? Yes, according to some scientists. At a conference
in 2017, researchers _____________________________ (prove)
                                            (4)
this. One researcher watched a movie, and the brain scanning
software _____________________ (show) the basic pictures that he
                        (5)
was looking at.

How _____________________ scientists _____________________ (use) this technology in the
            (6)   (6)
future? Some scientists say they are already using brain scan technology. They say that
brain scans _____________________________ (tell) if someone is lying.
                            (7)
Scientists are not the only ones who plan to use technology like this in the future.
Some companies think they _____________________________ (use) brain scanners for
                                            (8)
advertising as well. Advertisers hope they _____________________________ (see) the way
                                                            (9)
people respond to their products.

What do you think? How _____________________ we _____________________ (use) these
                                    (10)   (10)
technologies in the future?

B Pair Work **What do you think about the article? Are brain scanners a good thing or a bad thing? Discuss with a partner.**

A *I think brain scanners are good because police will be able to tell if someone is lying.*

B *Perhaps the police will be able to catch more criminals with brain scanners.*

🌐 DATA FROM THE REAL WORLD

The simple past forms (*was/were able to*) are more frequent than the simple present forms (*am/is/are able to*). However, *be able to* is most common after modal verbs like *will* and *should* and after verbs like *going to* and *want to*.

Be Able To

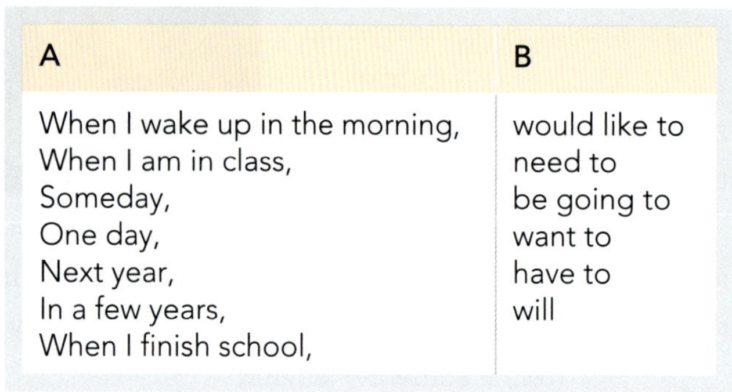

A Over to You Write five sentences about yourself. Write about work, school, technology, free time, or other ideas. For each sentence, choose one expression from Column A and one from Column B. Add *be able to*.

A	B
When I wake up in the morning,	would like to
When I am in class,	need to
Someday,	be going to
One day,	want to
Next year,	have to
In a few years,	will
When I finish school,	

Someday, I want to be able to buy a house.
When I finish school, I'm going to be able to get a better job.

1 ____

2 ____

3 ____

4 ____

5 ____

B Group Work Compare your sentences. Give more information. Who has similar experiences and dreams?

4 Avoid Common Mistakes ⚠ 

1 ***Cannot*** **is one word.**

       cannot
This technology ~~can not~~ do everything, but it can help.

2 **Don't forget the *be* or *to* in *be able to*.**

  wasn't   *to*
I ~~not~~ able ˄ understand the instructions for my new phone.

3 **In an affirmative sentence, use *was*/*were able to* for a specific action that someone completed successfully in the past. Do not use *could*.**

                   was able to
My grandmother fell yesterday, but she ~~could~~ get up.

Editing Task

Find and correct 11 more mistakes in this online review of an electronic translator. Some sentences have more than one mistake.

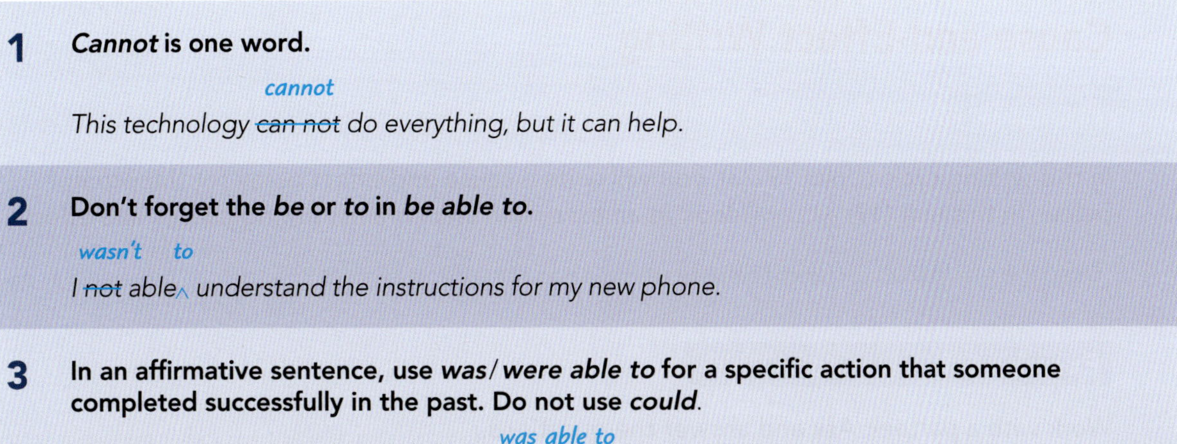

TECHNOLOGY TUESDAY REVIEW:
The Instant Interpreter

                             be
     Will people really need to ˄ able to speak other languages in the future? That is a question language students ask after they hear about the Instant Interpreter. This little machine translates for you when you visit a foreign country. It listens to what you say and is able translate your speech into eight world languages. It is also easy to

5 use. If you are able use a smart phone, you will able to use this.

     I tried the Instant Interpreter last week and I liked it. I able to order a cup of coffee in a restaurant. When the server asked me a question, the Interpreter gave me the translation, and I was able to answer. In the end, we were able to have a simple conversation. However, we not able understand everything we said to each other.

10   One problem with this machine is that it can not work quickly when your conversation becomes more complex. It needs time to able to learn your voice, too. I could solve the problem by talking to it a lot, so it learned my voice.

     If you need to be able get around in a foreign city, this is a good buy. You can not find a better translating machine on the market today.

5 Academic Writing

Cause-and-Effect Writing

Brainstorm > Organize > Write > Edit

In this writing cycle (Units 19-23), you will write a cause-and-effect essay for the prompt below. In this unit (19), you will look at an essay and start brainstorming causes and effects.

Describe the human causes of climate change and the effects climate change can have on the planet.

Exercise 5.1 Preparing to Write

Work with a partner. Ask and answer the questions.

1 What scientific breakthroughs have been good for the environment? Explain your answers.
2 Why do people cut down trees? What can happen when forests are destroyed?
3 What are some ways that governments are able to protect trees and forests?

Exercise 5.2 Focusing on Vocabulary

Read the definitions. Then complete the sentences with the correct form of the words in bold.

> **absorb** (v) to take in a liquid or gas through a surface and hold it
> **affect** (v) to cause a change in someone or something
> **construction** (n) the process of building something, usually large structures such as buildings, roads, or bridges
> **destruction** (n) the act of causing so much damage to something that it stops existing because it cannot be repaired
> **effect** (n) result; a change that happens because of something
> **habitat** (n) the natural environment of an animal or plant
> **logging** (n) the activity or business of cutting down trees for wood
> **rainforest** (n) a forest in a tropical area that gets a lot of rain

1 Clothes made from plants, like cotton or bamboo, can ________________ water more easily than man-made materials like polyester.

2 The ________________ of polar bears is shrinking due to the melting ice in the Arctic region.

3 ________________ of ancient forests hurts wild animals because it destroys their food and shelter.

4 The Amazon ________________ in South America receives 60 to 118 inches (150 to 300 centimeters) of rain every year.

5 Twenty acres of woods and fields were destroyed before the ________________ of the new office building and parking lot could start.

6 One dangerous _________________ of increasing temperatures is the melting of ice in the Arctic and Antarctica.

7 Huge fires around the world, from South America to California, are causing the _________________ of forests that are essential to the life of our planet.

8 Studies show that pollution from cars and factories _________________ people in many harmful ways.

The Causes and Effects of Deforestation

Forests, which cover almost one-third of the surface of the Earth, are able to produce oxygen and provide **habitats** for plants, animals, and humans. These days, many of
5 the world's great forests are threatened by deforestation: the process of removing trees from large areas of land. The **destruction** of forests can occur for several reasons: Trees are used as fuel or for **construction**, and cleared
10 land is used as pasture for animals and fields for planting food. The main harmful **effects** of deforestation are climate change and damage to animal habitats.

The main causes of deforestation are
15 commercial and local farming. Huge commercial farms have taken over large areas of forest in many countries. In Indonesia, for example, industrial **logging** is carried out to clear huge areas for the production of palm
20 oil, while in Brazil, large areas of the Amazon **Rainforest** are cleared to grow soybeans and vegetables for cooking oil. At the same time, local farmers may cut down and burn trees to clear an area just big enough to graze cattle
25 or grow crops. However, after two or three years, the land can no longer be used, so the farmer moves to another piece of land. In both cases, it can take ten years for cleared land to recover, but in populated areas the
30 land is often unable to recover at all. The constant clearing and reuse of land leads to heavy erosion—the loss of the top layer of soil that protects the ground. Erosion, in turn, can cause flooding in heavy rain.
35 One serious effect of deforestation is climate change. Normally tropical rainforests help control the Earth's temperature by **absorbing** carbon dioxide. As an example, the vast rainforest of the Amazon covers an
40 area of more than 2.6 million square miles— about 10 times the size of Texas—and is able to absorb an estimated 1.5 billion tons of carbon dioxide annually. However, in areas where deforestation has taken place, the
45 carbon dioxide goes into the atmosphere and traps heat in a process called the greenhouse effect. The result is global warming. These increasing global temperatures result in less rain. This can cause the rainforests to dry
50 out and can lead to fires that cause more emissions of carbon dioxide. Clearly, the loss of the rainforests, especially by fire, is a major problem to slowing down or ending global warming.
55 Forest destruction can also negatively **affect** biodiversity. Deforestation causes the loss of habitats and damage to land where plants and animal species live, leading to the extinction of many species. A decrease in
60 biodiversity can threaten entire ecosystems and destroy future sources of food and medicine.

In conclusion, damage to the world's forests is leading to changes in the natural
65 environment and causing global warming. Looking to the future, governments should plant more trees that will absorb carbon dioxide and protect forests from illegal logging while they are still able to make a
70 difference. Otherwise, deforestation on such a large scale will have terrible effects on the environment and our future.

Read the text on page 257, and answer the questions. Compare your answers with a partner's.

1 What negative effect can too much farming have on soil?

2 How are animals affected by deforestation?

3 Why are rainforests important for the planet?

4 According to the writer, what can governments do about deforestation?

Exercise 5.4 Noticing the Grammar and Structure

Work with a partner. Complete the tasks.

1 Underline the verb phrases that describe ability and possibility.
2 What is the main topic of the essay? Circle the thesis statement.
3 Highlight the topic sentences in paragraphs 2-4.
4 What causes and effects of deforestation does the writer mention?

Organizing a Cause-and-Effect Essay

Cause and effect is a common type of academic writing. Sometimes the causes and effects are discussed in different body paragraphs. Writers often do this when there is:

One cause with several effects

urban rooftop garden → (1) keeps building cool; (2) collects rainwater; (3) creates oxygen

One effect with several causes

large amount of plastic in the ocean ← (1) too much packaging; (2) low cost; (3) weak regulations

Exercise 5.5 Applying the Skill

Work with a partner. Use the text on page 257 to complete the chart.

DEFORESTATION

CAUSES		EFFECTS
	→	

Describing Causes and Effects

Writers use certain linking phrases to show the relationship between the causes of a problem and its effects.

Cause	Linking word or phrase	Effect
Deforestation	*leads to / causes / results in*	habitat destruction.

Effect	Linking word or phrase	Cause
Habitat destruction is	*caused by / due to / the result of*	deforestation.

Exercise 5.6 Applying the Skill

Complete the sentences with possible causes or effects. Use a different linking word or phrase in each sentence.

1 Planting trees ____.

2 Air pollution ____.

3 Rising sea levels ____.

4 Alternative energy sources ____.

My Writing

Exercise 5.7 Brainstorming

Work in a small group. Brainstorm at least three human causes of climate change and three effects of climate change. Compare your lists with another group's.

Human Causes of Climate Change		Effects of Climate Change	
1 ________________ ↘		↗ 1 ________________
2 ________________ → climate change		climate change → 2 ________________
3 ________________ ↗		↘ 3 ________________

Exercise 5.8 Writing Sentences

Use the information in Exercise 5.7 to write six cause-and-effect sentences about climate change.

1 ____

2 ____

3 ____

4 ____

5 ____

6 ____

1 Grammar in the Real World

A What kinds of volunteer work are common in your city or town? Read Lisa's e-mail about a volunteer project. What is she trying to do?

B Comprehension Check Match the person with his / her work assignment.

1 Professor Rodriguez __d__   a is going to bring plates.

2 Wei _____   b will do the vegetables.

3 Lara _____   c will pick up all the food.

4 Marcus _____   d is going to pick up the turkey.

5 Mohammed _____   e will make pumpkin pies.

C Notice Find the questions in the e-mail and complete them.

1 Professor Rodriguez, ___________________ please pick up the turkey on Wednesday evening?

2 Wei, ___________________ make the pumpkin pies on Wednesday?

3 Professor Rodriguez, ___________________ please contact your sister?

4 Mohammed, ___________________ get in touch with your roommate?

Which sentences ask permission to do something? Which sentences ask someone else to do something?

¹**give you a hand:** help with doing something

²**get in touch with:** communicate with

To Bay City Community College Student Volunteer Group
From Lisa Chen
Subject Subject: Volunteer Work Assignments for Thanksgiving

Hi Everyone!

Here are the volunteer work assignments for the Thanksgiving dinner at the Bay City Homeless Shelter. Please contact me if you have any questions.

5 Professor Rodriguez, **could** you please pick up the turkey on Wednesday evening? Then, **could** you take it to Ana's apartment?

Wei, **would** you make the pumpkin pies on Wednesday? That way, Ana can use the oven for the turkey.

Ana, **can** Eun give you a hand?[1]

10 Lara, **will** you do the vegetables? **Do you mind if** I help out? I make great sweet potatoes.

Marcus, you said you had plates and silverware. **Can** you please bring them? Let me know if you cannot.

Mohammed has offered to take all the food in his van. Mohammed, 15 **can** you go by Ana's around 11:00 on Thursday morning and pick everything up? **Can** I go with you? Then, Ana, **can** we go to the shelter together? **Do you mind if** we take your car?

I think that's everything. Let's all meet at the shelter and start serving at 1:00 p.m. Oh, wait! We really need a few more people to help 20 with serving. Professor Rodriguez, **may** I please contact your sister? Mohammed, **can** I get in touch with[2] your roommate?

Finally, would you like to get together at my apartment on Friday for a "thank-you" pizza party?

See you soon, and thanks! Enjoy the attached photo!

25 Lisa

2 Permission

Grammar Presentation

<table>
<tr>
<td>You can use can, could, may, and do you mind if to ask permission to do something.</td>
<td>"Could I go with you to Ana's?"   "Sure. No problem."
"Do you mind if we take your car?"   "No, not at all."</td>
</tr>
</table>

2.1 Can, Could, May: Yes/No Questions and Responses

Modal Verb	Subject	Base Form of Verb		Responses	
Can				Yes, you **can**.	No, you **can't**.
Could	I	go	in your car?	Yes, (of course).	No, (I'm afraid not).
May					

2.2 Do You Mind If: Yes/No Questions and Responses

Do you mind if	Subject	Verb	Responses	
Do you mind if	I	**drive**?	No, I don't. Not at all. Sure. No problem.	Well, actually, I prefer to drive.

2.3 Asking for Permission

A Less formal ↑ / More formal ↓

can	*Can* is very common in conversation and informal writing. Use *can* in most situations.	*Can I get in touch with your roommate?*
could	*Could* is more formal and more polite than *can*.	*Could we ride to the shelter with you, please?*
may	*May* is very formal and polite.	*May I please contact your sister, Professor Rodriguez?*

B Use the base form of the verb after modal verbs, including *can*, *could*, and *may*. Do not use other forms of the verb.

Can I be part of your volunteer group?
Can I ~~am~~ part of your volunteer group?
Can I ~~being~~ part of your volunteer group?

C Use *Do you mind if . . .* to be polite or when you think the request is inconvenient for the other person.

Do you mind if we take your car?

With *Do you mind if . . . ?*, the verb agrees with the subject.

Do you mind if Eun gives you a hand?

You can also use *Do you mind?* alone.

Can we go to the shelter together?
Do you mind?

2.3 Asking for Permission *(continued)*

D You can say *please* with requests for permission, especially in formal situations. Use it at the end of the sentence or after the subject.

*Could I drive your car, **please**?*

*May I **please** drive your car?*

2.4 Answering Requests for Permission

A Use *can* and *may* in short answers to requests for permission. Do not use *could*.

"Can I come with you in your car?" *"Yes, you **can**."*
"Yes, you ~~could~~."

"Could I call you later?" *"Yes."* / *"Yes, you **can**."*
"Yes, you ~~could~~."

May is more formal.

"May I sit here, please?" *"Yes, you **may**."*

B In conversation, you can use other expressions such as *Sure, no problem.* / *Certainly.* / *Of course.*

"Could I use your cell phone?" *"**Sure, no problem.**"*

Use *Certainly* and *Of course* in formal situations.

"May I contact your sister?" *"**Of course.**"* / *"**Certainly.**"*

C You can soften negative responses with an apology and/or a reason.

"Can I ride in your car?" *"**Sorry**, I don't have room."*
*"**I'm afraid** I don't have room."*
"~~I don't have room.~~"

Be careful with negative responses. *No, you can't* and other direct negative responses often sound rude.

D Say *No* or *No, not at all* to agree with requests with *Do you mind if.*

*"**Do you mind if** I borrow your cell phone?"*
*"**No, not at all**. Here you are."* / *"**Sure, no problem.**"*
(Yes = Yes, I do mind. You can't use it.)

No means "No, I don't mind." You can also say *Sure* or *Sure, no problem.*

*"**Do you mind if** I call you this evening?"*
*"**No, not at all.**"*
(No = It's OK to call.)

Notice: *No* in response to *Do you mind if* means the opposite of *No* in response to *can*, *could*, and *may*.

*"**Can** I call you this evening?"*
"No, I'm afraid I'm busy."
(No = It's not OK to call.)

 Grammar Application

Exercise 2.1 Asking and Answering Requests for Permission

Lisa's volunteers reply to her e-mail, and their plans change. Correct the mistake in each request.

1 Dear Lisa: Yes, I can make the pies on Wednesday. Could I ~~to~~ borrow a pie pan from you?

Thanks, Wei

2 Hi, Lisa: Do you mind if I picks up the turkey on Wednesday morning?
Thank you, Professor Rodriguez

3 Dear Lara: Ana's oven is not working. Do you mind if she cook the turkey at your house?
Thanks! Lisa

4 Hello, Lisa: Can my roommate calls you about volunteering? Do you mind if I give him your number? Mohammed

5 Dear Ana: May please I call you early on Wednesday morning to arrange a time?
Professor Rodriguez

6 Dear Lisa: Yes, I can bring plates. Can you helping me carry them? Thanks! Marcus

7 Dear Professor Rodriguez: Yes, may you call on Wednesday morning. I'm available after 8:00 a.m. Ana

8 Hi, Ana: My car is not working. Could I please to ride to the shelter with you? Eun

Exercise 2.2 Formal Requests for Permission

 **A** Listen to a student asking a teacher for permission. Complete his requests in the chart.

		Yes	No
1	*Could I ask you* ________ a question, please?	✓	☐
2	________ class early on Wednesday?	☐	☐
3	________ the computer room?	☐	☐
4	________ your CD player?	☐	☐
5	________ our homework on Friday, not Thursday?	☐	☐

B Listen again. Does the teacher agree to the student's requests? Check (✓) Yes or No in the chart on page 264.

C Pair Work Now compare your answers with a partner.

Exercise 2.3 Asking for Permission

A Write two requests for permission to each person. Use the ideas in the box or your own ideas.

You want to:

ask a question about …	discuss an idea for …	get help with …	take a day off …
borrow something	get a ride somewhere	sit down	talk after class about

Your Teacher	A Friend	A Stranger in the Cafeteria	Your Boss
1 *Could I please talk to you after class about my paper?*	3	5	7
2	4	6	8

B Pair Work Choose three of your requests. Read them to a partner. Do not identify the person you wrote the request to. Can your partner guess?

A *May I take a break now?*
B *Are you asking your boss?*

(To a stranger in the cafeteria)

A *Do you mind if I sit down here?*
B *No, not at all.*

3 Requests and Offers

Grammar Presentation

You can use *can*, *could*, *will*, and *would* to ask people to do things. You can use *can*, *could*, *may*, and *will* to make offers.

"*Could* you give me a hand?"
"*Yes, of course.*"

"*I'll help you with that.*"
"*Thank you.*"

3.1 Requests and Responses with *Can*, *Could*, *Will*, and *Would*

Modal Verb	Subject	Base Form of Verb	Responses	
Can **Could** **Will** **Would**	you	help?	Yes, I **can**. / Sure. No problem. Of course. / All right. / OK. Yes, I **will**. Yes, I'd be happy to. / I'd love to.	Sorry, I **can't**. I'm afraid I **can't**.

3.2 Asking People to Do Things with *Can*, *Could*, *Will*, and *Would*

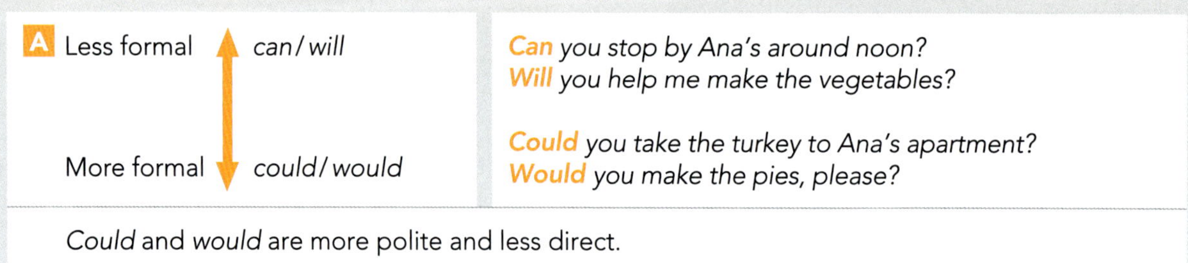

A Less formal — *can / will*

More formal — *could / would*

Can you stop by Ana's around noon?
Will you help me make the vegetables?

Could you take the turkey to Ana's apartment?
Would you make the pies, please?

Could and *would* are more polite and less direct.

3.2 Asking People to Do Things with *Can, Could, Will,* and *Would* (continued)

B You can say *please* to ask people to do things, especially in formal situations. Use it at the end of the sentence or after the subject.

*Would you help prepare the dinner, **please**?*
*Can you **please** arrive at the shelter by noon?*

C You can use *will* and *would* to ask if someone is willing to do something. *Would* is more polite than *will*. Use *would* in formal situations, and use *will* only with people you know well.

***Will** you buy the vegetables?*
***Would** you help us, Professor Rodriguez?*

3.3 Answering Requests to Do Things

A Use *can* and *will* in short answers. Do not use *could* or *would*.

"Could you drive me there?"   *"Yes, I **can**."*
"Yes, I ~~could~~."

"Would you help?"   *"Yes, I **will**."*
"Yes, I ~~would~~."

B In conversation, you can use other expressions, such as *Sure, no problem. / Certainly. / Of course.*

"Will you clean up after dinner, please?"
"Sure, no problem."

Certainly and *Of course* show emphasis. They can also sound more formal.

"Would you please help me with this?" "Certainly."

C You can soften negative responses with an apology and / or a reason.

"Can you help?"
*"**I'm sorry**, I don't have time this week."*

Be careful with negative responses. *No, I won't* and other direct negative responses often sound rude.

~~No, I won't,~~ I don't have time this week.

3.4 Making Offers with *Can, Could, May,* and *Will*

A You can use questions with *can, could,* and *may* to make offers.

Less formal	↑	can
		could
More formal	↓	may

***Can** I help you with dinner?*
***Could** I help you clean up after dinner?*
***May** I help you with that?*

B You can also use statements with *I'll*, *We'll*, *I can*, and *We can* to make offers.	*I'll cook* the turkey this year. *We'll make* dinner tonight. *I can drive* you to the shelter. *We can prepare* the vegetables.

3.5 Responding to Offers

A You can say *Thank you* or *No, thank you* to respond to an offer. *Thanks* and *No, thanks* are less formal.	"I can give you a ride." "Thank you." / "Thanks." "Could I help you with that?" "No, thank you."
You can also respond with *That would be great* or *OK*.	"I'll cook the turkey this year." "That would be great." / "OK, thank you."
B You can respond *Yes, please* or *That would be great* to an offer that is a question.	"Can I make the vegetables?" "Yes, please."

Grammar Application

Exercise 3.1 *Can*, *Could*, *Will*, and *Would*: Requests and Answers

A You need your co-workers' help to plan a charity raffle (an event where everyone who donates to the charity has a chance to win a prize). Use the words to write requests with *please*.

1 could/buy snacks and drinks *Could you please buy snacks and drinks? / Could you buy snacks and drinks, please?*

2 would/set up tables

3 can/sell raffle tickets

4 will/buy prizes for the raffle

5 would/decorate the room

6 could / serve snacks and drinks

7 will / give a speech about the charity

8 would / everyone / help clean up after the party

B Pair Work Take turns asking and answering the requests in A.

A *Could you please buy snacks and drinks?*
B *Yes, of course. / I'm sorry. I don't have time to do that, but I can …*

A It is the evening of the charity raffle. Listen. Complete the offers. Listen again. Complete the responses.

1 **A** Hi, Tony. ___*I'll drive*___ to the raffle tonight. OK?

  B Oh, that would be great. Thanks.

2 **A** Sarah, _________________________ carry those bags.

  B _________________________ . They're really heavy.

3 **A** _________________________ move those tables, Mr. Lee?

  B _________________________ . I just finished.

4 **A** _________________________ the snacks and drinks out now?

  B _________________________

5 **A** Jordy, _________________________ you take tickets.

  B _________________________

6 **A** Ms. Moncur, _________________________ with the decorations?

  B _________________________

7 **A** Oh, no!

  B _________________________

  A _________________________

8 **A** _________________________ that for you, Paula?

  B _________________________

B Which two conversations are the most formal?

_________________________   _________________________

DATA FROM THE REAL WORLD

Research shows people also use *Do you want to* to make requests. These requests sound less direct.

Do you want to help me with the dishes?

Do you want to drive now?

A Pair Work You and a partner are organizing a project for a good cause. Choose one of the projects below or use your own idea. Make a list of six to eight things you need to do.

- clean up a local park
- organize a party at a children's hospital
- organize a party at a senior center
- raise money for charity

B Pair Work Take turns. Offer to do jobs on your list from A. Write your name or your partner's name under the jobs you each offer to do.

C Group Work Work with another pair. Take turns making and responding to requests for help with your project. Ask questions with *can*, *could*, and *Do you want to . . . ?*

4 Avoid Common Mistakes ⚠ 

1 Use the base form of the verb after *can*, *could*, *may*, *will*, or *would*.

Could Lin ~~to~~ ride with you tomorrow?

2 Use *please* in a request at the end of the sentence or after the subject.

       please   *party, please*

Can ~~please~~ I ˄ride with you to the party? **or** Can ~~please~~ I ride with you to the ~~party~~ ?

3 Don't use *could* in short answers to requests for permission.

                                          can

"Could I use your phone, please?" "Yes, you ~~could~~."

4 Don't use *could* or would to respond to requests to do things.

                                          will

"Would you carry this bag for me?" "Yes, I ~~would~~."

Editing Task

Find and correct six more mistakes in the e-mail messages.

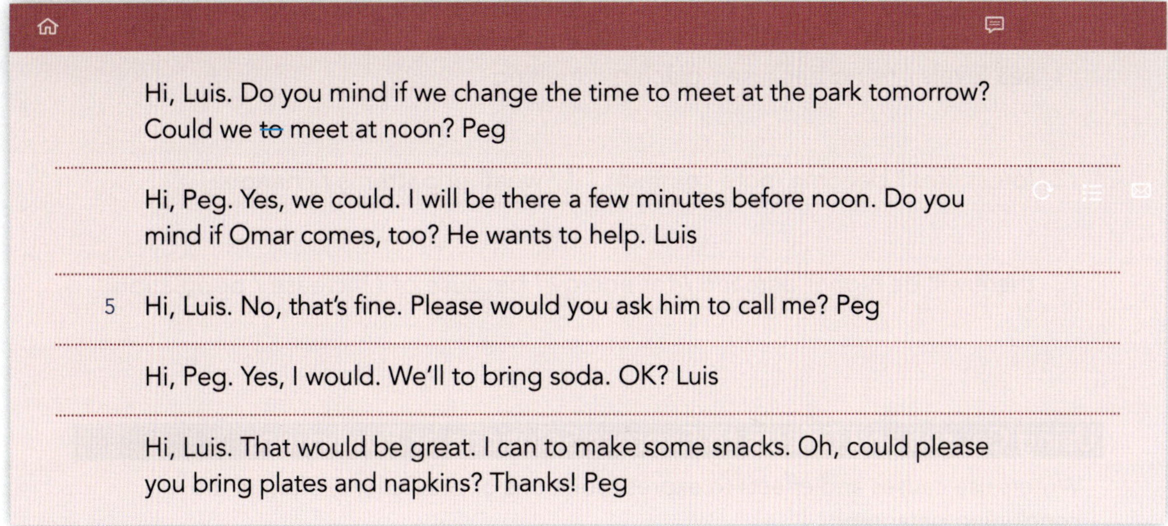

Hi, Luis. Do you mind if we change the time to meet at the park tomorrow? Could we ~~to~~ meet at noon? Peg

Hi, Peg. Yes, we could. I will be there a few minutes before noon. Do you mind if Omar comes, too? He wants to help. Luis

5   Hi, Luis. No, that's fine. Please would you ask him to call me? Peg

Hi, Peg. Yes, I would. We'll to bring soda. OK? Luis

Hi, Luis. That would be great. I can to make some snacks. Oh, could please you bring plates and napkins? Thanks! Peg

5 Academic Writing

Cause-and-Effect Writing

Brainstorm > Organize > Write > Edit

In Unit 19, you looked at the organization and language of a cause-and-effect essay and brainstormed ideas to answer the prompt below. In this unit (20), you are going to learn more ways to describe causes and effects, and begin organizing your ideas.

Describe the human causes of climate change and the effects climate change can have on the planet.

Describing Causes and Effects

Writers use *because-* and *if-* clauses to introduce causes and to show cause-and-effect relationships. The cause can come before or after the effect in a sentence.

Effect	Cause
Modern airplanes use less fuel	**because** they are made from lighter materials.

Cause	Effect
If this new technology is successful,	we may be able to clean our oceans.

Because of can also introduce a cause. However, it is followed by a noun or noun phrase, not a clause.
Some animals will not be able to survive **because of** higher temperatures.

Exercise 5.1 Applying the Skill

Make sentences that show cause-and-effect relationships. Add words as necessary.

1 sea levels / rising because / glaciers / melting

____

2 forest fires / become more common / if / weather patterns / change

____

3 there will be higher demand / for energy / because of / increase / population

____

Using Causes and Effects to Express Solutions or Predictions

Writers use causes and effects to express solutions or predictions, often in the concluding paragraph.
If we reduce the pollution in neighborhoods near airports, → residents in those areas will have healthier lives.

Exercise 5.2 Applying the Skill

Reread the concluding paragraph of the essay on deforestation on page 257. Then complete the tasks with a partner.

> In conclusion, damage to the world's forests is leading to changes in the natural environment and causing global warming. Looking to the future, governments should plant more trees that will absorb carbon dioxide and protect forests from illegal logging while they are still able to make a difference. Otherwise, deforestation on such a large scale will have terrible effects on the environment and our future.

1 Underline the solution the writer proposes.
2 Circle or highlight the writer's prediction.

My Writing

Making Requests in Academic Writing

Making requests and offers are not common in academic writing. They are normally used in spoken English or in emails. When writers make requests to professionals like professors or government officials, they use more formal language. For example:

Dear Mayor Thompson,

Our local environmental group is concerned about air pollution from buses picking up and dropping off students at schools. This is not good for our children's health. If the school district changes to electric buses, the air will be cleaner. As a result, our children will breathe cleaner air and be healthier.

Could we present our idea to the City Council? **Would you support** us? I'm afraid we can't do this alone.

Sincerely,
Lori Mishel, Moms for Clean Air

Exercise 5.3 Applying the Skill

Work in a small group, and complete the tasks.

1 Review your work in My Writing in Unit 19.
2 Brainstorm any additional causes and effects of climate change you can think of.
3 Brainstorm three possible solutions for the problem of climate change.
4 Discuss the positive effects of each solution.
5 Choose one of the solutions. Write an email to a government official. Present the solution and ask for help or support from that person. Include the cause and its positive effects.

1 Grammar in the Real World

A What are some important things to think about when you plan your career or look for a job? Read the article on advice for people looking for jobs. Which suggestion do you think is the most useful?

B Comprehension Check Circle the correct words.

1 Everyone wants **the same things / different things** from a job.

2 Looking at your personal relationships **can / cannot** help you learn more about how you relate to co-workers.

3 It is **easy / difficult** to make changes after you have started a new job.

4 **Everyone / Not everyone** uses common sense when they look for a job.

C Notice Find the sentences in the article and complete them.

1 According to experts, you _________________ think about these things.

2 You _________________ ask yourself exactly what you want from a job.

3 You _________________ also call the company.

In these sentences, do *ought* to and *should* show advice or show ability? Does *could* show ability or make a suggestion?

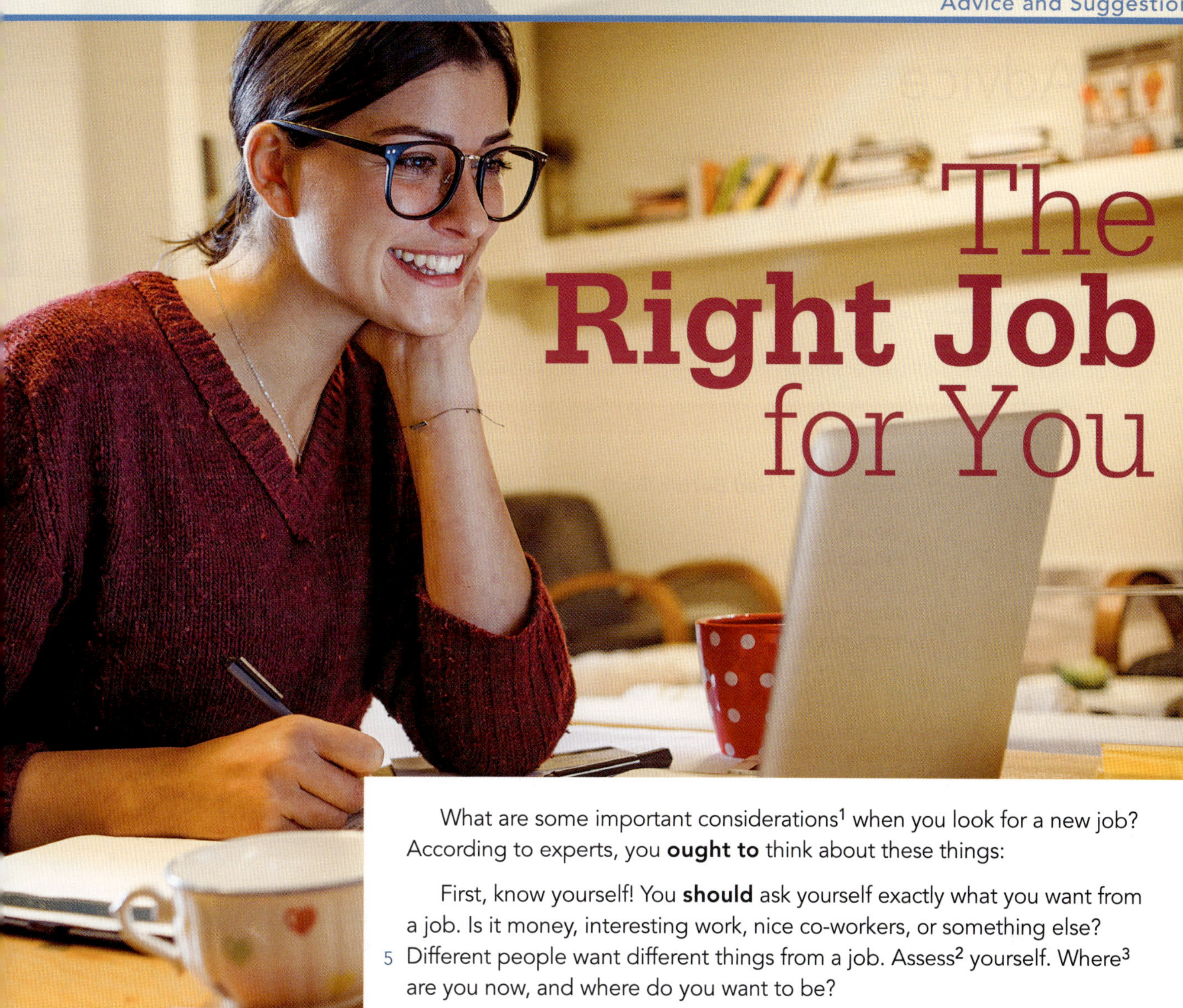

The Right Job for You

What are some important considerations[1] when you look for a new job? According to experts, you **ought to** think about these things:

First, know yourself! You **should** ask yourself exactly what you want from a job. Is it money, interesting work, nice co-workers, or something else?
5 Different people want different things from a job. Assess[2] yourself. Where[3] are you now, and where do you want to be?

You also **might want to** think about your personal relationships. Consider which relationships are going well, which ones are not, and, most importantly, why. This will help you understand how you relate to people you
10 work with.

Make changes! If you had problems in another job (maybe you were always late, or you did not finish projects), then you **should** make changes before you take a new job. It is too late when you are in the job.

Decide what you don't want! If you just want a nine-to-five[4] job, you **had**
15 **better not** work for a company that expects you to be on call 24-7.[5]

If you have an interview, prepare! You **should** find out about an employer's business before your interview. Study the company's website. You **could** also call the company. Ask to speak with someone about the job.

Of course, many of these ideas are common sense,[6] but a lot of people
20 just don't think about them. As a result, they are very unhappy in their jobs.

[1]**consideration:** something to think about when making decisions

[2]**assess:** judge or decide about

[3]**where:** in what situation

[4]**nine-to-five:** 9:00 a.m. to 5:00 p.m., a typical workday

[5]**24-7:** twenty-four hours a day, seven days a week, all the time

[6]**common sense:** the ability to use good judgment in making decisions and to live in a safe way

2 Advice

Grammar Presentation

Should, ought to, and *had better* are often used to give advice.	You **should** ask yourself exactly what you want from a job. You **had better** make changes before you take a new job.

2.1 Statements

Subject	Modal Verb / *Had Better (Not)*	Base Form of Verb	
I You He / She / It We They	**should shouldn't / should not ought to ought not to had better (not) 'd better (not)**	make	changes.

2.2 Yes / No Questions and Responses

Should	Subject	Base Form of Verb		Responses	
Should	I you he / she / it we they	take	a different job?	Yes, you **should**. Yes, she **should**.	No, you **shouldn't**. No, she **shouldn't**.

2.3 Information Questions

Wh- Word	Should	Subject	Base Form of Verb
When Who	should	I you he / she / it we they	call?

Wh- Word	Should	Base Form of Verb	
What Who	should	come	next?

2.4 Using *Should, Ought to,* and *Had Better* for Advice

A	Use *should* and *ought to* for general advice.	You **should** assess yourself before you look for a job. *She* **ought to** look for a new job.
B	Use *had better (not)* only for very strong advice and warnings. *Had better (not)* is much stronger than *should* or *ought to.* It suggests that something negative will happen if you don't take the advice. We usually only use it in speaking.	You **had better** finish this project, or you might lose *your job!*
C	Use *should* in questions. *Ought to* and *had better* are not common in questions.	**Should** I ask about the salary at the interview?
D	Use *maybe, perhaps,* or *I think* to soften advice. These expressions usually go at the beginning of the sentence.	**Maybe** you should be more careful when you write *your résumé.* **I think** he ought to look for a different job.
E	You can also use *probably* to soften advice. It can go before or after *should.* It goes before *ought to.*	She **probably** should take the job. / She should **probably** take the job. She **probably** ought to take the job. She ~~ought to probably~~ take the job.

🌐 *Should not* is much more common than *ought not to.* You can use *should not* in both speaking and writing.

DATA FROM THE REAL WORLD

Research shows that people often make advice stronger by adding *really.*

Really can go before or after *should/shouldn't.* When *really* goes before *should/shouldn't,* it is stronger.	You should **really** get advice from a career adviser. You **really** shouldn't quit your job before you've found another one.
Really goes before *ought to* and *had better.*	You **really** had better try to keep your current job. You **really** ought to update your résumé. You ~~ought to really~~ update your résumé.

Grammar Application

Exercise 2.1 Statements

Unscramble the words and add *you* to write sentences that give advice. Sometimes more than one answer is possible.

1 decide what you want from a job / should / really / .

You really should decide what you want from a job. / You should really decide what you want from a job.

2 had better / think about the hours you prefer / really / .

____

3 ought to / decide if you want to be on call 24-7 / perhaps / .

____

4 maybe / look for job advertisements online / should / .

____

5 tell your family about your plans / ought to / probably / .

____

6 really / shouldn't / get discouraged / .

____

7 should / ask for advice from a career counselor / I think / .

____

8 really / take a job you don't like / had better not / !

____

Exercise 2.2 Asking for and Giving Advice

A Complete the requests for job advice from an online forum. Add *should*. Sometimes you also need to add a *Wh-* word.

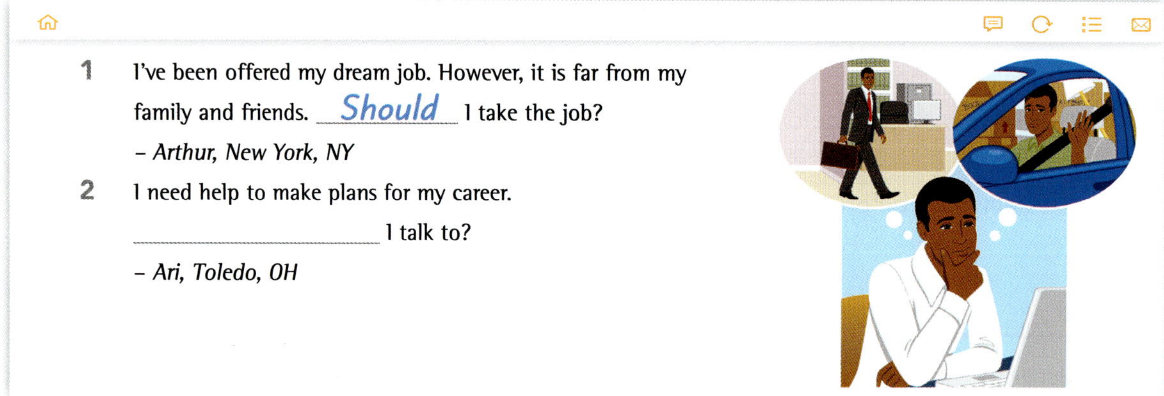

1 I've been offered my dream job. However, it is far from my family and friends. ___*Should*___ I take the job?

– *Arthur, New York, NY*

2 I need help to make plans for my career. ________________ I talk to?

– *Ari, Toledo, OH*

3   I've been looking for a job for several months. I finally have an offer, but it's not the perfect job for me.
    However, I really need money. _________________________ I take the job?
    – Camilla, San Francisco, CA

4   I absolutely hate my job! I want to look for another one, but I have lots of student loans.
    _________________________ I do?
    – Samuel, Miami, FL

5   I would like to change careers, but I don't have experience in the career I like. My friend told me to
    do volunteer work to get experience. _________________________ I do this?
    – Eleni, Austin, TX

6   I'm almost finished with school and I don't know what kind of job I want. _________________________ I do?
    – Katya, Denver, CO

7   My parents think money is the most important thing in a job. I want to look for a job that makes
    me happy. _________________________ I listen to my parents?
    – Helen, Seattle, WA

B Pair Work **Discuss the situations in A with a partner. What do you think each person
should do? Compare your answers.**

A *I think Arthur ought to talk to his family about his decision.*

B *I think he should just take the job. It's his dream job.*

C Listen to a career counselor give advice for each situation. Write the advice you hear.

1 Arthur *had better not take* the job and move.

2 Ari _________________________ to a career counselor.

3 _________________ Camilla _________________________ the job.

4 _________________ Samuel _________________________ for
   another job.

5 Yes, Eleni _________________________ some
   volunteer work.

6 Katya _________________________ talking to people.

7 _________________ Terry _________________________ looking
   for another job. It doesn't sound good, but he
   _________________________ to his boss, too.

8 Helen _________________________ what makes her happy.

A Write two to four questions asking for advice about jobs/work or school.

B Pair Work Exchange your questions from A with a partner. Write responses to your partner's requests for advice. Then read and compare the advice. Do you agree with the advice? Why or why not?

A *I need to find a part-time job. Where should I look?*

B *I think you should ask at the school cafeteria. They often need help there.*

3 Suggestions

Grammar Presentation

Might (want to), could, why don't / doesn't, and *why not* are often used to make suggestions. Suggestions are not as strong as advice.

You **might want to** schedule your interview in the afternoon.

Why don't you prepare questions for the interview?

3.1 Suggestions with *Might Want To* and *Could*

Subject	Modal Verb	Base Form of Verb	
I You He/She/It We They	**might want to** **might not want to** **could**	call	the company.

3.2 Suggestions with *Why Don't/Doesn't . . . ?*

Why Don't/Doesn't	Subject	Base Form of Verb
Why don't	I you we they	ask?
Why doesn't	he/she/it	

3.3 Suggestions with *Why Not . . . ?*

Why Not	Base Form of Verb	
Why not	buy	a new suit for the interview?

3.4 Making Suggestions

A Use *might (want to)* and *could* to make suggestions. They often express a choice of possible actions.	You **might** schedule your interview in the morning, or you **could** wait until the afternoon.	
Might is often used with *want to*.	You **might want to** think about volunteer work. You **might not want to** ask that question in an interview.	
Do not use *could not* in negative suggestions. Use *might not want to*.	You ~~could not~~ ask that question in an interview.	
B *Why not* and *Why don't / doesn't* are both question forms and end with a question mark.	**Why don't you** prepare questions for your interview? **Why not** prepare questions for your interview?	
🌐 *Why don't / doesn't* and *Why not* are very common in conversation. Do not use them in academic writing.	Say: "**Why don't** you practice for your interview?" Write: Interviewees **might want to** practice for their interviews.	

Complete the conversations. Circle the correct words.

1 **A** I sent my résumé in for a job a few weeks ago, but I haven't had any response.

   B *You could* / Why don't you call the company.

2 **A** I have an interview next week, and I'm worried about getting there on time. Traffic is so bad.

   B **You might / Why not** schedule the interview for the middle of the day, when traffic isn't as bad?

3 **A** I can't find a job in my field. I really need some work, any work!

   B You **why not / might want to** look for temporary work. That's often easier to find.

4 **A** I have an interview tomorrow, but I don't know a lot about the company.

   B **You might want to / Why don't you** do some research online. I'll help you.

5 **A** I'm nervous about my interview on Monday. I don't know what they'll ask me.

   B Well, **we could / why not** practice together. I can ask you questions.

6 **A** I'm going to dress casually for my interview tomorrow. It's a very informal company.

   B You **could not / might not want to** dress too casually. It's still a job interview.

7 **A** I have to drive to my interview tomorrow, and I always get lost when I drive.

   B **You might want to / Why don't you** print out directions or use a GPS.

8 **A** I just had a good interview, and I'm really interested in the job.

   B **Why don't / Why not** you follow up with a thank-you note? It's always a good idea.

A Pair Work   Read about Alex. He has a job interview in a few days. Write three more suggestions for him. Then compare answers with a partner.

You could go to bed early.

B Pair Work Tell a partner what you worry about in job interviews. Give each other suggestions.

A *I worry about the questions they might ask.*
B *You might want to research the job and the company. Maybe that will help you.*

4 Avoid Common Mistakes ⚠ 

1 **Do not forget *had* or *'d* when you write *had better*.**

had
You ∧ better start looking for another job.

2 **Use *had better (not)* only for very strong advice and warnings.**

should
At an interview, you ~~had better~~ speak clearly and look interested in the questions.

3 **Do not use *could not* in negative suggestions. Use *might not want to*.**

might not want to
You ~~could not~~ wear jeans for the interview.

4 **Do not use an *-ing* form or a *to-* infinitive after *Why not*.**

go
Why not ~~going~~ to a career adviser?
Why not ~~to~~ leave at 6:00 a.m.?

Editing Task

Find and correct five more mistakes in the conversation.

Jordan There are a lot of changes happening at my company. I'm worried I might lose my job.

Isabela Well, you ∧*had* better probably start looking for something else.

Jordan I guess so.

5 Isabela At the same time, you better try to keep your current job. They say it's a lot harder to find a new job when you're unemployed.

Jordan Is there anything I can do?

Isabela Yes, there's a lot you can do. First, why not to talk to

10 your boss? You get along well, right? Why not asking for feedback on your work? Then, you probably ought to tell your boss you're working on those things. You might want to keep in touch with her by e-mail.

Jordan OK. What else?

15 Isabela Well, do extra work. You ought to take on extra tasks whenever you can. And you could not complain about anything.

Jordan That makes sense. Thanks, Isabela. I'd better ask you for advice more often!

5 Academic Writing

Cause-and-Effect Writing

Brainstorm > Organize > Write > Edit

In Unit 20, you looked at more ways to describe causes and effects and continued brainstorming ideas for the prompt below. In this unit (21), you are going to focus on paragraph coherence and supporting details to strengthen your writing.

Describe the human causes of climate change and the effects climate change can have on the planet.

Maintaining Paragraph Coherence

A well-written paragraph has just one main idea. All sentences in the paragraph should explain or give information about the main idea. They should not include any unrelated ideas. Any sentences that are not about the main idea should be deleted or moved to a different paragraph in the essay. When a paragraph has these characteristics, it is coherent. Paragraph coherence is essential to good academic writing.

Exercise 5.1 Applying the Skill

Read the paragraph and complete the tasks.

The fight against climate change has affected the job market for college graduates outside traditional careers in science or engineering. For example, college graduates with teaching degrees can now find work training people and companies about how their behavior affects climate change. In my opinion, teachers should be comfortable talking with groups of all ages. There are also new job opportunities for journalism students. The *New York Times*, for instance, has had employees who specialize in climate change since 2017. In 2018, the *New York Times* won an award for its environmental journalism. Finally, business majors can apply for positions that help companies adapt to climate change by making environmentally friendly products and services. Clearly, "green" jobs are no longer just for graduates with science degrees.

1 Underline the main idea.
2 Cross out two sentences that do not support the main idea. Explain your reasons to a partner.

Choosing Strong Supporting Details

Good writers use strong supporting sentences to develop and explain the main idea of a paragraph. These sentences state important points about the main idea. Often, writers provide details such as *facts*, *examples*, *reasons*, and *explanations* for each supporting sentence.

Look at an annotated version of the first body paragraph of "The Causes and Effects of Deforestation" in Unit 19. Notice the kinds of details that are included.

Topic sentence: The main causes of deforestation are commercial and local farming.

1st supporting sentence: Huge commercial farms have taken over large areas of forest in many countries.

Details (examples): In Indonesia, for example, industrial logging is carried out to clear huge areas for the production of palm oil, while in Brazil, large areas of the Amazon Rainforest are cleared to grow soybeans and vegetables for cooking oil.

2nd supporting sentence: At the same time, local farmers may cut down and burn trees to clear an area just big enough to graze cattle or grow crops.

Details (facts / explanation): However, after two or three years, the land can no longer be used, so the farmer moves to another piece of land. In both cases, it can take ten years for cleared land to recover, but in populated areas the land is often unable to recover at all.

Details (reasons): The constant clearing and reuse of land leads to heavy erosion—the loss of the top layer of soil that protects the ground. Erosion, in turn, can cause flooding in heavy rain.

Exercise 5.2 Applying the Skill

Re-read the paragraph in Exercise 5.1 on page 284. Complete the notes below.

Topic sentence: _______________________________________

1st supporting sentence: _______________________________________

Details: _______________________________________

2nd supporting sentence: _______________________________________

Details: _______________________________________

3rd supporting sentence: _______________________________________

Details: _______________________________________

Using Formal Modals for Advice and Suggestions

When writing about effects or solutions, academic writers use more formal modals for advice and suggestions. Use *should* or *ought to* instead of *had better*, *why doesn't*, or *why not*.

Exercise 5.3 Applying the Skill

Edit the sentences. Use more formal modals for advice and suggestions.

1 Why doesn't the government require cars to use less gas?
2 People had better not expect the government to solve this problem alone.
3 Why not start a student environmental action group to find solutions?

My Writing

Exercise 5.4 Organizing Your Writing

Review your list of causes and effects from My Writing in Units 19 and 20. Write a topic sentence, two supporting sentences, and some details for two body paragraphs in your cause-and-effect essay. Use the outline in Exercise 5.2 as an example to organize your writing.

Necessity, Prohibition, and Preference

How to Sell It

1 Grammar in the Real World

A What are three different kinds of advertising you see every day?
Read the article about advertising companies. What are two difficulties
for advertisers?

B Comprehension Check **Answer the questions.**

1 How did people advertise in the past?
2 Why is it difficult for advertisers to appeal to consumers?
3 How many advertisements do people see or hear each day?
4 What must advertisers not do?

C Notice **Find the sentences in the article and complete them.**

1 Companies ___________________ appeal to consumers so they buy their
products.

2 Companies ___________________ not spend a lot of money on it.

3 They ___________________ to save their money.

4 Each one ___________________ be clever.

**Which of these sentences talk about something that is necessary?
Which talk about something that is preferred?**

The Challenges[1] of Advertising[2]

Advertising is not a new idea. Long ago, sellers called out to people on the street. They tried to persuade[3] people to buy their products. Now advertising is everywhere. It is on the street, on the Internet, in magazines, and on phones.

5 Although there are now many ways to advertise, it is not an easy business. There are many challenges. Companies **need to** appeal[4] to consumers so they buy their products. This can be quite difficult because people have so many choices these days. Each advertiser **must** make its choice seem better than all the others.

10 Advertising is also very expensive. Companies **would rather** not spend a lot of money on it. They **would prefer** to save their money. However, to sell their products, companies often **need to** spend large amounts of money on ads. Consumers see or hear up to 3,000 advertising messages each day. Each one **has to** be clever.[5] This means 15 companies **have to** pay to show the ads on TV, online, or in other places, and they also **need to** pay creative people to make them.

There is another challenge for companies when they advertise. Today, there are numerous rules they **must** follow. For example, they **must not** lie. Companies also **need to** be careful when they try to sell 20 products to children.

Advertisers **must** do a number of different things at once. This is not easy, but it is also a big business with big rewards. Just one good advertisement can convince millions of people to buy a product.

[1]**challenge:** something that needs great mental or physical effort to be done well

[2]**advertising:** making something known generally in public, especially in order to sell it

[3]**persuade:** cause someone to do or believe something, especially by explaining why they should

[4]**appeal (to):** be attractive or interesting

[5]**clever:** showing quick intelligence in doing something

Grammar Presentation

Have to, have got to, need to, and *must (not)* are used to say what is necessary, not necessary, or prohibited.

An ad **has to** appeal to consumers. (necessary)

They **do not need to** advertise abroad. (not necessary)

Companies **must** follow rules when they create ads. (necessary)

They **must not** lie in their advertising. (prohibited)

2.1 *Have To, Have Got To*, and *Need To*: Statements

Subject	*Have To / Have Got To / Need To*	Base Form of Verb	
I You We They	**have to / do not have to have got to need to / do not need to**	be buy	clever. advertising.
He / She / It	**has to / doesn't have to has got to needs to / doesn't need to**		

2.2 *Must*: Statements

Subject	Modal Verb	Base Form of Verb	
I You He / She / It We They	**must must not / mustn't**	be buy	clever. advertising.

2.3 *Have To* and *Need To*: Yes / No Questions

Do / Does	Subject	*Have To / Need To*	Base Form of Verb
Do	you	**have to need to**	advertise?
Does	he / she / it		

2.4 *Have To* and *Need To*: Information Questions

Wh- Word	*Do / Does*	Subject	*Have To / Need To*	Base Form of Verb
When Why Where	do	you	**have to need to**	advertise?
	does	he / she / it		

2.4 *Have To* and *Need To*: Information Questions (*continued*)

Wh- Word	*Have To / Need To*	Base Form of Verb
Who	**has to** **needs to**	advertise?

2.5 Expressing Necessity and Prohibition

A Use *have to* and *need to* to say something is necessary.	*Advertisers **have to** think about consumers.*
Have to is twice as common as *need to*.	*The company **needs to** be more creative.*
B You can also use *have got to* in affirmative statements. It is usually less formal. The contraction for *has* is *'s*.	*The ad **has got to** appeal to a lot of people.* *It**'s got to** be interesting.*
Have got to is not usually used in negative sentences.	*The ad hasn't got to appeal to children.*
C *Must* is very strong and sounds formal or official. It is often used in writing to state rules or laws and is rare in speaking.	*Advertising companies **must** follow these rules.* *He **must** report this immediately.*
D You can use *don't have to* and *don't need to* to say something is not necessary.	*She **doesn't need to** finish that.*
However, use *must not / mustn't* to express strong prohibition or to forbid something.	*Companies **must not** lie in their advertising.*
Be careful: *have to* and *must* have a similar meaning in the affirmative, but they are very different in negative sentences.	*You **must / have to** use a pen. (A pen is necessary.)* *You **don't have to** use a pen. (A pen is not necessary. You have a choice.)* *You **must not** use a pen. (A pen is prohibited. You have no choice.)*
E Use *have to* and *need to* to ask about necessity. Use a form of *do* in the question and answer.	*"**Do** we **have to** follow this rule?"* *"Yes, we **do**."* *"**Does** this ad **need to** appeal to kids?"* *"No, it **doesn't**."*
🌐 We often use *can't* instead of *must not* to express prohibition, especially in spoken English.	Say: *"You **can't** do that. It's against the rules."* Write: *Drivers **must not** exceed the speed limit.*

Pronunciation Focus: *Have To, Has To, Have Got To*

In informal conversation:	*have to* is often pronounced "hafta." *has to* is often pronounced "hasta." *got to* is often pronounced "gotta."

Grammar Application

A Listen to an advertising manager discuss plans with his employees. Complete the sentences with the verbs you hear.

1 We _**'ve got to**_ do this quickly, so we really _**have to**_ work together.

2 Each team _______________ choose a leader.

3 The leader _______________ organize the team.

4 Then, you'll all _______________ work together to make a plan for the project.

5 I absolutely _______________ have all plans by the end of the week.

6 You really _______________ e-mail a report of your progress to me at the end of each week.

7 The report _______________ be long, but it _______________ explain your progress clearly.

8 You _______________ forget this because I _______________ report to the president every week.

9 We _______________ create some really interesting ads.

10 But remember, we _______________ be honest in all of the ads.

B Which sentence says that something is not necessary? Which sentence says that something is prohibited?

Exercise 2.2 Questions and Answers

Complete the e-mail messages with the correct form of the verbs in parentheses.

<table>
<tr><td>⌂</td><td style="text-align:right">💬 ↻ ☰ ✉</td></tr>
</table>

Hi team,   October 21, 10:00 a.m.

Remember, we are meeting tomorrow to discuss our plan. I _____**need to**_____ (need to) get
                                                                    (1)
your ideas on it. I _______________ (have to) hand the plan in on Friday. Let me know if you have
                         (2)
questions.   – Nick

Nick,   October 21, 10:15 a.m.

_______________ we _______________ (have to) bring specific ideas for ads to the
        (3)   (3)
meeting?   – Blanca

Hi Blanca,   October 21, 10:30 a.m.

No, you _________________ (not need to) have specific ideas. But, we _________________
                (4)   (5)
(must) start brainstorming soon. I _________________ (have to) give Mr. Gomez an update on our
                                              (6)
ideas next week.   – Nick

Dear Nick,   October 21, 10:45 a.m.

I have specific ideas. Is it OK if I start to work on them?   – Jason

---

Hi Jason,   October 21, 11:00 a.m.

It's better to wait. Mr. Gomez _________________ (have to) approve our ideas before we begin
                                        (7)
work on them. He _________________ (need to) put them all together. Bring them tomorrow, and
                          (8)
we can discuss them.   – Nick

Hi Nick,   October 21, 11:15 a.m.

When _________________ Mr. Gomez _________________ (need to) have the ideas? I will
          (9)   (9)
be on vacation for a few days next week. _________________ I _________________ (have to)
                                                  (10)   (10)
finish them before I leave?   – Claire

Dear Claire,   October 21, 11:30 a.m.

Yes, I'm afraid so. We _________________ (have got to) do them quickly.
                              (11)
He _________________ (need to) have them sometime next week.   – Nick
        (12)

Exercise 2.3 More Questions and Answers

A Over to You **Write answers to the questions.**

1 What is one thing you have to do every day?

____

2 What is something you need to do but haven't done yet?

____

3 What is something you do at work or school that you don't have to do?

____

4 What is something that you must do at work or school?

____

5 What is something that you must not do at work or school?

____

B Pair Work **Ask and answer the questions in A with a partner. Try to add extra information.**

A *What is one thing you have to do every day?*

B *I have to take my children to school every day. Their school starts at 7:30,
   so I have to get up at 6:15.*

C Group Work Tell the class about your partner.

Raul has to take his children to school every day. Their school starts at 7:30, so he has to get up at 6:15.

3 Preference

Grammar Presentation

Would rather, *would like to*, and *would prefer* are used to express preferences.	I **would rather not watch** those commercials. They **would like to see** some new and interesting ads. I**'d prefer to turn** the TV off.

3.1 *Would Rather*: Statements

Subject	*Would Rather (Not)*	Base Form of Verb
I You He / She / It We They	**would rather (not)**	advertise.

3.2 *Would Like* and *Would Prefer*: Statements

Subject	*Would (Not) Like / Would Prefer (Not)*	Infinitive
I You He / She / It We They	**would (not) like** **would prefer (not)**	to advertise.

3.3 *Yes / No* Questions

Would	Subject		Infinitive
Would	you	**like** **prefer**	to advertise?

Would	Subject		Base Form of Verb
Would	you	**rather**	advertise?

3.4 Information Questions

Wh- Word	*Would*	Subject		Infinitive
What	would	you	**like** **prefer**	to advertise?

Wh- Word	*Would*		Infinitive
Who	would	**like** **prefer**	to buy this product?

3.4 Information Questions (*continued*)

Wh- Word	Would	Subject	Base Form of Verb
What	**would**	you	**rather** advertise?

Wh- Word	Would		Base Form of Verb
Who	**would**	**rather**	buy this product?

3.5 Expressing Preferences

A You can use *would rather, would like,* and *would prefer* to express preference. *Would prefer* is more formal.

I **would rather** spend a little money on advertising.
I **would prefer** to listen to the radio.

Use *would rather* with a base form of the verb.
Use *would like* and *would prefer* with an infinitive.
The contraction of *would* is '*d.*

I **would rather** see more interesting advertising.

I **would like** / **would prefer** to see more interesting advertising.
I**'d like** to see more interesting advertising.

B In negative sentences, *not* goes between *would* and *like*. It goes after *would prefer* and *would rather*.

He **wouldn't like** to work at that advertising company.
He **would prefer not** to work at that advertising company.
We**'d rather not** watch all the commercials.

C You can use the verb *prefer* without *would*. When used without *would, prefer* takes -s with *he* / *she* / *it*.

She **would prefer to** watch shorter commercials.
She **prefers** to watch shorter commercials.
She ~~prefer~~ to watch shorter commercials.

D *Would prefer* and *prefer* can be followed by a noun, an infinitive, or a verb + *-ing*.

He prefers / would prefer **a TV channel** without ads.
He prefers / would prefer **to watch** TV without commercials.
He prefers / would prefer **watching** TV without commercials.

E Use *or* in questions about preference to offer a choice. The verb after *or* is usually in the base form.

Would you like to go out **or** (to) stay home?
Would you rather go out **or** stay home?

F You can use *I'd rather not* to respond to suggestions or requests.

A We could go out tonight.
B **I'd rather not.** I'm tired.

G You can make a comparison with *would rather* and *than*. If there is a verb after *than*, it is also in the base form.

I**'d rather see** one long ad **than** a few short ones.
I**'d rather see** ads on the Internet **than watch** them on TV.

Grammar Application

Complete the conversation between two colleagues at an advertising agency. Use the correct form and the correct order of the words in parentheses. Add words if necessary.

A Let's discuss the ad for the new music player. What do you think? What _____*would*_____ (1)
consumers _____*like to see*_____ (1) (would like / see)?

B Well, we need to give some detail about the size, weight, memory – things like that. Not too much, though. People ________________ (2) (not / would rather / get)
all the details in an ad. I think a consumer usually ________________ (3) (prefer / get) a general idea and then research it more if they're interested.

A OK, good point. ________________ (4) they ________________ (4) (would rather / see) an ad that's more informative or one that's more fun?

B Well, I ________________ (5) (not / would like / see) an ad that's just informative.
I ________________ (6) (would rather / see) one that's really fun than one that's really informative. That seems a little boring.

A OK, but I think we need to do both – entertain and inform.

B True. Now, what do you think? ________________ (7) people ________________ (7) (would prefer / see) a man or a woman in the ad?

A Let's include both.

B I ________________ (8) (not / would rather). It costs a lot to hire two actors.

A Both men and women buy music players.
I ________________ (9) (would prefer / hire) both. I think it's worth the cost.

B Let's think about that. This is a good start. We can discuss all of this tomorrow.

Unscramble the words to make questions.

1 see a lot of ads on TV / would / rather / not / you / ?
   Would you rather not see a lot of ads on TV?

2 prefer / e-mail ads / you / advertising by mail / do / or / ?

____

3 a lot of ads before you buy things / to see / like / would / you / ?

____

4 you / to watch TV / prefer / without commercials / would / ?

____

5 not / have advertising / would / you / online / rather / ?

____

6 ads on the radio / you / ads on TV / do / prefer / or / ?

7 more informative ads or more funny ads / you / like / to see / would / ?

8 not / rather / would / any advertising at all / you / have / ?

4 Avoid Common Mistakes ⚠ 

1 Use *don't have to* or *don't need to* to say something is not necessary, not *must not*.

    don't need to
You ~~must not~~ take notes. I'll give you a copy at the end of the meeting.

2 Do not use an infinitive with *would rather*. Use an infinitive with *would like* and *(would) prefer*.

We would rather ~~to~~ use this idea for the ad.

3 Use *would* before *rather*.

    would
I∧rather not start work at 7 o'clock.

Editing Task

Find and correct seven more mistakes in the e-mail messages.

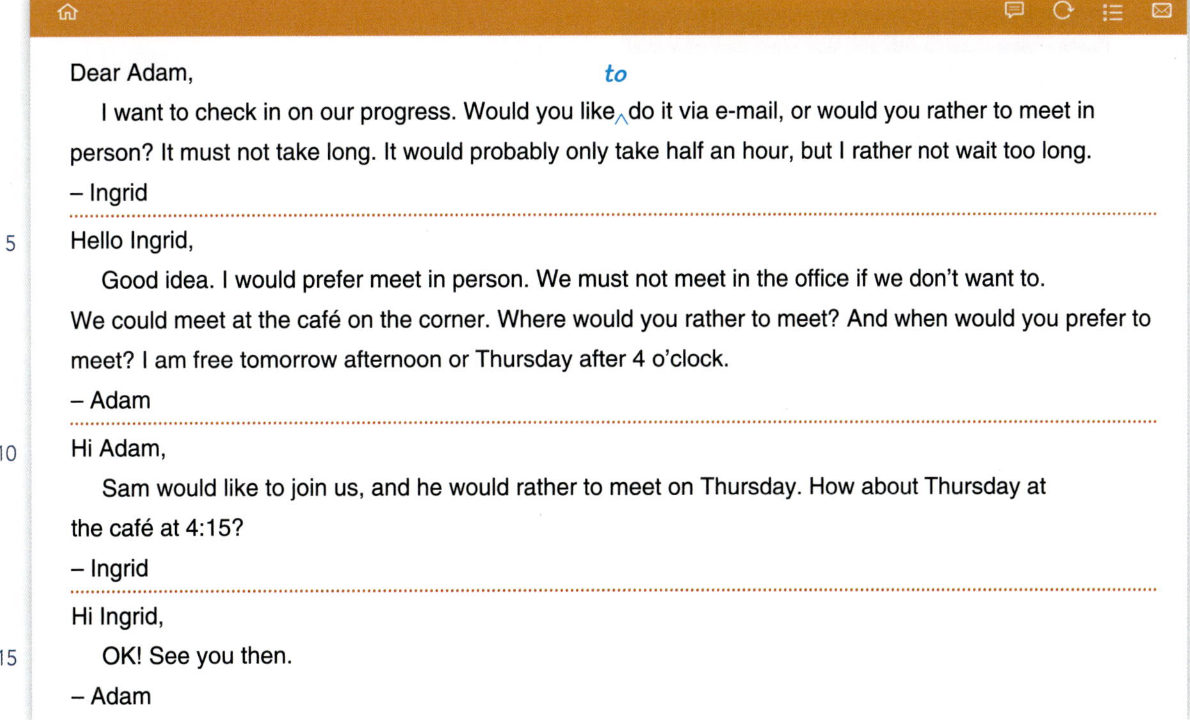

Dear Adam,

    I want to check in on our progress. Would you like *to* ∧do it via e-mail, or would you rather to meet in person? It must not take long. It would probably only take half an hour, but I rather not wait too long.

– Ingrid

5   Hello Ingrid,

    Good idea. I would prefer meet in person. We must not meet in the office if we don't want to. We could meet at the café on the corner. Where would you rather to meet? And when would you prefer to meet? I am free tomorrow afternoon or Thursday after 4 o'clock.

– Adam

10 Hi Adam,

    Sam would like to join us, and he would rather to meet on Thursday. How about Thursday at the café at 4:15?

– Ingrid

Hi Ingrid,

15   OK! See you then.

– Adam

5 Academic Writing

Cause-and-Effect Writing

Brainstorm > Organize > Write > Edit

In Unit 21, you looked at coherence and the importance of adding appropriate supporting details to strengthen your writing. In this unit (22), you are going to organize and write the first draft of your essay to answer the prompt below.

> *Describe the human causes of climate change and the effects climate change can have on the planet.*

Writing an Effective Hook

Many writers start an essay with a **hook**. Think of it as catching a reader, like catching a fish. When the hook is interesting or humorous, people want to keep reading. Writers often use amazing facts and statistics, quotations, or questions the reader would relate to. Most importantly the hook must be related to the topic of the essay.

Interesting fact: Worldwide, one third of the world's food -1.3 billion tons- is thrown away every year.

Relevant quotation: Steve Jobs once said, "The only way to do great work is to love what you do."

Relatable question: Do you drink from plastic bottles? If you do, you might want to think about changing your habit.

Exercise 5.1 Understanding the Skill

Work with a partner. Read and evaluate each hook to begin an essay about the effects of advertising. Choose the three best hooks. Explain your reasons.

1 Everywhere you look you see advertisements.
2 Are you influenced by television ads? You don't think so?
3 Young Spotify listeners don't mind advertising if the music is free, unlike their parents who will pay the subscription fee to avoid ads.
4 There should not be advertisements about cigarettes or alcohol on TV.
5 "Advertising is the art of convincing people to spend money they don't have for something they don't need." -Will Rogers

Exercise 5.2 Applying the Skill

Write a hook to introduce an essay about the effects of advertising.

____

____

Using Modals of Necessity and Prohibition

Academic writers often use modals of necessity and prohibition: *must, must not, need to, should*. Some words are more common in spoken language and are less formal, such as *have got to, can't*, and *had better*. Do not use less formal modals in academic writing.

Exercise 5.3 Applying the Skill

Work with a partner. Choose the sentences that are acceptable in academic writing. Discuss your reasons for your choices.

- ☐ **1** Television stations must limit the number of minutes of advertising during children's programs.
- ☐ **2** Advertisers had better not use bad language in television advertisements.
- ☐ **3** The volume of advertisements on TV can't be louder than the regular program.
- ☐ **4** In political ads, they have to say the name of the sponsor or group that paid for the ad.

My Writing

Exercise 5.4 Writing Your First Draft

Follow the steps to write the first draft of your cause-and-effect essay.

1 Write the introductory paragraph. Include a hook, background information, and a thesis statement.

2 Write about the human causes of climate change in your first body paragraph. Include a topic sentence, supporting sentences, and specific details.

3 Write about the effects of climate change in your second body paragraph. Include a topic sentence, supporting sentences, and specific details.

4 Write a concluding paragraph. Summarize your main ideas and offer at least one solution or recommendation.

Present and Future Probability

Life Today, Life Tomorrow

1 Grammar in the Real World

A What is one way you think society will be different in the future? Read the article about trends in the United States. What is happening in the United States now? What might happen in the future?

B Comprehension Check **Answer the questions.**

1 What are two possible reasons for the decline in the yearly birthrate?
2 How much does it cost to raise a child in the United States?
3 What is one possible positive result of the change in the birthrate?
4 What is one possible negative result of this change?

C Notice **Find the sentences in the article and complete them.**

1 The economy ___________________ also affect birthrates.

2 Even small changes in the economy ___________________ increase this cost.

3 For example, cities ___________________ become less crowded.

4 There ___________________ be fewer people in the workforce.

Do these sentences describe something that is certain or uncertain? Are *could* and *might* used to talk about the present, the future, or both?

The UNITED STATES of TOMORROW

[1] **trend:** direction of changes or developments

[2] **decline:** a decrease in amount or quality

[3] **yearly birthrate:** a measure of how many children are born each year

[4] **predict:** say that an event will happen in the future

Which current trends[1] are likely to affect us most? Which trends **might** be important for society in the future? One trend that **could** be important in the United States is a decline[2] in the yearly birthrate.[3]

5 The birthrate has been going down for several years. Why is this happening? According to experts, there **may** be more than one reason for this change. Women **might** be choosing to have fewer children because more women now have careers. The economy **might** also
10 affect birthrates. Today, it costs more than $300,000 to raise a child from birth to age 17. Even small changes in the economy **could** increase this cost. As a result, couples **may** worry about having children during unsure economic times.

15 How **could** a lower birthrate today affect U.S. society in the future? This is not completely clear. Some effects **could** be positive. For example, cities **could** become less crowded, and there **may** be less pollution. However, other effects **could** be negative. There **might** be fewer
20 people in the workforce. This **could** cause economic difficulties. In addition, as people age, there **could** be fewer doctors and other health professionals to care for them. This **could** cause a decline in the general health of the population.

25 No one can predict[4] exactly what society will be like in the future. However, when experts study trends like the yearly birthrate, they can learn important facts to help us plan for a better tomorrow.

2 Present Probability

Grammar Presentation

The modals *can't, cannot, could (not), may (not), might (not), must (not),* and *should (not)* talk about probability in the present. These modals express how certain you are that something is true.

This **could** be because more women now have careers.

The economy **might** also affect birthrates.

2.1 Affirmative Statements

Subject	Modal Verb	Base Form of Verb	
I You He / She / It We They	**must** **should** **may** **might** **could**	be	important.

2.2 Negative Statements

Subject	Modal Verb	Base Form of Verb	
I You He / She / It We They	**must not / mustn't** **could not / couldn't** **cannot / can't** **should not / shouldn't** **may not** **might not**	be	important.

2.3 Expressing Present Probability

Certain ↑

A When you are **certain** that something is true in the present, you do not need a modal. Use a present form.

The birthrate this year **is** not the same as last year.

The birthrate **is declining**.

Almost Certain

B Use *must (not)* to draw a conclusion about the present, often because you have evidence. You are **almost certain** about your conclusion.

She **must not live** nearby. She never walks to work.

Do not use the contraction *mustn't* in this case.

She ~~**mustn't**~~ live nearby. She never walks to work.

2.3 Expressing Present Probability *(continued)*

Fairly Certain	**C** Use *could not*, *couldn't*, *cannot*, or *can't* when you are **almost certain** that something is impossible. These modals usually express strong disbelief or surprise. We usually use *can't* or *couldn't*.	The birthrate statistics **can't be** right. They look completely wrong. They **couldn't be** at home. They left for vacation yesterday.
	D Use *should*, *should not*, or *shouldn't* when you are **fairly certain** that something is true, often because you have evidence. We often use *shouldn't*.	They **should be** at work. They usually are at this time of the day. They **shouldn't be** at work. It's Saturday.
Not Certain	**E** Use *may (not)*, *might (not)*, or *could* when you are **not certain** that something is true. You are uncertain, but you are making an "educated guess."	The economy **may (not) be** the reason for the declining birthrate. Experts are not sure.
	Do not use *mightn't*. It is very rare.	The economy **might not be** the reason for the declining birthrate. The economy ~~mightn't~~ be the reason for the declining birthrate. Experts are not sure.
	F *Can* is not usually used for present probability. Use *may*, *might*, or *could*.	They ~~can~~ be related. They look similar. They **might be** related. They look similar.

2.4 Answers to Questions About the Present

A You can use modals of present probability to answer questions about the present. Use them when you are not 100 percent sure about your answer.	*"Where are they?"* *"They* **might be** *at home."* *"What does this information mean?"* *"It* **could mean** *society is changing."*
B In short answers to *Yes/No* questions, you can use the modal alone.	*"Do they know about this?"* *"They* **must**.*"*
C If *be* is the main verb in *Yes/No* questions, use the modal + *be* in short answers.	*"Are they correct?"* *"They* **must be**.*"*

Grammar Application

A Listen to the conversation about a trend for young adults. Complete the sentences you hear.

1 The economy _____*must*_____ be part of the reason.
2 It ______________ be easy if you have a lot of debt and college loans.
3 And it ______________ be hard for young people to find a good job these days.
4 Yes, but there ______________ be other reasons, too.
5 They ______________ be able to afford an apartment.
6 It ______________ be better financially for them to live at home.
7 It ______________ always be easy for them.
8 Maybe, but it ______________ be nice, too.
9 Some parents ______________ like to have their children around as they get older.
10 I guess it ______________ depend on the family.
11 Of course. It ______________ .

B Listen again. How certain are the speakers about each statement? Check (✓) the correct box.

	Not Certain	Almost Certain
1 The economy is part of the reason young adults move back home.	☐	✓
2 It isn't easy if you have a lot of debt and college loans.	☐	☐
3 It is hard for young people to find a good job these days.	☐	☐
4 There are other reasons students move home.	☐	☐
5 Students can't afford apartments.	☐	☐
6 It is better financially for them to live at home.	☐	☐
7 It isn't always easy for parents.	☐	☐
8 It is nice when children return home, too.	☐	☐
9 Some parents like to have their children around as they get older.	☐	☐
10 It depends on the family. (female speaker)	☐	☐
11 It depends on the family. (male speaker)	☐	☐

Circle the correct words. Add *be* where necessary.

1 A Is this information correct?

  B It (**must**)/ could _____*be*_____ . We checked it very carefully.

2 **A** Is the birthrate changing?

   B It **must not**/**may** ________ . We'll know when we have all the statistics.

3 **A** Does he have children?

   B He **shouldn't**/**must** ________ . I see him walking with a little boy every morning.

4 **A** Does she know him?

   B She **should**/**can't** ________ . They work in the same office.

5 **A** Do they know about this?

   B They **couldn't**/**might not** ________ . I'm not sure if anyone has discussed it.

6 **A** Is she away on vacation?

   B She **might not**/**can't** ________ . I just saw her a few minutes ago.

7 **A** Does he live far away?

   B He **might**/**can't** ________ . He's sometimes late for work.

8 **A** Does the birthrate affect society?

   B It **may**/**must** ________ . It's hard to know.

Exercise 2.3 Using Modals of Present Probability

A Over to You Write possible reasons for these trends. Use modals of present probability.

1 More people are going to college.
   This might be because there are fewer jobs.

2 More young adults live with their parents. __________________________

3 People have more credit card debt. __________________________

4 Fewer people have phones at home. __________________________

5 People are getting married later. __________________________

6 Couples are having children later. __________________________

B Pair Work Compare your reasons with a partner. Are they similar or different?

3 Modals of Future Probability

Grammar Presentation

Cannot, could (not), may (not), might (not), and *should (not)* talk about future probability.

*Society **might change** a lot in the future.*
*It **shouldn't be** difficult to see how things change.*

Subject	Modal Verb	Base Form of Verb	
I You He/She/It We They	will should may might could	be	different in the future.

3.2 Negative Statements

Subject	Modal Verb	Base Form of Verb	
I You He/She/It We They	will not/won't could not/couldn't cannot/can't should not/shouldn't may not might not	be	different in the future.

3.3 Expressing Future Probability

Certain ↑	**A** Use a future form (*will* or *be going to*) when you are **certain** about the future.	More people **will live** in cities in the future. A lot of cities **are going to be** bigger in the future.
Almost Certain	**B** Use *cannot* or *can't* when you are **almost certain** that something is impossible in the future. They usually express strong disbelief or surprise. We usually use *can't*.	The economy **can't** get any worse!
Fairly Certain	**C** Use *should (not)* or *shouldn't* when you are **fairly certain** about the future, often because you have evidence. In the negative, we usually use *shouldn't*.	The changes in society **should be** clear. It **shouldn't be** difficult to see the changes.
Not Certain ↓	**D** Use *may (not)*, *might (not)*, or *could* when you are **not certain** about the future. You are uncertain, but you are making an "educated guess."	More people **may live** with their families in the future. It **could be** more difficult to find affordable housing.
	Do not contract **may not**. **Mayn't** is rare.	There **may not** be any changes in the statistics next year. There ~~mayn't~~ be any changes in the statistics next year.

3.3 Expressing Future Probability *(continued)*

E *Must, can,* and *couldn't* are not usually used for future probability.

They ~~must~~ be tired tomorrow.
They ~~can~~ be tired tomorrow.
They ~~couldn't~~ be tired tomorrow.

3.4 Questions and Answers About Future Probability

A *Should, may, might,* and *could* are not usually used to ask questions about the future. Use a future form instead. You can use modals of future probability to answer questions about the future.

"**Are** you **going to** go to the lecture?"
"Yes, but I **might be** late."

"When **is** the lecture **going to** start?"
"It **should start** in a few minutes."

"How long **will** the economy have problems?"
"It **could be** a long time."

B In short answers to *Yes / No* questions, you can use the modal alone.

"Will society change?"
"It **should**."

C If *be* is the main verb in *Yes / No* questions, you can use the modal + *be* in short answers.

"Is the economy going to be different?"
"It **should be**.

Grammar Application

Exercise 3.1 Future Probability

A Listen to an interview about what schools and education might be like in the future. Complete the sentences with the words you hear.

1 Schools and education _____*will*_____ be quite different.

2 There _____________ be small changes.

3 There _____________ be larger ones.

4 Technology _____________ be the most important thing.

5 It _____________ be necessary to have physical schools in the future.

6 For example, parents and schools _____________ organize social activities in new places.

7 In some ways, we _____________ need libraries.

8 There _____________ always be some people who want to read real books.

B Listen again. How certain is Professor Li about each idea? Check (✓) the correct box.

		Not Certain	Certain
1	Schools and education will be quite different.	☐	✔
2	There will be small changes.	☐	☐
3	There will be larger changes.	☐	☐
4	Technology will be the most important thing.	☐	☐
5	There will not be physical schools in the future.	☐	☐
6	There will be new places to learn social skills.	☐	☐
7	There will not be libraries in the future.	☐	☐
8	Some people will want books in the future.	☐	☐

Exercise 3.2 Practicing Future Probability

Complete the online postings about future family trends. Circle the correct words.

Family Life in the Future: What Do You Think It Might Be Like?

Family life in the future will be more like it was in the past. Grandparents will live with their children and grandchildren. This **may** / **must** be for economic reasons, or it **may not** / **might** just be easier. Grandparents
(1)   (2)
could help raise the grandchildren. Also, it **might** / **should not** be nice for grandparents to have young people
(3)
in the same house.

Couples are having children later, when they are older. This **can't** / **may** cause problems. Older parents
(4)
could / **might not** find it difficult to deal with children, especially during their children's teenage years.
(5)
– Jake P.

Technology **couldn't** / **might** affect families in the future. We're all busy texting, talking on smartphones,
(6)
or using computers. We don't have time to just talk anymore. It shouldn't surprise us if families communicate less in the future. This **could** / **can't** change family life a lot.
(7)
– Pete N.

Young adults are going to live at home longer. It **could** / **should not** be more difficult for them to find
(8)
jobs in the future, so they **should** / **may** need to live with their parents. This is not necessarily a bad thing. It
(9)
may / **may not** make families stronger over time.
(10)
– Darla B.

Exercise 3.3 Using Modals of Future Probability

A Over to You Write three predictions about the future. Use these topics or your own ideas.

- family life
- transportation
- jobs and the workplace
- living situations
- technology
- schools

I think family life could change a lot. More people may live in one house together.
We might have better public transportation in the future.

B Group Work Compare your predictions as a class or group. How similar or different are your ideas?

4 Avoid Common Mistakes  

1 Do not use *can* for present or future probability.

could
It's after 5 o'clock, but they ~~can~~ still be at work.

2 Do not confuse *maybe* with *may be*.

may be   *Maybe*
The situation ~~maybe~~ different in the future. ~~May be~~ things will change.

3 Do not use *couldn't* when you aren't certain. Use *may not, might not,* or *shouldn't*.

may not
She ~~couldn't~~ be in a meeting right now. I'll check and see.

4 Do not use *must* or *must not* to talk about probability in the future.

will
The situation ~~must~~ be different next year. It always changes.

5 Use the modal alone in short answers to *Yes/No* questions. Use the modal + *be* in short answers when *be* is the main verb in a *Yes/No* question.

"Do they work together?"   "They might ~~work~~."

be
"Is the meeting at 11:00 a.m.?"   "It may∧."

Editing Task

Find and correct 11 more mistakes in the discussion about a class presentation.

Jim OK. The trend we're going to discuss in our presentation is the increase in the number of people going to college. We have to start by discussing reasons.

Lucy Well, it ~~can~~ *might* be because a lot of people are unemployed. They can be getting a degree because they don't have work. They're in school.

5 **Alex** Yes, that maybe the most important reason, but is it the only reason.

Lucy No, it can't.

Alex May be students are also preparing for a better job.

Lucy Yes, that can be another reason.

Jim OK, good. May be we'll add more reasons later. What about the future effects of this

10 trend, though? Will they be good or bad?

Alex There must be a lot of good effects in the future I'm sure. because it must be good to have more educated people in the workplace in the future.

Lucy Yes, but there can be some problems in the future, too. People could have a lot of debt when they finish school.

15 **Jim** Hmm. Good point. I think So it couldn't be difficult to think of several more effects. We're doing very well so far. Let's summarize our ideas and see if we need any more information. We couldn't have enough, or we might have just what we need.

Cause-and-Effect Writing

Brainstorm > Organize > Write > Edit

In Unit 22, you wrote the first draft of an essay for the prompt below. In this unit (23), you are going to review, revise, and edit your essay.

> *Describe the human causes of climate change and the effects climate change can have on the planet.*

My Writing

Exercise 5.1 Revising Your Ideas

1 Work with a partner. Use the questions to give feedback on your partner's essay.
   - Which of your partner's ideas seem strongest to you?
   - Which of your partner's ideas need to be explained more clearly?
   - What could your partner add or remove to make the essay stronger and easier to understand?

2 Use the feedback from your partner to revise the ideas and content of your essay.

Using Modals to Express Future Probability

Cause-and-effect essays often end with statements or predictions about the future. Using different modals of probability shows the writer's level of certainty.

Certain: *If the global population continues to grow, by 2050 there will be 9.5 billion people on the planet.*

Fairly Certain: *Some areas should/will likely see drier conditions, leading to more drought.*

Not Certain: *There may/could be technological solutions to many of today's urban problems.*

Exercise 5.2 Applying the Skill

Review your concluding paragraph. Use one or more modals of probability to clarify your level of certainty about your solution or recommendation.

Exercise 5.3 Editing Your Writing

Use the checklist to review and edit your essay.

Did you completely answer the prompt?	
Did you use an effective hook to catch the reader's attention?	
Did you describe causes in the first body paragraph and effects in the second body paragraph?	
Did you include strong supporting details to support your ideas?	
Did you use linking phrases and clauses to show the relationship between the causes of a problem and its effects?	
Did you use causes and effects to express solutions or recommendations?	
Is each paragraph coherent?	

Exercise 5.4 Editing Your Grammar

Use the checklist to review and edit the grammar in your essay.

Did you use formal modals and expressions of ability correctly to talk about the present or future?	
Did you use formal modals of advice and suggestions to make recommendations to your reader?	
Did you use any modals of necessity to make your viewpoint stronger?	
Did you use formal modals of future probability to clarify your level of certainty?	
Did you avoid the common mistakes in the charts on pages 255, 283, 295, and 307?	

Exercise 5.5 Writing Your Final Draft

Apply the feedback and edits from Exercises 5.2 to 5.4 to write the final draft of your essay.

1 Grammar in the Real World

A How often do you read advice columns? Where do you read them: in newspapers, in magazines, or online? Read the advice column about problems in the workplace. What do you think is the best advice for getting along at work?

B Comprehension Check **Answer the questions.**

1 According to the advice column, why is it a bad idea to wear perfume in the workplace?

2 Why does Jorge think his co-worker is angry?

3 According to the advice column, why should people avoid telling jokes to people they don't know well?

4 Why does Mei Lee have a problem with her boss?

C Notice **Find the sentences in the advice column and complete them.**

1 A new employee _____________________ yesterday.

2 Something terrible _____________________ last week!

3 I _____________________ a joke at work.

4 I think I _____________________ him.

Which verbs are followed by a noun or pronoun?

Ask the **EXPERT**

Welcome to our advice column, where you can **ask an expert for** advice on all your workplace problems. Here are this week's questions and our expert's answers.

Dear Expert: A new employee **arrived** yesterday. She **wears too**
5 **much perfume**, and it **distracts**[1] **the other employees**. I'm her boss. What should I do? – Rosa M.

Dear Rosa: You should **discuss this with** your employee. You can tell her that most offices ask employees not to **use perfume** because some people are allergic[2] to it.

10 Dear Expert: Something terrible **happened** last week! I **told a joke** at work, and now a co-worker from China is angry with me. I think I **offended him**. – Jorge P.

Dear Jorge: **Apologize for** your behavior. Humor is very different in different cultures, so you probably shouldn't **tell jokes** to people you
15 don't know well. It's also not a good idea to **talk about** politics, religion, or how much money a person has.

Dear Expert: I have a very difficult boss. She constantly **makes outrageous**[3] **demands**. For example, she asked me to **get her suit** from the dry cleaners the other day. This is a personal task, not a work-
20 related task, and she shouldn't ask me to do this. How can I handle this? – Mei Lee W.

Dear Mei Lee: This is a difficult situation to **deal with**. It might help to **make a list** of things you are working on for your boss. When she asks you to run an errand,[4] **show the list** to her. Then she will know how
25 busy you already are.

---

[1]**distract:** take someone's attention away from what the person is doing

[2]**allergic:** having an illness from eating, touching, or breathing something specific

[3]**outrageous:** shocking and unacceptable

[4]**run an errand:** make a short trip to do something, such as buy groceries

2 Transitive and Intransitive Verbs

Grammar Presentation

A transitive verb needs an object. The object completes the meaning of the verb. An intransitive verb does not need an object.

VERB OBJECT
The new employee **wears perfume**. *(transitive)*

VERB
The new employee **arrived**. *(intransitive)*

2.1 Transitive Verbs

Subject	Verb	Object
I You We They	**wear**	**perfume**.
He / She / It	**wears**	

2.2 Intransitive Verbs

Subject	Verb
I You We They	**arrived**.
He / She / It	**arrived**.

2.3 Using Transitive and Intransitive Verbs

A The object after a transitive verb is often a noun or an object pronoun.

*She wears **perfume**.*
*My boss doesn't like **me**.*

B An intransitive verb does not have an object. However, it is often followed by an expression of time, place, or manner.

*The flight arrived **at 5:30 p.m.***
*How many people work **at your office**?*
*She resigned **unexpectedly**.*

C Some verbs can be transitive or intransitive.

Sometimes the meaning of the verb is the same.

TRANSITIVE
*He **drives a truck**.*

INTRANSITIVE
*He **drives** badly.*

Sometimes the meaning of the verb is different.

TRANSITIVE
*She **runs a company** in Phoenix. (manages)*

TRANSITIVE
*She can **run** fast.*

DATA FROM THE REAL WORLD

Most English verbs are transitive.

*He **died** in 1998.*

The most common intransitive verbs in speaking and writing are *come, die, fall, go, happen, live, remain, rise, stay,* and *work.*

*Gas prices **are rising**.*

The most common verbs that can be transitive or intransitive are *begin, call, change, leave, move, open, run, start, stop,* and *study.*

OBJECT
*Could you **move** your car, please?* (transitive)
*We all sat very still. No one **moved**.* (intransitive)

Grammar Application

Exercise 2.1 Transitive or Intransitive?

Read the e-mail. Label each underlined verb *T* (transitive) or *I* (intransitive) according to how it is used in the e-mail. Circle each object.

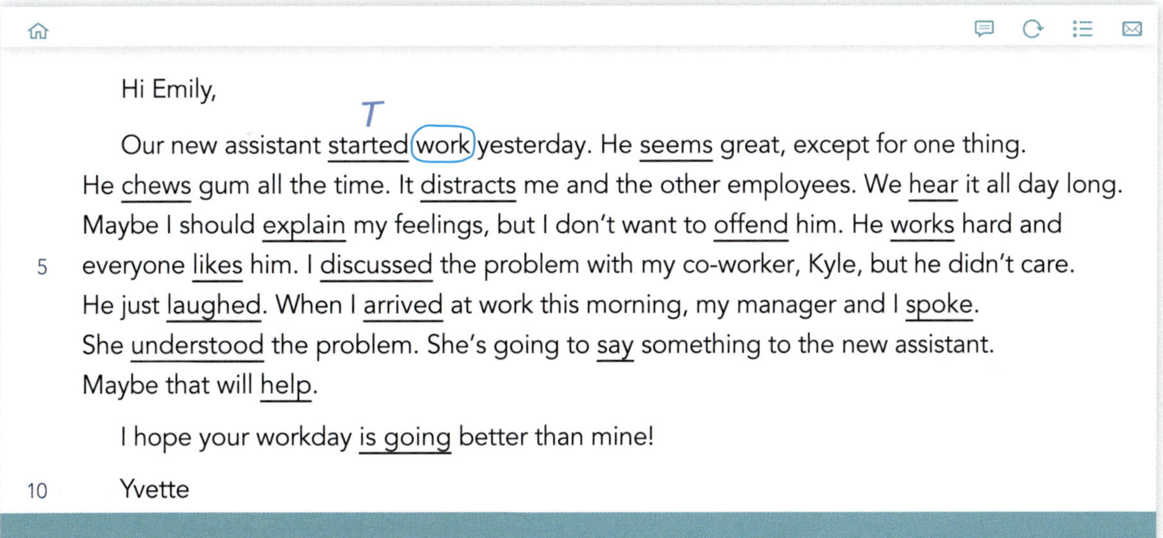

Exercise 2.2 Questions and Answers

A Underline all of the transitive verbs in the questions. Circle all of the intransitive verbs.

1 What distracts you most when you are studying?

2 How often do you stay late at work (or school)?

3 What time do you usually leave for work (or school)?

4 What has changed in your work (or school) life recently?

5 What time do you usually begin your workday (or school day)?

6 What time does your workday (or school day) usually end?

Getting Along at Work **313**

A *What distracts you most when you are studying?*

B *Nice weather really distracts me. I always want to go outdoors.*

3 Verb + Object + Preposition Combinations

Grammar Presentation

Some verbs are followed by an object and a prepositional phrase.

VERB	OBJECT	PREPOSITION
She **discussed**	**company policies**	**with** the new employees.

VERB	OBJECT	PREPOSITION
He **borrowed**	**a laptop**	**from** his co-worker.

3.1 Some Verb + Object + Preposition Combinations

A Verb + object + *about*

remind … about

We **reminded** them **about** the meeting at 3 o'clock.

B Verb + object + *for*

ask … for
thank … for

He **asked** me **for** advice.
I **thanked** him **for** his help.

C Verb + object + *from*

borrow … from
get … from
learn … from
take … from

She **borrowed** the book **from** me.
We **got** some good feedback **from** our manager.
Have you **learned** a lot **from** her?
They **took** the information **from** the new employees.

D Verb + object + *to*

explain … to

She **explained** the problem **to** her boss.

E Verb + object + *with*

discuss … with
help … with
spend … with

I **discussed** the project **with** my manager.
He **helps** her **with** the mail.
Does she **spend** a lot of time **with** him?

Grammar Application

Exercise 3.1 Verb + Object + Preposition Combinations

Listen to the conversation about a woman's day at work. Complete the sentences with the verbs and prepositions you hear.

1 I _explained_ company policies _to_ them.

2 I ___________________ some time ______________ them after the meeting.

3 I ___________________ everything _______________ them one more time.

4 I couldn't fix them, so I ___________________ a laptop ______________ the technology department.

5 I ___________________ Robert ________________ some information.

6 I had to wait and ___________________ it _______________ Carrie.

7 Carrie ___________________ me ______________ a department meeting at 11:30.

8 Robert and Carrie both had time to ___________________ me ______________ it then.

9 I ___________________ Carrie and Robert _______________ their help.

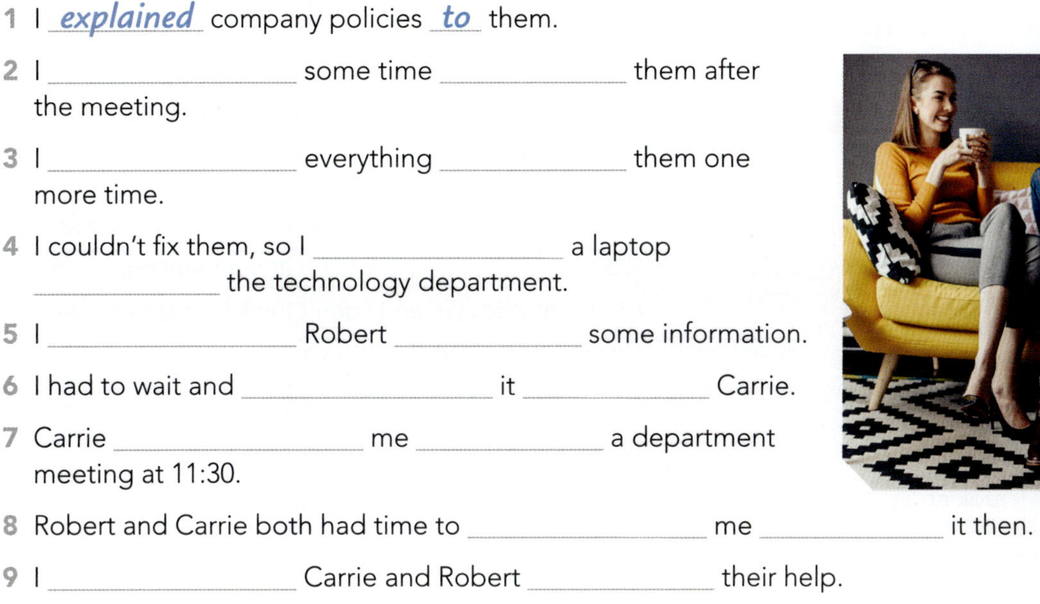

Exercise 3.2 More Verb + Object + Preposition Combinations

A Over to You Write three sentences about things you have to do or have recently done at work or school. Choose from these topics.

- discuss something with someone
- explain something to someone
- get something from someone
- remind someone about something
- borrow something from someone
- help someone with something

I had to discuss a problem at work with my boss yesterday.

____

____

____

B Pair Work Read a partner's sentences. Tell the class about your partner.

Nuria borrowed some books from her teacher, and then she lost them. She doesn't know what to do about this.

4 Verb + Preposition Combinations

Grammar Presentation

Some verbs are often followed by specific prepositions.	I always **listen to** my co-workers during meetings. Don't **worry about** the project. I'll help you.

4.1 Some Verb + Preposition Combinations

A Verb + about

ask about	The new employees **asked about** company policies.
talk about	We **talked about** the problem at our meeting.
think about	I **thought about** it, and I don't think it's a good idea.
worry about	Do you **worry about** work problems?

B Verb + at

laugh at	She is **laughing at** us.
look at	Could you **look at** this report and tell me what you think?

C Verb + for

apologize for	I **apologize for** my behavior.
ask for	Did she **ask for** a raise?
look for	I'm **looking for** my boss. I have a question for him.
wait for	We've been **waiting for** you.

D Verb + on

count on	You can **count on** me in a crisis.
depend on	A company's success **depends on** every employee's hard work.
rely on	He **relies on** me for help.

E Verb + to

belong to	Does this **belong to** you?
happen to	What **happened to** Tom's boss? I haven't seen her lately.
listen to	We **listened to** the discussion.
talk to	Our boss **talked to** all the employees on Monday.

F Verb + with

agree with	No one **agrees with** him.
argue with	It's not a good idea to **argue with** your co-workers.
deal with	I can't **deal with** her.

▸▸ Verb and Preposition Combinations: See page A5.

4.2 Using Verb + Preposition Combinations

A Verb + preposition combinations often include verbs for communication and verbs for thinking and feeling.

*You should **ask about** the new job.* (communication)
*Don't **worry about** it.* (thinking and feeling)

B The preposition can come at the end of an information question.

*"What did you talk **about**?" "We talked about work."*
*"Who does this bag belong **to**?" "It belongs to me."*

C Some verbs can combine with more than one preposition. The meaning may be different.

*I **talked to** him yesterday.* (had a conversation with)
*We **talked about** our new project.* (discussed)

Grammar Application

Exercise 4.1 Verb + Preposition Combination in Statements

Complete the text about company policies with the correct form of the verbs in parentheses and the correct preposition from the box.

about	about	for	~~to~~	to	with
about	at	to	to	with	

Yesterday, our boss __*talked to*__ (talk) the new
(1)
employees on their first day. He ______________
(2)
(talk) company policies. The employees
______________ (listen) him attentively. He said
(3)
everyone should ______________ (think) the policies.
(4)
He told them to ______________ (ask) anything that
(5)
was unclear.

One employee asked if it was acceptable to speak
his first language at work. The boss said, "We prefer
everyone to speak English, but we think it's important to ______________ (look)
(6)
each situation. Sometimes it's acceptable to use your first language, for example, if
you're ______________ (talk) a customer who speaks your language."
(7)

At the end of the meeting, he said, "We all ______________ (belong) the
(8)
same organization and have the same goals. If you need help, please don't hesitate to
______________ (ask) it." It seemed like everyone ______________ (agree) the
(9)   (10)
boss's views. Nobody ______________ (argue) him.
(11)

A Use the words to write questions. Add the correct preposition.

1 Who / you / talk / most at work (or school) / ?

   Who do you talk to most at work?

2 What / you / usually talk / at work (or school) / ?

3 What / you / worry / at work (or school) / ?

4 Who / you / depend / for help / ?

5 Whose advice / you / listen / most / ?

6 Who / you / sometimes argue / ?

7 Who / you / usually agree / ?

8 What / clubs or professional organizations / you / belong / ?

B Pair Work Ask and answer the questions in A with a partner.

   A *Who do you talk to most at work?*
   B *I talk to my co-worker, Sandra.*

 # Avoid Common Mistakes 

1 **A transitive verb needs an object. Don't forget the object.**

it

I went to see the movie, but I didn't like ∧.

2 **Some verbs need a preposition. Don't forget the preposition.**

to

My co-workers often don't listen ∧ me.

3 **Use the correct preposition with verbs that need them.**

about

Don't worry ~~on~~ the presentation. I'll help you finish it.

4 **Don't use a preposition with verbs that don't need them.**

Let's discuss ~~about~~ the problem.

Editing Task

Find and correct eight more mistakes in this magazine article.

NOT APPRECIATED AT WORK?

Do these problems sound familiar to you? If so, you are not alone. These are the common problems our readers sent to us in our recent survey. Try our solutions! They could help you change your work life forever!

› Problem: Some people do not appreciate me, or even like *me* ∧.

Solution: Maybe you should talk your boss about the problem.

5 › Problem: My co-workers often argue me. I don't like it.

Solution: You could talk with the problem with your co-workers.

› Problem: Nobody listens me when I have a new idea.

Solution: Maybe you need to explain your ideas more clearly to them.

› Problem: I always thank my co-workers for their help, but they never thank.

10   Solution: You could discuss about the problem with them, but it may not change.

› Problem: My co-worker always asks me help. I don't mind helping him, but then I don't finish my own work.

Solution: Discuss this him. Tell him you want to help, but you must also do your work. I think he'll understand.

5 Academic Writing

Description and Analysis

Brainstorm > Organize > Write > Edit

In this writing cycle (Units 24-27), you will write a description-and-analysis report using a multiple line graph. In this unit (24), you will look at a report and study ways to understand, interpret, and describe line graphs.

Describe the trends in a multiple line graph, and analyze the data. Do some additional research to discuss the trends you identify.

Exercise 6.1 Preparing to Write

Work with a partner. Discuss the questions.

1 Who do you go to for financial advice? Why?
2 If your income fell, how would your spending habits change?
3 What are the three biggest expenses for households?

Exercise 6.2 Focusing on Vocabulary

Read the sentences. Use the context to match the words in bold to their definitions.

1 My family has a comfortable **standard of living**. We have enough money to pay for everything we need, and we are able to save a little bit of money every month.
2 Lawyers usually have higher **incomes** than teachers.
3 The weather is one **factor** that influences the price of food. For example, if there is not enough rain, crops are smaller and the price of food goes up.
4 Wars and natural disasters often **drive up** the cost of gasoline and heating oil.
5 Between 2008 and 2009, the number of unemployed people **doubled** in the United States, from five to ten percent.
6 The price of the company's stock **soared** when the CEO announced excellent earnings last week.

a _________________________ (n) the amount of money and comfort someone has

b _________________________ (v) to increase quickly by a lot

c _________________________ (v) to cause to increase

d _________________________ (n) money that you earn by working or investing

e _________________________ (n) something that affects a particular situation or decision

f _________________________ (v) to become twice the original size or amount

What Has Happened to the American Dream?

One common definition of the "American Dream" is the belief that each generation will do better than the one before it. Unfortunately, many Americans today do not enjoy the same **standard of living** as their parents. This means many people are actually poorer today than they were 20 years ago. Experts tell us that there are several reasons for this trend.

Over time, **incomes** change. Between 1999 and 2014, real incomes fell almost 8%. Lower incomes lead to a declining standard of living because people do not have as much money to spend on themselves and their children. Fortunately, incomes have been increasing since 2014. However, another key **factor** in determining people's standard of living is expenditure[1]. Unfortunately, since 1999, American have also been spending more income on several important products and services (Figure 1). There are many reasons for increasing expenditures over time, but two important ones are the high cost of housing and health care. In many cities, a shortage of houses and apartments to buy and rent has **driven** up costs. Also, healthcare expenses have **doubled** as prescription drugs and hospital costs have become more and more expensive. Transportation and food prices have also **soared** in recent years. As a result, real incomes - incomes after inflation[2] - have been falling for most Americans (Figure 2).

In the end, the combination of rising prices and falling incomes has left many Americans with less money. Because people must pay more for essentials like housing and food, they have less money for education, investment, savings[3], and small luxuries like eating in restaurants. Many people have had to sell their homes, use their savings, or borrow money in order to meet their monthly expenses. For these people, the American Dream must seem very far out of reach. Sadly, no one seems to know how or when their situation will improve.

---

[1]**expenditure** (n) the total amount of money that a business, group, or person spends on something
[2]**inflation** (n) an increase in prices
[3]**savings** (n) money that you put away, usually in a bank, to use later

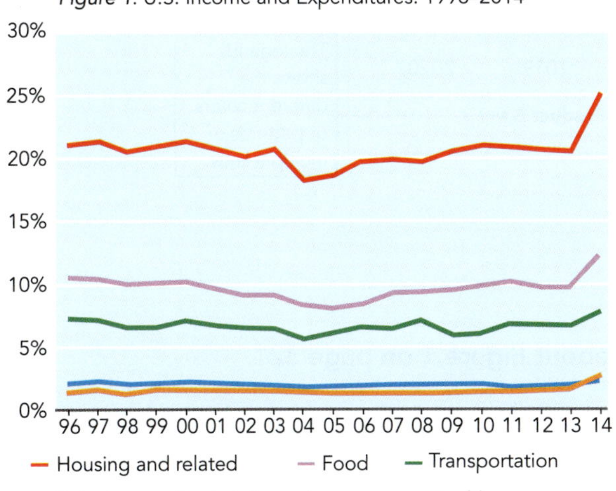

Figure 1: U.S. Income and Expenditures. 1996–2014

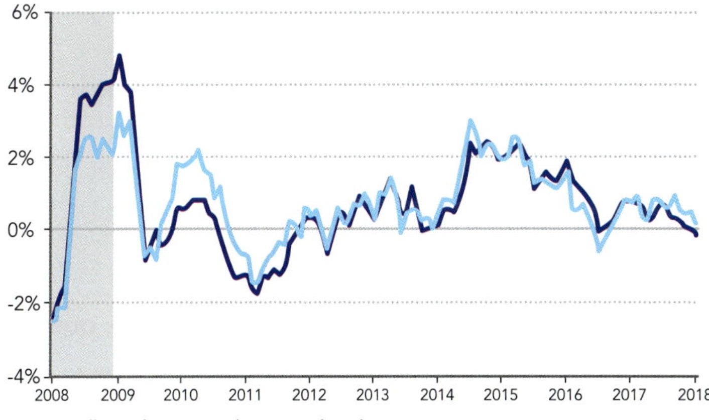

Figure 2: 12-month percent change in real hourly and weekly earnings, private sector employees, seasonally adjusted, July 2008–July 2018

Read the text on page 321. Work with a partner. Ask and answer the questions.

1 How has the American standard of living changed in the last 20 years? Why?
2 What do Americans spend the most money on?
3 Why are Americans spending more of their earnings today than in the past?
4 What are three ways that struggling Americans survive financially?

Work with a partner. Complete the tasks.

1 In paragraph 1, underline the trend that is discussed in the essay. How are the two graphs related to the trend?
2 Circle all the verbs in paragraph 2 that indicate a change, up or down. Identify each verb as transitive or intransitive.
3 Highlight two verb + preposition combinations in paragraph 2. What do they mean?

Understanding Line Graphs

A **line graph** uses points on a line to show a trend. A trend is a general change in a situation. This is similar to a "main idea" in other essays. Here is a guide to understanding a multi-line graph.

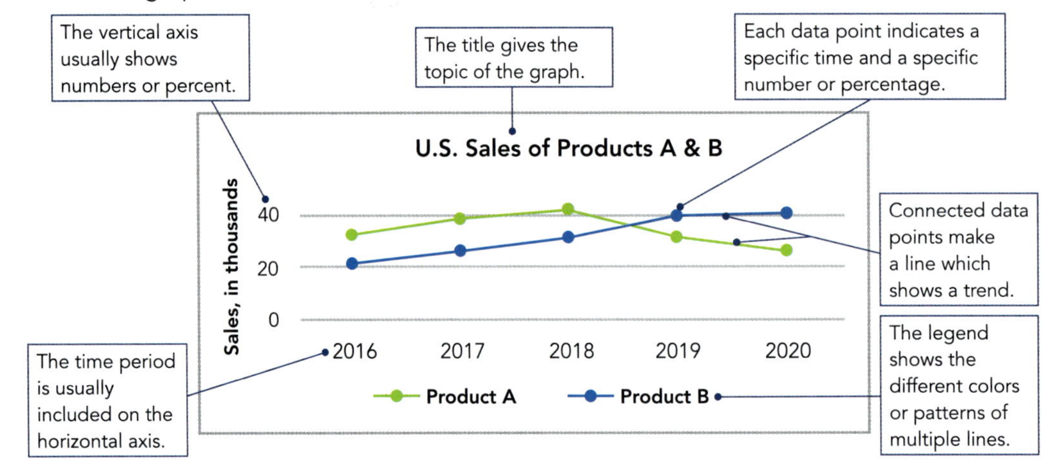

Work with a partner. Ask and answer the questions about Figure 1 on page 321.

1 What is the topic of the graph?
2 What do the numbers on the vertical axis show?
3 What is the time period of the graph?
4 Why does the graph have 5 lines of different colors? What does each color mean?

Interpreting a Line Graph

After reading a graph, the writer's task is to identify and explain the trend it shows. If the graph has more than one line, the writer should explain the relationship between them. The most important trend is generally included in the writer's thesis.

From 2016 to 2018, Product A had higher sales than Product B. However, by 2018, sales of Product A dropped while Product B was stronger.

The line graph provides facts. In a description-analysis report, the writer identifies a trend, presents the facts, and provides explanations. Writers often do more research to explain the reasons for the trends.

In 2018, the global economy weakened. Customers generally lost interest in luxury products, so sales of Product A began to fall. Product B was good quality and well-priced, so its sales continued to grow slowly.

Exercise 6.6 Applying the Skill

Work with a partner. Ask and answer the questions about Figure 1 on page 321.

1 What is the overall trend of the graph?

2 Why might housing become more or less expensive?

3 Of the five expenditures, which do you think are necessary?

4 How do you think people deal with increased expenses?

My Writing

Using Noun and Verb Phrases to Describe Graphs

You can use certain noun and verb phrases to describe changes in a line graph.

Noun Phrase: From 2016 to 2018, there was a **sharp rise** in the number of job opportunities.

Verb Phrase: After 2010, communication skills in the workplace **increased gradually.**

Below are a list of common noun and verb phrases used to describe economic or business trends. The verbs in these verb phrases are intransitive.

Adjective	Noun		Verb	Adverb
slight	rise		rise	slightly
gradual	increase		increase	gradually
sharp	decrease		decrease	sharply
dramatic	fall		fall	dramatically

Exercise 6.7 Applying the Skill

Look at Figure 2 on page 321. Write five sentences to describe the graph using noun and verb phrases. Then compare your sentences with a partner's.

Phrasal Verbs

Money, Money, Money

1 Grammar in the Real World

ACADEMIC WRITING

Description and analysis

A What are some good habits for managing money? What are some bad habits? Read the article about managing money. What two steps does the author's plan include?

B Comprehension Check **Answer the questions.**

1 Why should you write down your expenses?
2 According to the article, which expenses are the most important ones?
3 According to the article, what are some expenses that are not important?
4 What are two financial goals that the article mentions?

C Notice **Find the sentences in the article and complete them with the missing verbs.**

1 If this describes you, you might want to _______________ your finances now, before bad habits _______________ .

2 _______________ with a notebook.

3 Over the next month, _______________ all your monthly expenses.

How many words are there in each blank, one or two? Which words are followed by an object (transitive)? Which words are not followed by an object (intransitive)?

MONEY MATTERS

Does your money usually **run out** before the end of the month? Do you spend more money than you earn? Are you starting to **build up** credit card debt? Have you **taken out** a loan and can't **pay** it **off**? If this describes you, you might want to **sort out**[1] your finances now, before bad habits **set in**.[2] Do not **put** it **off** until tomorrow. Here is a plan to help you get control of your money.

Step 1: **Figure out** your income and your spending habits. **Sit down** with a notebook and **write down** how much you make every month. Then **find out** where your money goes. Over the next month, **write down** all your monthly expenses and **add** them **up**. Include everything you buy or spend money on. The purpose of this exercise is to get a clear picture of your usual spending habits. Do you **eat out** too much? What do you need to **give up**?

Step 2: **Set up** a budget. Use your notebook to **work out** what you can spend. Then, prioritize[3] your expenses. Rent, food, electricity, and gas are the most important. These are high-priority[4] expenses. Movies and dinners out are not. You can allow yourself some treats, but remember to **put** money **away** for unexpected expenses, such as repairs when your car **breaks down**.

Once you are in control of your finances, you can set a goal like **paying off** your credit card or saving for a large purchase. You can also relax, enjoy life more, and worry less.

---

[1]**sort out:** organize something or solve a problem
[2]**set in:** begin and continue for a long time
[3]**prioritize:** put things in order of importance
[4]**high-priority:** important

2 Intransitive Phrasal Verbs

Grammar Presentation

Phrasal verbs are two-word verbs. They include a verb and a particle. A particle is a small word like *up*, *down*, *back*, *out*, *on*, *off*, or *in*.

VERB PARTICLE
*Does your money usually **run out** before the end of the month?*

VERB PARTICLE
***Sit down** with a notebook.*

2.1 Intransitive Phrasal Verbs

Subject	Verb	Particle
I You We They	**sit** **sat**	**down.**
He / She / It	**sits** **sat**	

2.2 Using Intransitive Phrasal Verbs

A	Intransitive phrasal verbs do not need an object to complete their meaning.	***Sit down** with a notebook.* *Do you **eat out** too much?*
B	The particle comes after the verb.	*They **came back** from vacation today.*
	Note: Do not put a word or phrase between the verb and the particle of an intransitive phrasal verb.	*They came ~~from vacation~~ back today.*
C	The meaning of some phrasal verbs is easy to understand.	*I **go out** every night.* *Can you **stand up** for a moment?* *She **went away** for a month and then **came back**.*

2.2 Using Intransitive Phrasal Verbs *(continued)*

D Some intransitive phrasal verbs have more than one meaning. The meaning of some phrasal verbs is not easy to understand.

She walked into the room and then **ran out**. (left)
Does your money **run out**? (be completely used)

Her plane **takes off** *at 12:00.* (leaves)
Debt counseling has **taken off**. (grown; been successful)

My car **broke down** *last week.* (stopped working)
He **broke down** *in tears.* (started to cry)

We **work out** *at a gym.* (exercise)
My job **didn't work out**. (didn't go as planned)

E Many everyday spoken commands use intransitive phrasal verbs.

Hold on./Hang on. (Wait.)   *Go ahead!* (Do it!)

Come on. (Hurry. Let's go.)   *Go on.* (Continue.)

Look out!/Watch out! (Be careful!)   *Sit down.* (Sit.)

2.3 Some Intransitive Phrasal Verbs

break down (1. stop working 2. lose control)

come back (return)

come on (1. hurry 2. start)

eat out (eat in a restaurant)

get along (have a good relationship)

give up (stop)

go ahead (start or continue)

go away (leave; go to another place)

go on (continue)

go out (not stay home)

go up (rise; go higher)

grow up (become an adult)

hang on (1. wait 2. keep going)

hold on (1. wait 2. persist)

look out (be careful)

move in (1. take your things to a new home 2. begin living somewhere)

run out (1. leave 2. be completely used)

set in (begin and continue for a long time)

sit down (sit; take a seat)

stand up (stand; rise)

take off (1. leave on an airplane 2. grow; be successful)

watch out (be careful)

work out (1. exercise 2. go as planned)

▶▶ Phrasal Verbs: Transitive and Intransitive: See page A10.

DATA FROM THE REAL WORLD

In general, phrasal verbs are less common in academic writing, but writers often use these verbs: *grow up, go on, go back, turn out, break down, come up, work out.*

Talks between the two countries have **broken down**.

One question **came up** *in the discussion.*

🖱️ Grammar Application

Exercise 2.1 Intransitive Phrasal Verbs

Underline the phrasal verbs in the conversations. Circle the particles.

1 A Come on! We're going to be late.
  B Hold on. I'm coming.
2 A It's Friday night. Let's eat out somewhere.
  B I can't. My money's already run out, and I don't get paid until next week.
3 A I have some new neighbors. They moved in last week.
  B Are they nice? Do you think you'll get along?
4 A I want to go out now. Do you want to come?
  B No, go ahead. I'm tired. I'm going to stay home.

Exercise 2.2 Using Phrasal Verbs

A Complete the story. Use the particles from the boxes.

along	away	back	in	~~up~~

    Peter and Carlos grew **_up_** in the same neighborhood.
(1)
They were good friends and got ___________ really well.
(2)
Carlos went ___________ to college when he was 18, but they
(3)
kept in touch. When Carlos came ___________ , they decided
(4)
to share an apartment. Peter found an apartment, and they
moved ___________ .
(5)

on	out	out	out	up

    It all worked ___________ well for a while. They shared
(6)
the bills. They went ___________ for pizza or to see a movie
(7)
after work. Then Carlos got a great job in a bank and
wanted to eat ___________ more often and in more expensive
(8)
restaurants. Peter couldn't afford it, but he used his credit
card and tried not to worry. Life went ___________ as normal,
(9)
but Peter's spending was going ___________ every day.
(10)

down	down	on

    One morning, Peter sat ___________ to have coffee and pay some bills online while
(11)
Carlos was at work. He saw his high credit card bill and broke ___________ . "I can't go
(12)
___________ like this," he said. He called Carlos's voice mail and left a message. He said . . .
(13)

B Pair Work Study the story for two minutes. Tell it to your partner using the phrasal verbs.

Two boys grew up together. They were good friends and . . .

C Group Work What do you think Peter said in his voice mail to Carlos? What do you think Carlos said to Peter in his response? Discuss in a group.

I think Peter said, "Hi Carlos, it's Peter calling. I read my credit card bill this morning. It's very high. I can't go on like this . . ."

Exercise 2.3 Questions and Answers

A Complete the questions with the correct particle. Use Chart 2.3 on page 265 to help you.

1 Do you go _out_ on weekends very often?
2 Do you eat ___________ for lunch, or do you bring your own lunch?
3 Do you exercise at home or work ___________ at a gym?
4 Has your computer or car broken ___________ lately and needed expensive repairs?
5 Have prices for anything been going ___________ lately? If so, what has been getting more expensive?
6 After this course, would you like to go ___________ and study more? If so, what would you study?
7 Do you make a budget? If so, does it usually work ___________ ?

B Pair Work Ask and answer the questions with a partner. How similar or different are your answers?

3 Transitive Phrasal Verbs

Grammar Presentation

<table>
<tr><td>Transitive phrasal verbs need an object.</td><td>VERB   PARTICLE   OBJECT
Have you **taken** **out** a **loan**?

VERB   OBJECT   PARTICLE
Can you **pay** **it** **back**?</td></tr>
</table>

3.1 Transitive Phrasal Verbs

Subject	Verb	Particle	Object (Noun)
I You We They	**figure** **figured**	**out**	the budget.
He / She / It	**figures** **figured**		

Subject	Verb	Object (Noun or Pronoun)	Particle
I You We They	**figure** **figured**	the budget it	**out.**
He / She / It	**figures** **figured**		

3.2 Using Intransitive Phrasal Verbs

A Some phrasal verbs are transitive. They need an object to complete their meaning.

He paid back **the money he owed**.

She added up **her expenses**.

B Most transitive phrasal verbs are "separable." This means that noun objects can come **before** or **after** the particle.

VERB   PARTICLE   OBJECT
Write   *down*   *your expenses.*

VERB   OBJECT   PARTICLE
Write   *your expenses*   *down.*

Object pronouns come **before** the particle.

Write *them* *down.*

Do not put an object pronoun after the particle.

Write down ~~*them.*~~

C Indefinite pronoun objects (e.g., *something, nothing, someone, no one, everyone*) can come before or after the particle.

She *throws away* *everything.*

She *throws* *everything* *away.*

D Longer objects usually go after the particle.

Is he *setting up* *a new financial management company?*

Is he *setting* ~~*a new financial management company*~~ *up?*

E Some transitive phrasal verbs have more than one meaning.

They are *bringing up* *three children.*
(raising a child)

I'd like to *bring up* *the subject of money.*
(introduce a topic)

Please *turn down* *the radio. It's too loud.*
(lower the volume)

I *turned down* *the invitation to the party because I had to work.* (rejected)

3.2 Using Intransitive Phrasal Verbs *(continued)*

F Some phrasal verbs have one meaning when they are transitive. They have a different meaning when they are intransitive.

*I **worked out** a budget.* (transitive; solved or calculated something)
*I **work out** at a gym every day.* (intransitive; exercise)

3.3 Some Transitive Phrasal Verbs

add up (add together; combine)
bring up (1. raise a child
         2. introduce a topic)
build up (accumulate)
figure out (find an answer; understand)
find out (discover information; learn)
give up (quit)
pay back (repay money)
pay off (repay completely)
put away (1. save for the future
         2. put in the correct place)

put off (delay, postpone)
set up (1. arrange 2. plan 3. build)
sort out (1. organize 2. solve)
take out (1. remove
         2. obtain something officially)
throw away (get rid of something; discard)
turn down (1. lower the volume 2. reject)
work out (solve; calculate)
write down (write on paper)

▸ Phrasal Verbs: Transitive and Intransitive: See page A10.

DATA FROM THE REAL WORLD

Research shows that the following transitive phrasal verbs are common in academic writing:

break off	cut off	point out	sum up
carry out	find out	set up	

Grammar Application

Exercise 3.1 Transitive and Intransitive Phrasal Verbs

Label the phrasal verbs *T* (transitive) or *I* (intransitive) according to their use in the sentences. Circle the objects.

1 Experts say you should work on your money problems now. Don't **put** (them) **off**. _____*T*_____

2 Most experts say it's a good idea to **write down** all your expenses. ________

3 For example, Mariah S., from Chicago, **adds up** everything she's spent at the end of the month. ________

4 After Mariah **worked out** a budget, she changed some of her spending habits. ________

5 She used to pay for an expensive gym membership, but now she **out** at home. ________

6 She also decided to **give up** expensive dinners in order to save money. ________

7 Mariah didn't **give up** and eventually saved enough money to start a business. ________

8 She also **paid back** some money her family had loaned her. ________

Listen to the expert give advice about money. Complete the list of advice.
Use phrasal verbs.

Dana's Money Advice

1 _Put away_ a little money each month.

2 Even a small amount will _______________ over time.

3 You need to _______________ a budget.

4 _______________ your expenses.

5 Don't _______________ receipts.

6 Don't _______________ a lot of debt.

7 _______________ your credit card every month.

8 You need to _______________ the topic _______________ and discuss it.

9 Don't _______________ money matters.

A Complete the conversations. Unscramble the words in A's questions. Use the verb given and an object pronoun in B's answers.

1 A Do you usually _write your expenses down / write down your expenses_
      (your expenses / write down)?

   B No, I don't. I _don't add them up_ (not add up) every month, either.

2 A Do you _______________ (your receipts / throw away),
      or do you keep them?

   B I usually _______________ (throw away).

3 A Do you ever _______________ (things / put off), like doing your finances?

   B I do. I know I should _______________ (sort out).

4 A Do you think it's a good idea to _______________ (a loan / take out)?

   B Yes, but only if you can _______________ (pay off) quickly.

5 A Do you think it's difficult to _______________ (a budget / work out)?

   B I don't think so. You just need to _______________ (figure out).

B Pair Work Ask and answer the questions in A with a partner. Answer with your own opinion or information.

A *Do you usually write down your expenses?*
B *Yes, I do. I write everything down. Then I add it up at the end of the month.*

4 Avoid Common Mistakes ⚠ 

1   **Don't forget a particle when you need one. Be especially careful with these verbs:** *pick up, break down,* **and** *point out.*

He's picked ^*up* *bad spending habits, like eating out every night.*

2   **Don't use a particle when you don't need one. Be especially careful with these verbs:** *fall, rise, go, find.*

Gas prices fell ~~down~~, then rose ~~up~~.
Things are going ~~on~~ well for me.

3   **Don't confuse** *grow up* **and** *grow. Grow up* **means to grow from a child to an adult.** *Grow* **means get bigger.**

Before the children grew ^*up*, *we didn't have any savings.*
Now our savings have grown ~~up~~.

4   **Do not put object pronouns after particles. They go before particles.**

She summed ~~up it~~. ^*it up*

Editing Task

Find and correct eight more mistakes on this website.

Debt Help Website

It is easy to get into debt. Prices are going ^*up* all the time.
Maybe you have to change jobs and your income decreases.
Maybe you've picked bad habits, like ordering a pizza
instead of cooking. You are using your credit card more and
5   more. Soon your debt has grown up, and it is more than
you can afford. Or maybe you have a loan and you cannot
pay back it. If you do not watch, you may find that you have
thousands of dollars of debt. It is hard to know what to do
with debt that has risen up. We can help! Our website is full
10   of financial advice. It points the things you must and must
not do when you get into debt.

Do you have difficulty with your budget? Read our **Budget**
15   **Guide**. It will help you figure out it.

Do you want to get married? First, find how your partner
20   feels about money. Read our **Money and Relationships Guide**.

5 Academic Writing

Description and Analysis

In Unit 24, you looked at a report about the American dream and learned how to understand and interpret line graphs. In this unit (25), you will continue interpreting graphs and then write the introductory and concluding paragraphs of a report that answers the prompt below.

Describe the trends in a multiple line graph, and analyze the data. Do some additional research to discuss the trends you identify.

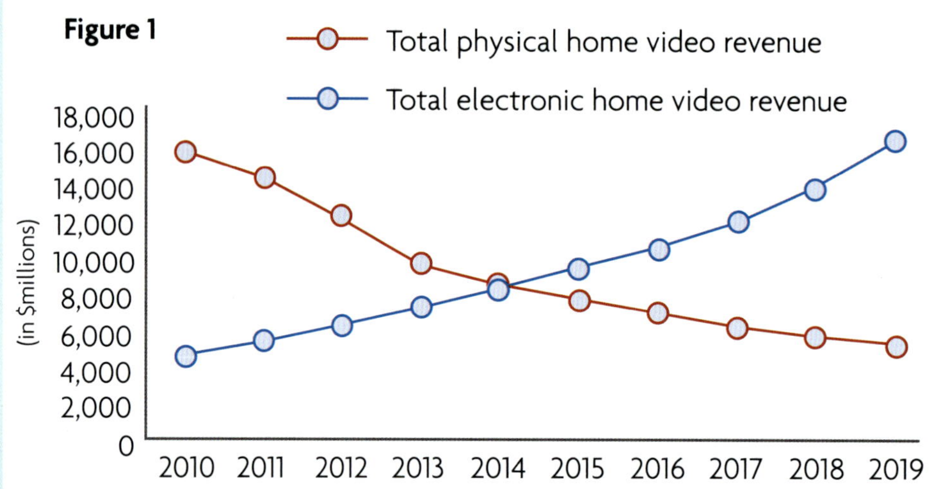

Exercise 5.1 Understanding and Interpreting a Line Graph

Work with a partner. Ask and answer the questions about Figure 1.

1 What is the topic of the graph?
2 What do the numbers on the vertical axis show?
3 What is the time period of the graph?
4 What trends do you see in the graph? What might explain these trends?

Choosing the Important Details from a Graph

When you write about a line graph, include details that support a trend.

- Include dates and / or numbers.
- Compare the beginning and end of each line in the graph.
- Compare different lines. Write about where they are similar or different.
- Point out major changes, not small ones.
- Do not include every data point.

Exercise 5.2 Applying the Skill

Work with a partner. Look at Figure 1 on page 334. Complete the sentences with important details.

1 According to the figure, revenues from physical home video sales and electronic home video sales have moved in opposite directions. As revenue from sales of _______________ has risen, revenue from sales of _______________ has fallen.

2 In 2010, sales from physical home videos were worth about $ _______________, compared to only about $_______________ for electronic home videos. Revenues from these two types of home video were exactly the opposite in the year _______________.

Writing the Concluding Paragraph

The concluding paragraph usually has three parts:

- **a transition phrase** such as *In conclusion* or *To sum up*
- **a restatement of the trend or thesis statement** using different words
- **a final comment** - an opinion, prediction, or recommendation

Exercise 5.3 Applying the Skill

Work with a partner. Re-read "What Has Happened to the American Dream?" on page 321. Then ask and answer the questions.

1 What is the thesis statement in the introductory paragraph?
2 Which sentence in the concluding paragraph restates the thesis statement?
3 What is the transition phrase in the concluding paragraph?
4 What is the writer's final comment? What type is it?

My Writing

Exercise 5.4 Writing Your Introductory and Concluding Paragraphs

Review Figure 1 on page 334. Complete the tasks.

1 Discuss the trends in the graph about home video revenue with a partner or small group.
2 Write your introductory paragraph. Include the general trend of the graph.
3 Write your concluding paragraph. Include a transition phrase, thesis summary, and final comment.
4 Review the Data from the Real World sections on pages 327 and 331. Use at least two of the phrasal verbs common in academic writing.

Comparatives

We Are All Different

1 Grammar in the Real World

ACADEMIC WRITING

Description and analysis

A Think of a family you know with more than one child. How similar or different are the children's personalities? Read the web article about birth order and personality. Do you agree with the results of the research it describes?

B Comprehension Check Match the child with the description.

1 The first-born child _________   a can be good at resolving conflicts.
2 The younger child _________   b often has an easy time.
3 The middle child _________   c often wants to be a leader.
4 The last-born child _________   d can often be creative and break rules.

C Notice Find the sentences in the article and complete them.

1 Because first-born children are usually _______________ and

_______________ _______________ their younger siblings,

they can try to dominate them.

2 Younger children are often _______________ _______________ and

_______________ _______________ _______________ older children.

Look at the adjectives and other words you wrote. The sentences show two ways to make comparisons. How are the two ways similar? How are they different?

Does Birth Order[1] Affect Personality?

Some researchers believe that birth order affects people's personalities. According to Dr. Frank Sulloway, professor of psychology, birth order differences are **as strong as** gender differences.[2]

First-born children, he says, are often **more responsible** and **more**
5 **conservative**. They are also **more likely** to be successful, and many first-born children are presidents and CEOs. Because first-born children are usually **bigger** and **stronger** than their **younger** siblings,[3] they can try to dominate[4] them.

As a result, says Sulloway, **younger** children can be rebellious and
10 **less likely** to obey rules. Younger children are often **more adventurous** and **more creative than older** children. They are also **more independent**. They may **try harder** to get attention from their parents, and parents often do not discipline **younger** children **as strictly as** their **older** siblings.

15 Not all researchers agree with these ideas, but most do agree that middle children can have a very difficult time. They are **more likely** to have to repeat a grade in school. Middle children often worry that they are **not** loved **as much as** their siblings. However, middle children are often the peacemakers in the family and are **more easygoing** as
20 a result.

Parents are often **less strict** with the "baby," or last-born child of the family. Last-born children are **more often** spoiled. Parents are usually **more relaxed** with them, and they often seem to have an easy time. However, if you are from a large family, that may be something you
25 already know!

[1]**birth order:** order in which children were born

[2]**gender difference:** difference between men and women

[3]**sibling:** brother or sister

[4]**dominate:** control

2 Comparative Adjectives and Adverbs

Grammar Presentation

Comparative adjectives and adverbs show how two things or ideas are different.

COMPARATIVE ADJECTIVE
First-born children are usually **bigger than** their siblings.

COMPARATIVE ADVERB
Younger children try **harder** to get their parents' attention.

2.1 Comparative Adjectives

Subject	Verb	Comparative Adjective	Than	
First-born children	are	**stronger** **more responsible** **less easygoing**	**than**	their siblings.

2.2 Comparative Adverbs

Subject	Verb (+ Object)	Comparative Adjective	Than	
First-born children	do things obey rules get spoiled	**better** and **more easily** **more often** **less often**	**than**	their siblings.

2.3 The Spelling of Comparative Adjectives and Adverbs

A Add *-er* to one-syllable adjectives and adverbs.

fast → *fast**er***
hard → *hard**er***
strong → *strong**er***

For one-syllable adjectives that end in a vowel + consonant, double the consonant.
Do not double the consonant *w*.

big → *big**ger***
hot → *hot**ter***
low → *low**er***

B Remove the *-y* and add *-ier* to two-syllable adjectives ending in *-y*.

early → *earl**ier***
funny → *funn**ier***
heavy → *heav**ier***

C Use *more* with most adjectives and adverbs that have two or more syllables.

hardworking → ***more** hardworking*
intelligent → ***more** intelligent*
quickly → ***more** quickly*
often → ***more** often*

2.3 The Spelling of Comparative Adjectives and Adverbs *(continued)*

D Some comparative adjectives and adverbs are irregular.

Adjectives			Adverbs		
good	→	*better*	*well*	→	*better*
bad	→	*worse*	*badly*	→	*worse*

▸▸ Adjectives and Adverbs: Comparative and Superlative Forms. See page A12.

2.4 Using Comparative Adjectives and Adverbs

A You can use comparative adjectives to describe how two nouns are different.

NOUN · ADJECTIVE · NOUN
*First-born children are sometimes **taller than** their siblings.*

You can use comparative adverbs to compare the way two people do the same action.

VERB · ADVERB · VERB
*My son **works harder** in school **than** my daughter works.*

B *Less* is the opposite of *more*.

*Julia is **more independent than** her brother Lucas.*
*Lucas is **less independent than** Julia.*
*He plays **more quietly than** his sister does.*
*His sister plays **less quietly**.*

Less is not usually used with one-syllable adjectives or adverbs, except *clear*, *safe*, and *sure*.

*My daughter is **younger than** my son.*
My daughter is ~~less old~~ than my son.

C You can use a pronoun after *than* instead of repeating the noun. In academic writing, use a subject pronoun + verb.

*Tim's sister is more creative than **he is**.*

When both verbs are the same, you do not need to repeat the verb after *than*.

*She works harder than **Tim**.*

You can also use an auxiliary verb.

*Tim's sister works harder than **he does**.*
*She did better in college than **he did**.*
*She's gone further in her career than **he has**.*

D You do not need *than* plus the second part of the comparison when the meaning is clear.

*Older children **are** often **more conservative**.*
(than younger children)

E You can also use a comparative adjective without *than* before a noun when the comparison is clear.

*Parents are strict with **older** children.*
(older than other children)

We Are All Different **339**

F In speaking, you can use an object pronoun after *than*. In formal speaking or academic writing, use a noun or subject pronoun and a verb or auxiliary verb.

Say: *"Tim's sister works harder than* **him**.*"*

Write: *Tim's sister works harder than* **Tim** / **he does**.

DATA FROM THE REAL WORLD

Some two-syllable adjectives have two comparative forms. However, one form is usually more frequent, especially in writing.

Use *-er* to form these comparative adjectives: *easier, narrower, quieter, simpler*	Mateo is **quieter** than his sister.
Use *more* to form these comparative adjectives: *more likely, more friendly*	Do you think she is **more friendly** than her brother?

 **Grammar Application**

Exercise 2.1 Comparative Forms

Listen to the news report about birth order and intelligence. Fill in the blanks with the words you hear.

A Norwegian study says that there may be differences in intelligence between brothers. The study showed that older siblings are <u>*more intelligent than*</u> their (1) younger siblings. The researchers gave intelligence tests to 60,000 pairs of brothers. They found that the older siblings did _________________________ their brothers (2) on the tests. The _________________________ boys' scores were definitely (3) _________________________ , although not by very much. (4)

Researchers say one reason for this may be that older siblings have _________________________ (5) language skills. Their language may develop _________________________ because they have (6) been in an adult environment _________________________ . It is possible that younger siblings are (7) _________________________ in other ways, for example, in emotional intelligence. (8)

The Norwegian study did not look at age differences. However, _________________________ (9) research suggests that when the age difference between two brothers is _________________________ , (10) the difference in intelligence is _________________________ . (11)

Exercise 2.2 More Comparative Forms

A Complete the sentences with the correct comparative forms. Use the information in the chart.

	Tom Mason	Dave Mason
Age	32	28
Height	6 feet, 3 inches tall	5 feet, 11 inches tall
Weight	200 pounds	152 pounds
Work style	hardworking	doesn't work hard
Personality	very conservative, serious, not very friendly	a little conservative, easygoing, funny, friendly
Hobbies and skills	good at sports, especially tennis; not good at guitar	plays tennis but not very athletic; plays guitar well

1 Dave is _younger than_ (young) Tom.

2 Tom is Dave's ____________________ (old) brother.

3 Tom is ____________________ (tall) Dave.

4 Tom is ____________________ (heavy) Dave.

5 Dave is ____________________ (hardworking) Tom.

6 Tom works ____________________ (hard).

7 Tom is a ____________________ (conservative) person.

8 Tom is ____________________ (athletic) Dave.

9 Tom is ____________________ (friendly) Dave.

10 Dave plays the guitar ____________________ (good) Tom.

B Write three more sentences about Tom and Dave. Use comparatives.

Dave is shorter than Tom.
Tom is better at sports than Dave.

____

____

____

We Are All Different **341**

Exercise 2.3 Comparatives with Be and Do

A Rewrite the sentences about Sarah and Louisa, two sisters who go to the same college. Use comparatives with the correct form of *be* or *do*.

1 In Biology 101, Sarah works really hard, but Louisa doesn't.

Sarah works harder than Louisa does.

2 Louisa is very creative. Sarah isn't.

3 Sarah lives very far from school. Louisa doesn't.

4 Louisa is good at writing. Sarah isn't.

5 Sarah learns quickly. Louisa doesn't.

6 Louisa is very quiet. Sarah isn't.

B What happens when you cross out *be* or *do*? Is the meaning still clear?

C Pair Work Rewrite the sentences in A so they are true for you and your partner. Give reasons. Tell the class about your partner.

Virginia works harder than I do. She has three jobs!

Exercise 2.4   More Comparative Practice

A How have you changed? Answer the questions. Use comparatives and try to give extra information.

1 Are you more or less shy than you used to be?

I'm less shy than I used to be. Now I enjoy parties because I'm more confident.

2 Do you work or study harder than you did when you were younger?

3 What can you do more easily now than last year?

4 What do you do on weekends more often than you used to?

5 What has been more difficult about studying English than you thought? What has been easier?

B Group Work **Discuss your answers in a group. Have you changed in similar or in different ways?**

I am less shy than I used to be, but Leona is more shy. She doesn't like speaking in front of the class. We've changed in different ways.

3 Comparisons with *As . . . As*

Grammar Presentation

<table>
<tr><td>You can use as . . . as to say that two ideas are the same or similar.
Not as . . . as means "less."</td><td>Birth order differences are as strong as gender differences.

Older children are sometimes not as creative as younger children. (= Older children are less creative.)</td></tr>
</table>

3.1 *As . . . As* with Adjectives

Subject	Verb	*As*	Adjective	*As*	
Younger children	are are not aren't	**as**	**smart creative good**	**as**	older children

3.2 *As . . . As* with Adverbs

Subject	Verb	*As*	Adverb	*As*	
The younger boys	learned didn't learn	**as**	**easily quickly well**	**as**	their older brothers.

A You can use *as* + adjective + *as* to show that two nouns are similar or the same.	*Max is **as intelligent as** his brother.*
You can use *as* + adverb + *as* to show that the way two people do things is the same or the way that two events happen is the same.	*Max **works as hard as** his brother.* *(How Max works = how his brother works.)*
B *Not as . . . as* shows that two ideas are not similar. It means "less than."	*Andreas is **not as ambitious as** his brother.* *(= Andreas is less ambitious than his brother.)*
Use *not as . . . as* instead of *less* with short adjectives and adverbs, such as *bad, easy, high, great,* and *big.*	*My brother's test score **was not as high as** my score.* *(= My brother's score was lower than my score.)*
C *As . . . as* can be followed by a noun or a subject pronoun + a verb or auxiliary verb.	*Kate's brother is as intelligent as **Kate/she is**.* *Kate's brother did as well in college as **she did**.* *He works as hard as **she does**.* *He's gone as far in his career as **she has**.*
D You do not need to use *as* + the second part of the comparison when the meaning is clear.	*Middle children feel their parents **don't love them as much** (as the other children).*
E In speaking informally, you can use an object pronoun after *as . . . as.*	*Say: "Kate's brother isn't as creative as **her**."*
In formal speaking or academic writing, use a noun or subject pronoun and a verb or auxiliary verb.	*Write: Kate's brother is not as creative as **Kate/she is**.*

 **DATA FROM THE REAL WORLD**

Research shows that these are some of the most common adjectives and adverbs with (*not*) as . . . as in speaking and writing:

adjectives: *bad, big, easy, good, great, hard, high, important, popular, simple, strong*
adverbs: *easily, fast, hard, much, often, quickly, well*

Grammar Application

Exercise 3.1 Forming (*Not*) As . . . As Sentences

A Rewrite the sentences in the article with (*not*) *as . . . as.* Keep the same meaning.

How Much Gender Difference Is There?

The following statements are common beliefs about gender differences:

1 Boys are better than girls at math.

Girls _are not as good as_ boys at math.

2 Women are better than men at communication.

Men________________________________ women at communication.

3 Teenage boys are more confident than teenage girls.

Teenage girls ________________________teenage boys.

4 Men solve problems more easily than women.

Women ________________________ men.

A study by psychologist Janet Shibley Hyde (2007) showed that these beliefs may not all be true. According to her study:

5 People think the differences between boys and girls are big, but they aren't.

The differences ________________________ people think.

6 Young girls and boys do equally well in math.

Young girls ________________________ boys in math.

7 Communication is equally hard for men and women.

Communication for women ______________ ________________________ it is for men.

8 Girls and boys are equally likely to have low confidence.

Boys ________________________ girls to have low confidence.

Hyde found that in 78 percent of tests, men and women were about the same. She did find some differences.

9 Boys are more aggressive than girls.

Girls ________________________ ________________________ .

10 Men get angry more quickly than women.

Women ________________________ ________________________ .

11 Men can throw objects further than women.

Women ________________________ ________________________ .

Hyde's study shows that most differences are in our beliefs, and not really in our gender. She hopes these beliefs will change.

B Pair Work Discuss the information with a partner. What did you know? What surprised you?

A *I didn't know that girls do as well as boys in math.*

B *I know. That surprised me, too.*

Exercise 3.2 Using *As . . . As*

A Pair Work Answer the questions. Then ask and answer the questions with a partner.

What is something . . .

1 you do as often as possible? Why?

I play soccer as often as I can because it is my favorite sport.

2 you can't do as often as you'd like? Why?

3 you do as quickly as you can each day? Why?

Who is . . .

4 as creative as you? Why do you think so?

5 as adventurous as you? Why do you think so?

B Group Work Tell the class about your partner.

A *Agnes plays soccer as often as possible. It's her favorite sport.*

B *Boris visits his parents as often as he can because he misses them.*

Exercise 3.3 Using *(Not) As . . . As*

A Over to You Think of a person you know who fits each description below. Write a sentence about each person using *(not) as . . . as* + a subject pronoun + verb.

1 works as hard as you　　*My sister works as hard as I do.*

2 doesn't talk as much as you

3 did as well as you in school

4 isn't as old as you

5 hasn't lived here as long as you

6 can speak English as well as you

7 doesn't drive as carefully as you

8 has studied as much as you

B Pair Work Discuss the people you know with a partner. Are your friends, relatives, and teachers similar or different?

A My sister works as hard as I do.
B What does she do?
A She's a nurse. We're both nurses.

4 Avoid Common Mistakes ⚠ 

1 **Do not use a comparative when you are not comparing two ideas.**

young
I have two very ~~younger~~ sons.

2 **Use *than*, not *that*, after a comparative.**

than
I am more patient now ~~that~~ I was.

3 **Do not use *more* and *-er* together.**
My work is ~~more~~ better than it used to be.
I work ~~more~~ harder now than I used to.

4 **Do not forget the second *as* in *as . . . as* comparisons.**

as
I do not see my family now as much ⌃ I did last year.

Editing Task

Find and correct 12 more mistakes in this student's personal essay.

How I Have Changed

I think I have changed in three important ways since high school. First, I have a ~~more~~ kinder personality now. I used to be less patient that I am now, especially with my grandparents. I have spent a lot of time with my grandparents in the last three years, and I have learned to be more patient with them and to understand them more better. I can see that getting old can be more difficult, so I try to
5 help my grandparents as often I can.

Second, I did not use to be as serious I am now about my education. I now realize that I need to study as much possible so I can get a diploma in engineering. Five years ago, I was very younger and did not study a lot. Now I'm studying more harder than I did then, and I do not skip classes as much I did in high school.

10 Finally, I worry less that I did because I have goals now. I know what I want and where I am going. In general, I have grown up and become more clearer about who I am and what I want out of life. I believe I am a better person that I used to be.

Description and Analysis

Brainstorm > Organize > **Write** > Edit

In Unit 25, you looked at line graphs and wrote a draft of the introductory and concluding paragraphs for your report that answers the prompt below. In this unit (26), you will use comparatives to describe and analyze a graph, and you will complete your report.

Describe the trends in a multiple line graph, and analyze the data. Do some additional research to discuss the trends you identify.

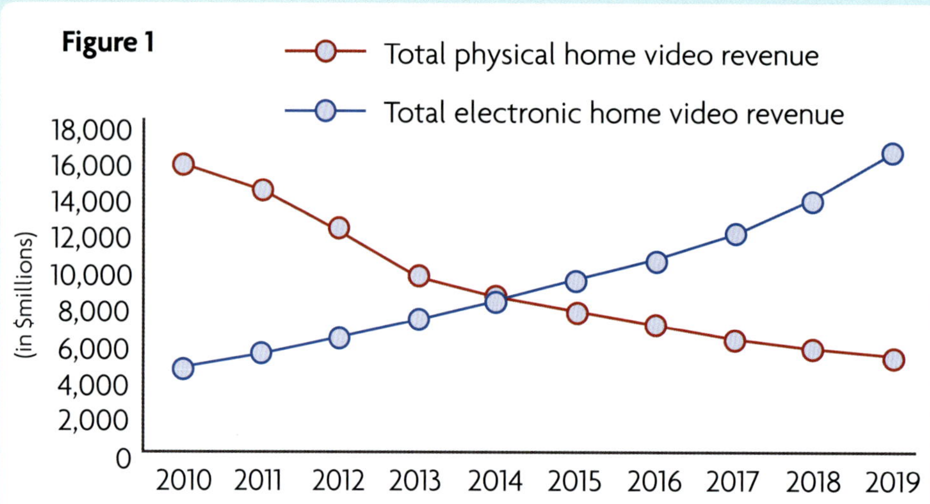

Using Comparatives to Describe and Analyze Graphs

Comparatives are very useful to describe and analyze multi-line graphs.

Majority of Americans now use Facebook, YouTube

% of U.S. adults who say they use the following social media sites online or on their cell phone

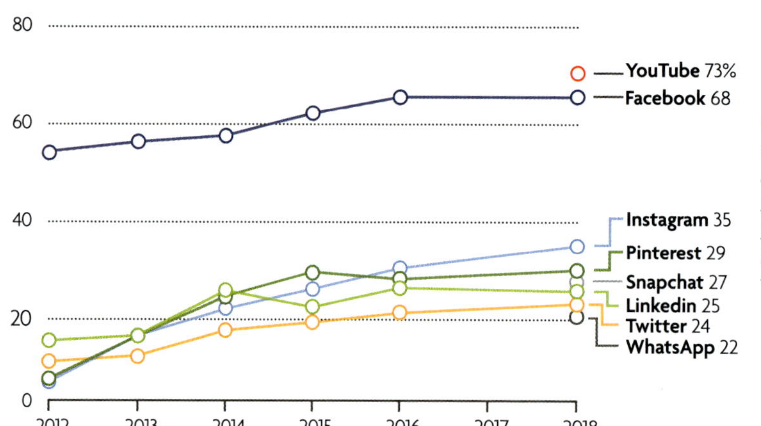

Note: Pre-2018 telephone poll data is not available for YouTube, Snapchat or WhatsApp.
Source: Survey conducted Jan. 3-10, 2018. Trend data from previous Pew Research Center surveys. "Social Media Use in 2018"

You can use comparatives to describe the changes between points on a line.

From 2012 to 2018, Instagram became **more and more popular.**

From 2015 to 2016, the use of Facebook increased **faster than** between 2017 and 2018.

You can also use comparatives to describe similarities and differences between data and trends in multiple-line graphs.

In 2014, Americans used Snapchat **as often as** Instagram.

However, by 2018, Snapchat was **less popular than** Instagram.

Instagram has grown **more quickly than** most other social media sites.

Exercise 5.1 Applying the Skill

Write four more comparative sentences about Americans' use of social media.

1 ____

2 ____

3 ____

4 ____

My Writing

Exercise 5.2 Writing Your First Draft

1 Review the prompt and Figure 1 on page 348.

2 Review your introductory and concluding paragraphs from My Writing in Unit 25.

3 Plan your body paragraph. Use the questions below to help you analyze the data.

- What is the relationship between the lines in the graph? Where are they similar or different?
- What trends can you identify? What are some reasons or explanations for them?

4 Write your body paragraph. Use comparatives to describe similarities and differences in the data.

5 When you are finished, revise your introductory and concluding paragraphs if necessary.

UNIT 27

Superlative Adjectives and Adverbs

The Best and the Worst

1 Grammar in the Real World

A What are some ways we can help people during disasters? Read the web article about technology and disaster relief. What is one way people use technology for disaster relief?

B Comprehension Check Answer the questions.

1 When did Hurricane Harvey happen?
2 Which hurricane hit hardest before Hurricane Harvey?
3 What is one way people used social media after the hurricane?
4 How did the Red Cross use social networking sites after the 2010 earthquake in Haiti?
5 What was special about the ice bucket challenge?

C Notice Read the sentences from the article and answer the questions.

1 "The heaviest rainfall was 51.88 inches in Cedar Bayou, making it a record for a single storm."

Was there heavier rain in another city?

2 "This (social media) seemed to be **the quickest** and **the most efficient** way to give and get information."
Did there seem to be a quicker and more efficient way to get and give information?

3 "The ALS ice bucket challenge became one of **the fastest** worldwide money-raising events in history."
Were there slower money-raising events before?

The TECHNOLOGY of RELIEF[1]

Natural disasters[2] can strike at any time and with no warning. However, **today's newest** technologies can help disaster victims in new and amazing ways. Here are a few examples.

When Hurricane Harvey hit Texas in August 2017, it was a terrible disaster. It was **the hardest** hurricane to hit the United States since Hurricane Katrina in 2005. **The heaviest** rainfall was 51.88 inches in Cedar Bayou, making it a record for a single storm. TV, newspapers, and radio all covered the storm, but **one of the best** sources of news about the disaster was social media. Soon after the storm hit, people began to post[3] reports of missing persons and to share news and stories. This seemed to be **the quickest** and **the most efficient** way to give and get information. The news on the radio and TV was often not **the most current.**[4] **One of the most important** roles of social media is to help raise money.[5] Soon after the major earthquake in Haiti in 2010, the Red Cross and other organizations that help people in disasters were trending topics on social networking sites. The Red Cross raised more than $8 million in fewer than 48 hours through these sites. Similarly, in 2014, the ALS ice bucket challenge became one of **the fastest** worldwide money-raising events in history. It raised $115 million dollars in just one summer!

Unfortunately, disasters will continue to happen. Hopefully, however, new technologies will continue to develop as well. They can help people to get and to give relief and funding in **the best** ways possible.

[1]**relief:** help
[2]**natural disaster:** a natural event (e.g., hurricane) that causes great damage
[3]**post:** announce; put something on the Internet
[4]**current:** up-to-date, present
[5]**raise money:** convince people to give money, usually for a charity

2 Superlative Adjectives and Adverbs

Grammar Presentation

Superlative adjectives and adverbs compare one idea to other ideas. They mean "more / less than all of the others."

SUPERLATIVE ADJECTIVE
*Social networking sites are **the newest** way to communicate after a disaster.*

SUPERLATIVE ADVERB
*The rainfall in Cedar Bayou was **the heaviest** ever recorded.*

2.1 Superlative Adjectives

Subject	Verb	*The*	Superlative Adjective	
The hurricane	was is	**the**	**biggest** **most expensive** **least damaging**	storm of the season.

2.2 Superlative Adverbs

Subject	Verb	(*The*)	Superlative Adjective	
Rescuers	worked	**(the)**	**hardest** **most quickly** **least efficiently**	right after the disaster.

2.3 Forming Superlative Adjectives and Adverbs

A Add *the* and *-est* to one-syllable adjectives and adverbs.

fast → *the* fast**est**
hard → *the* hard**est**
strong → *the* strong**est**

B For adjectives that end in a vowel + consonant, double the consonant.

big → *the* bi**gg**est
hot → *the* ho**tt**est

C Remove the *-y* and add *-iest* to two-syllable adjectives ending in *-y*.

busy → *the* bus**iest**
early → *the* earl**iest**
heavy → *the* heav**iest**

D Use *the most* with almost all adjectives that have two or more syllables and with adverbs ending in *-ly*.

expensive → **the most** expensive
frequently → **the most** frequently

2.3 Forming Superlative Adjectives and Adverbs *(continued)*

E Some superlative adjectives and adverbs are irregular.

Adjectives			Adverbs		
good	→	*the best*	*well*	→	*the best*
bad	→	*the worst*	*badly*	→	*the worst*

▶▶ Adjectives and Adverbs: Comparative and Superlative Forms: See page A12.

2.4 Using Superlatives

A Superlative adjectives show that a noun has the most or least of a certain quality. They compare one noun to the other nouns in a group.

*It was **the biggest** forest fire in the state.*
(Compares one forest fire to all others in the state.)

B Superlative adverbs show that a verb happens in the most or least of a certain way. They compare one action or situation to others in a group.

*That group worked **most effectively** after the disaster.*
(Compares the way that group worked to the way all other groups worked.)

C *The least* + adjective or adverb is the opposite of *the most* + adjective or adverb.

*This storm was **the least dangerous** one of the season. There wasn't much damage from it.*

The least is not usually used with one-syllable adjectives or adverbs.

*My daughter is **the youngest** of my children.*
My daughter is the ~~least old~~ of my children.

D You do not need to repeat words after the superlative when the meaning is clear.

*That disaster was **the biggest** (disaster).*
*Of all the technologies we use, this is **the easiest** (technology).*

E You can identify the group being compared with:

- a prepositional phrase (*in* and *of* are the most common prepositions).

*It was **the worst** storm **in** years.*

- a possessive form, like a possessive pronoun or noun. You do not need *the* before the superlative when you use possessives.

***Today's newest** technologies help us during disasters.*
***Our biggest** problem was raising relief money.*

F You can use *one of the* or *some of the* before a superlative adjective.	*It is* **one of the** *best ways to communicate quickly.*
Use a plural noun or a noncount noun with these expressions.	*These are* **some of the** *most interesting new technologies.*

DATA FROM THE REAL WORLD

The five most common superlative adjectives with *-est* in writing are *best, biggest, greatest, highest,* and *largest*.	*They are* **the best** *workers to have during a disaster.* *The disaster struck* **the largest** *city in the country.*
The five most common superlative adjectives with *most* in writing are *most common, most effective, most famous, most important,* and *most popular*.	*It's* **the most popular** *site for social networking.* *What is* **the most common** *problem after a disaster?*
Research shows that *the* is rarely used before superlative adverbs, except in formal speaking and writing.	*Rescue workers worked* **fastest** *in the first days after the event.*

Grammar Application

Complete the sentences with the superlative form of the adjectives or adverbs in parentheses. Use *most* or *-est* with ↑. Use *least* with ↓. Some forms are irregular.

1 The flood was **the largest** (↑ large) disaster of the past 10 years.

2 Rescue workers worked _______________________ (↑ hard) during the first few days.

3 It was one of _______________________ (↑ big) earthquakes in history.

4 This is _______________________ (↓ useful) way to help during a disaster.

5 This disaster was the state's _______________________ (↑ bad) storm.

6 People donated money _______________________ (↑ quickly) using websites.

7 It was the area's _______________________ (↓ damaging) hurricane of the year.

8 Medical staff worked _______________________ (↓ effectively) during the night.

Exercise 2.2 More Superlative Forms

A Write the superlative form of each of the words below. Then listen to the lecture about the eruption of Mount Vesuvius and the Great Chicago Fire. Listen for the superlative forms of the words in the chart, and check (✓) which event they describe.

		Eruption of Mount Vesuvius	Great Chicago Fire
1 bad	*the worst*	☐	☐
2 big		☐	☐
3 famous		☑	☐
4 fast		☐	☐
5 good		☐	☐
6 helpful		☐	☐
7 important		☐	☐
8 interesting		☐	☐
9 popular		☐	☐

B Listen again. Complete the sentences with the words you hear.

1 The eruption of Mount Vesuvius is ________________________ ________________ natural disasters in history.

2 It is also probably ________________________ disaster in history.

3 However, it has also been ________________________ events in history for archeologists.

4 It was ________________________ fire and ________________________ disaster in the history of the city.

5 ________________________ story is that a cow kicked over a lantern in a barn and started the fire.

6 The way people worked together after the fire was ________________________ result.

7 I think that has to be ________________________ building projects in history.

8 This also shows how people often work together ________________________ when they are helping one another.

Mount Vesuvius

The Great Chicago Fire

Exercise 2.3 More Superlative Practice

A Look at the information in the chart about three forest fires. Write eight more sentences about the information. Use superlative adjectives and adverbs from the box. Use some words more than once.

| ~~big~~ | damaging | expensive | long | quickly | short | small |

	Westland Fire	Highside Fire	Lakeview Fire
1 Size of fire	100 acres	25 acres	50 acres
2 How long the fire lasted	10 days	3½ days	4 days
3 Damage from the fire (+ = 20 cabins destroyed)	++++	++	+++
4 Cost of fighting the fire	$$$$$	$$	$$$
5 How quickly the firefighters arrived to fight the fire	5 minutes	7 minutes	8 minutes

The Westland fire was the biggest fire. The Highside fire was the smallest.

1 ____

2 ____

3 ____

4 ____

5 ____

6 ____

7 ____

8 ____

B Pair Work Check your partner's sentences. Are they similar or different from yours?

Exercise 2.4 Using Superlatives

A Over to You Write three superlative sentences about yourself or people you know. In each sentence, use one word or expression from each column.

Expressions	Adjectives		Nouns	
one of the	good	useful	job	technology
some of the	bad	funny	family	life
my friend's/brother's/family's . . .	interesting	enjoyable	story	pet
my/our/your	exciting	unusual	classes	hobby
	difficult		hometown	

This has been one of the least exciting years of my life.
My brother's most unusual pet was a spider.

B Over to You Write three more superlative sentences about yourself or people you know. In each sentence, use one word or expression from each column.

Verbs		Adverbs		Expressions	
study	run	well	easily	I know	in my life
work	speak English	badly	fast	of anyone I know	in my family
play	cook	carefully	quietly	of my life	in the world
learn	drive	quickly	creatively	of the year	
walk		slowly			

My friend Lisa cooks the best of anyone I know.

In my family, my mother drives the most carefully.

3 Avoid Common Mistakes ⚠

1 **Use *the most* with long adjectives. Do not use *-est*.**

    most helpful

They were the ~~helpfulest~~ *workers after the hurricane.*

2 ***Good*** **and** ***bad*** **have irregular superlative adjective and adverb forms.**

  worst   *best*

It was the ~~baddest~~ *fire of the year.*   *Everyone worked* ~~wellest~~ *early in the morning.*

3 **Use a possessive pronoun before a superlative. Do not use an object pronoun.**

        his

Cleaning up after the storm was ~~him~~ *biggest problem.*

4 **Do not put a superlative adverb between the verb and the object.**

       the fastest

They helped ~~the fastest~~ *those people* ∧ *after the storm.*

Editing Task

Find and correct nine more mistakes in the e-mail.

Hi Miko,

                                                   worst

We had a terrible storm last week. It was the ~~baddest~~ storm of the decade. It was probably the terrifyingest experience of my life. The children were home with me. All three of them were scared, but Alexis behaved the wellest. She was the helpfulest. She kept the other children calm. The dog was

5   probably the difficultest! He barked and barked.

    After the storm, we went outside. The damage to our house is the baddest. Me biggest problem is getting someone to help us fix it. There were some people injured, so rescue workers helped the fastest those people. After that, they started cleaning up the most quickly our neighborhood. A tree fell on our garage and is still there, so that's us biggest problem right now. We hope someone will

10   move it tomorrow.

Pat

Academic Writing

Description and Analysis

Brainstorm > Organize > Write > **Edit**

In Unit 26, you completed your first draft of a report that described and analyzed the graph in Figure 1. In this unit (27) you will revise and edit your draft.

Describe the trends in a multiple line graph, and analyze the data. Do some additional research to discuss the trends you identify.

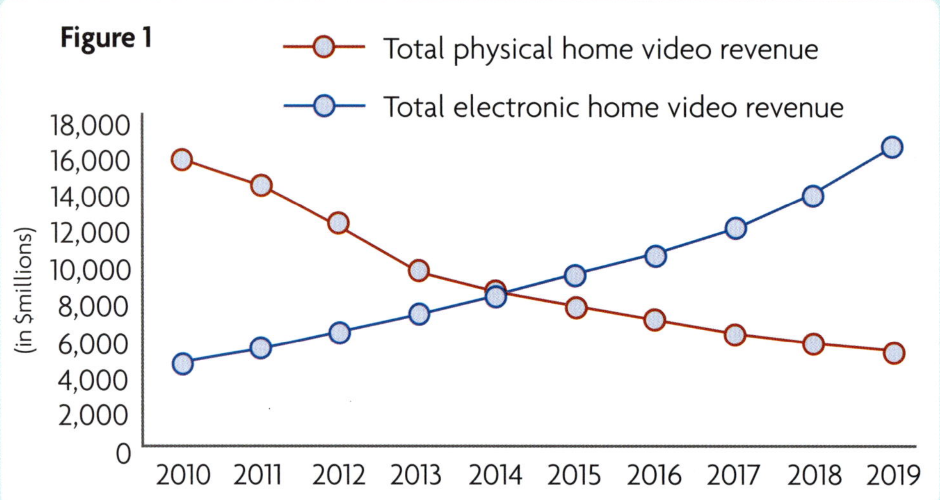

My Writing

Exercise 4.1 Revising Your Ideas

1 Work with a partner. Use the questions below to give feedback on your partner's report.
   - Which of your partner's ideas seem strongest to you?
   - Which of your partner's ideas need to be explained more clearly?
   - What could your partner add or remove to make the essay stronger and easier to understand?

2 Use the feedback from your partner to revise your report.

Using Superlatives in Academic Writing

Superlative adjectives and adverbs are often used to describe important events in news stories and history books. However, accuracy is important in academic writing, so academic writers must be careful when they use superlative forms.

Accurate superlative: In the last decade, 2019 was **the most successful** year for electronic home video products by revenue. (The information in the graph supports this statement.)

Inaccurate superlative: Electronic home video companies are **the most successful** entertainment companies in the world. (The information in the graph does not support this statement because it does not discuss other types of entertainment companies, which may be more successful.)

Exercise 4.2 Applying the Skill

Review the graph in Figure 1 and your report. Add at least one accurate superlative statement.

Exercise 4.3 Editing Your Writing

Use the checklist to review and edit your report.

Did you completely answer the prompt?	
Does your thesis statement include a general trend?	
Does your body paragraph describe and analyze the data to support your thesis?	
Did you use noun and verb phrases to describe changes and trends in the graph?	
Did you choose important details to describe and analyze the graph?	
Does your concluding paragraph include a transition phrase, summarize your thesis, and make a final comment?	

Exercise 4.4 Editing Your Grammar

Use the checklist to review and edit the grammar in your report.

Did you use transitive and intransitive verbs correctly?	
Did you use verb + preposition combinations correctly?	
Did you use academic phrasal verbs and avoid informal phrasal verbs?	
Did you use comparatives and superlatives correctly?	
Did you avoid the common mistakes in the charts on pages 319, 333, 347, and 357?	

Exercise 4.5 Writing Your Final Draft

Apply the feedback and edits from Exercises 4.1 to 4.4 to write the final draft of your essay.

Gerunds and Infinitives (1)

Managing Time

1 Grammar in the Real World

A Think of a time when someone made you wait. How did you feel? Read the web article about how different cultures think about time. What are some different ways that people see time?

B Comprehension Check Answer the questions.

1 Why does Joe feel frustrated?
2 If people like to control time, which view do they have?
3 If people don't expect to control time, which view do they have?
4 What are two tips for avoiding time problems with multicultural groups?

C Notice Underline the first verb (main verb) in the sentences below. Circle the second verb.

1 Joe needs to leave soon.
2 People from these cultures do not expect to control time.
3 Joe enjoys keeping a schedule.
4 How can Joe avoid experiencing problems with multicultural meetings?

Look at the second verb in the sentences. How are the second verbs in sentences 1 and 2 different from the ones in sentences 3 and 4?

VIEWS of TIME

Joe is a new manager at his company. He is leading his first team meeting today, and he is feeling frustrated. He **remembered to e-mail** everyone about the meeting, but one person is missing. Did she **forget to come**? Also, Joe **needs to leave** soon, but the group has not
5 discussed everything on the agenda.[1] He **remembers arranging** a two-hour meeting, and he has **tried to keep** the discussion moving forward. However, he has not succeeded. What is the problem? Many of Joe's team members are from different cultures, and different cultures see time very differently.

10 For people in some cultures, like Joe's, time is linear.[2] Events happen one after the other, along a time line, and each one has a beginning and an end point. People in these cultures **like to control** their time. For example, Joe **enjoys keeping** a schedule, and he **likes being** punctual.[3]

15 However, people from other cultures, like some of Joe's team members, see time as a cycle.[4] In this view, events do not have specific beginning and end points – they occur and then reoccur. People from these cultures do not **expect to control** time, so they often do not **like to make** schedules. Instead, they **prefer to be** flexible.

20 How can Joe **avoid experiencing** problems with multicultural meetings? Here are some tips: Get other people on the team to help plan the meeting. If they help create the agenda, it will be more realistic for them. Also, **try to be** flexible. Understand the reasons behind different ideas about time. **Try following** these tips, and you will have
21 more productive meetings.

[1]**agenda:** list of points to discuss
[2]**linear:** following a straight line; continuing in a clear way from one part to the next
[3]**punctual:** on time
[4]**cycle:** a process that repeats

2 Verbs Followed by Gerunds or Infinitives

Grammar Presentation

A gerund is the *-ing* form of a verb, used as a noun.

An infinitive is *to* + the base form of a verb.

VERB   GERUND
I **kept looking** at the clock during the meeting.

VERB   INFINITIVE
We **expected to finish** by 4:00 p.m.

2.1 Using Verbs with Gerunds and Infinitives

A Some verbs can be followed by a gerund, but not by an infinitive.

I kept looking at the clock during the meeting.
I kept to look at the clock during the meeting.

B Some verbs can be followed by an infinitive, but not by a gerund.

We expected to finish by 4:00 p.m.
We expected finishing by 4:00 p.m.

C Some verbs can be followed by an infinitive or by an object + an infinitive. These verbs include *expect*, *need*, and *want*.

VERB   INFINITIVE
Roberto   expects   to go   soon.

VERB   OBJECT   INFINITIVE
*Roberto   expects   **us**   to go   soon.*

D When a verb is followed by an infinitive or gerund, use *not* before the infinitive or gerund to form a negative statement.

*Jim suggested **not leaving** early today.*
*We agreed **not to work** after 5 o'clock.*

E You can use *and* or *or* to connect two infinitives or two gerunds. When you connect infinitives, you don't usually repeat *to*, especially when the sentence is short.

*We **suggested waiting and going** another day.*
*I **need to stop and think** about this for a minute.*

▸▸ Spelling Rules for Verbs Ending in *-ing*: See page A4.

2.2 Verbs Followed by a Gerund Only

avoid	involve
consider	keep (continue)
deny	mind (object to)
enjoy	recall (remember)
finish	suggest

2.3 Verbs Followed by an Infinitive Only

agree	plan
decide	refuse
expect	seem
hope	tend (be likely)
need	want

▸▸ Verbs + Gerunds and Infinitives: See page A5.

🌐 DATA FROM THE REAL WORLD

Research shows that these are the most common verbs followed by a gerund in speaking and writing:			These are the most common verbs followed by an infinitive in speaking and writing:		
avoid	finish	miss	agree	hope	seem
consider	involve	practice	decide	need	tend
deny	keep	risk	expect	plan	want
enjoy	mind	suggest	fail	refuse	

🖥 Grammar Application

Exercise 2.1 Listening for Gerunds and Infinitives

Listen to a podcast about how people think about time. Complete the sentences with the gerund or infinitive you hear.

Most people feel that time speeds up as they get older. At the end of each day, adults often ask themselves: Why haven't I done the things that I planned __to do__ (do) today? (1)

When you are a child, time seems ___________ (go) very slowly. As you get older, time tends (2)

___________ (pass) more quickly. Why do adults and (3) children see time differently?

According to psychologists, one theory is that children tend ___________ (look) forward. On a car trip, for (4) example, children always want ___________ (arrive). (5) They ask, "Are we there yet?" Children look forward, so time seems ___________ (last) longer. Adults, on the other hand, enjoy (6) ___________ (look) back and ___________ (think) about their (7) (8) memories.

In addition, adults tend ___________ (be) busy, so time often passes (9) more quickly for them. Also, most adults will keep ___________ (look) at (10) their watch throughout the day, and as a result, are more aware of time.

Finally, children have a lot of new experiences to process, but as people get older, they do not tend ___________ (have) so many new (11) experiences. This also speeds time up. Maybe experiencing new adventures as we get older can help us feel as if we can regain a little bit of that childhood sense of time.

Complete the e-mail about problems with time in multicultural business settings.
Circle the correct answer.

To productionteam@cambridge.org
From jj@cambridge.org
Subject Time Management Issues

Dear Team,

As you all know, yesterday morning we had an important meeting. I hoped **to finish** / **finishing** at noon. However, the meeting did not end until 1:30 p.m. In addition, (1) we did not finish **to discuss** / **discussing** everything on the agenda. I do not mind (2) **to end** / **ending** late. However, we need **to cover** / **covering** everything on the agenda. (3) (4)

At the end of the meeting, some of you suggested **to continue** / **continuing** our (5) discussions over lunch. I usually avoid **to combine** / **combining** work with meals, so I (6) suggested **not to do** / **not doing** that. We also considered **to stop** / **stopping** and (7) (8) **to continue** / **continuing** another day. In the end, we decided **to arrange** / **arranging** another (9) (10) meeting for next week.

I want **to feel** / **you to feel** good about coming to meetings when I ask you to come. (11) For this reason, I need **to help** / **the team to help** me plan meetings from now on. Can we (12) agree **to write** / **writing** the agenda for next week's meeting together? Can I expect (13) **to participate** / **everyone to participate** with me in this? (14)

Good time management involves **to agree** / **agreeing** on an agenda and then (15) **follow** / **following it**. I hope you all agree. (16)

Sincerely,

Joe

Exercise 2.3 Using Gerunds and Infinitives

A What can you tell the people in these situations? Give advice with gerunds or infinitives.

Situation	Advice
1 My friends always come late to my parties.	Your friends need _to call you and tell you that they are going to be late_ .
2 Heather is always late for class.	She should plan ___________ .
3 Roberto always turns his homework in late.	He should avoid ___________ .
4 Time goes so slowly for me at work. I look at the clock again and again, but it never changes!	You shouldn't keep ___________ .
5 Wei doesn't leave me a message when he's going to be late.	He should agree ___________ .
6 Lisa refuses to wear a watch.	She needs ___________ .

B Pair Work Compare answers in A with a partner. Is your advice similar or different?

A I think Heather should plan to get to class on time.
B I said Heather should plan to have a friend call her one hour before class starts.

3 Verbs Followed by Gerunds and Infinitives

Grammar Presentation

Some verbs can be followed by both a gerund and an infinitive. Sometimes the meaning is the same. Sometimes it is different.	I **stopped e-mailing** the agendas. (For a while, I e-mailed the agendas. Then I stopped doing that.) I **stopped to e-mail** the agendas. (different meaning) (First I stopped what I was doing. Then I e-mailed the agendas.)

A Some verbs can be followed by an infinitive or a gerund without a change in meaning. These verbs include *begin*, *continue*, *hate*, *like*, *love*, *prefer*, and *start*.

*Everyone **began to speak**/**speaking** at the same time.*

*Wei **loves to get up**/**getting up** early.*

B Some verbs can be followed by an infinitive or a gerund, but the meaning changes. These verbs include *forget*, *remember*, *stop*, and *try*.

*Luis **will** never **forget meeting** the president.* (Luis met the president, and he will never forget that he did this.)

*Luis **must** not **forget to enclose** his résumé with his application.* (Luis has not enclosed his résumé with his application yet, and he must not forget to do this.)

C In sentences with *forget*, *remember*, or *stop* + a gerund, the gerund tells what happens first.

SECOND EVENT   FIRST EVENT
*Jim **remembered making** an appointment.*
(First Jim made the appointment. Later, he remembered this.)

In sentences with *forget*, *remember*, or *stop* + an infinitive, the infinitive tells what happens second, after the action of the main verb.

FIRST EVENT   SECOND EVENT
*Jim **remembered to make** an appointment.*
(First Jim remembered that he needed to make an appointment. Then he made it.)

D In sentences with *try* + gerund, the action of the gerund generally happens.

*Marta **tried setting** her alarm for 6:00 a.m., but she was still late.* (She set the alarm.)

In sentences with *try* + infinitive, the action of the infinitive often does not happen or is not successful.

*Marta **tried to set** her alarm for 6:00 a.m., but the clock wasn't working.* (She didn't set the alarm.)

E You can use *and* or *or* to connect two infinitives or two gerunds. With infinitives, you don't usually repeat *to*, especially when the sentence is short.

*He **loves planning and attending** meetings.*

*He **loves to plan and attend** meetings.*

*I **like walking or riding** a bike to work.*

With verbs that can be followed by either a gerund or an infinitive, use the same form for both after the verb.

*I **like walking and riding** a bike to work.*

I like walking and ~~to ride~~ my bike to work.

Grammar Application

Exercise 3.1 Same or Different Meaning?

A Rewrite the sentences. Change the gerunds in **bold** to infinitives and the infinitives in **bold** to gerunds. If the meaning of the sentence stays the same, write *S* next to the sentence. If the meaning is different, write *D*.

1 I remembered **making** an appointment with the doctor.

   I remembered to make an appointment with the doctor.   D

2 My co-workers and I like **to learn** about how different cultures view time.

3 We began **discussing** our plans for next year.

4 To manage her time, our colleague Kelly tried **to buy** a calendar.

5 Our boss started **to accept** that different cultures see time differently.

6 Kelly and I love **having** a very long lunch break.

7 Our colleague Bill hates **mixing** work and social activities.

8 Our co-workers didn't stop **eating** lunch until 4:00 p.m.

9 We continued **to discuss** our problems until very late at night.

10 Jill forgot **to contact** Janet last week.

11 Bo remembered **writing** and **sending** the memo.

B Pair Work   In which sentences in A does the meaning change? Explain the difference in meaning to a partner.

The meaning is different in number 1. In the first sentence, he made the appointment and later remembered that. In the second sentence, he first remembered that he needed to make an appointment. Then he made it.

Exercise 3.2 *Forget*, *Remember*, *Stop*, and *Try*

Read the class discussion. Circle the correct answer.

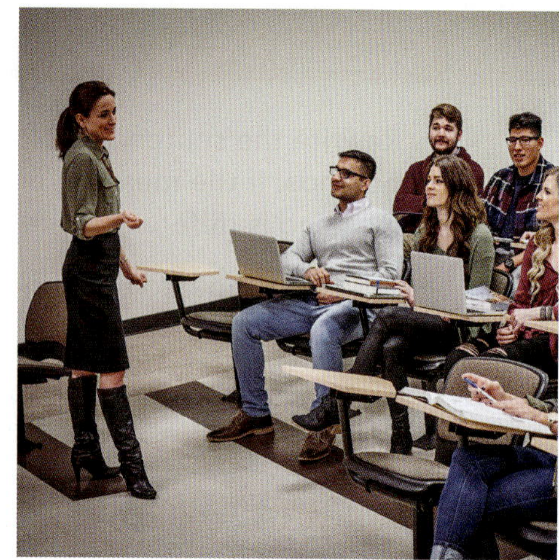

Ms. Vargas Class, tell me how you did research for this assignment. Did most of you use the web?

Laura Well, yes. I tried **reading** / **to read** a long article on the web. The conclusion was good, (1) but I didn't learn much from the rest of the article. I found another article on a website about linear time, but I stopped **reading** / **to read** it because it wasn't very academic. (2)

Wendy I tried **getting** / **to get** on to a website about time and psychology, but I (3) couldn't make it work. It kept shutting down.

Ms. Vargas Did anyone else have trouble?

Ahmet No. Not really. I remember **reading** / **to read** one article that wasn't very (4) good. I found another really good website, though, and I luckily remembered **bookmarking** / **to bookmark** it before I closed it. (5)

Wendy That was a good idea! I found one good site, but I forgot **bookmarking** / **to bookmark** it. I was reading an article, but then I stopped (6) **reading** / **to read** and answered the phone. When I got back, my computer was (7) off. That was weird because I don't remember it **crashing** / **to crash!** (8)

Diego I didn't use the web. In fact, I read a book. I prefer books. I read for a while and take notes, then I stop **thinking** / **to think** for a few minutes about my own (9) ideas. Then I add my ideas to the notes.

Exercise 3.3 Using Verbs Followed by Gerunds and Infinitives

A Over to You Answer the questions about time. Write complete sentences.

1 Where do you like to go when you have free time?

   I like to go / going to the beach when I have free time.

2 What do you prefer to do after work or school?

3 What do you try doing when you feel bored?

4 How do you remember not to miss appointments?

B Pair Work Ask and answer the questions in A with a partner. Are your answers similar or different?

4 Avoid Common Mistakes ⚠

1	**Do not use gerunds after verbs that require infinitives.**
	to discuss
	They did not expect ~~discussing~~ work during lunch.
2	**Do not use infinitives after verbs that require gerunds.**
	writing
	We finished ~~to write~~ our report at 5:00 p.m.
3	**Remember: Infinitives include to.**
	to
	I want⌃learn about other cultures.

Editing Task

Find and correct eight more mistakes in this paragraph from a web article about time and boredom.

FIGHTING BOREDOM

looking

Do you keep ~~to look~~ at the clock when you are bored? Does time seem going slowly for you? If you expect having a boring life, you will have a boring life. It is time to make a change! Here are things you can do to avoid to feel bored. First, try look at the clock less often. Time will go more quickly. Next, use your time differently. Start thinking

5 about things that interest you. Try do things that you know will be interesting. If you enjoy to do an activity, time will pass more quickly. In addition, do things that involve changing your daily habits. For example, try wearing your watch on the other wrist or to brush your teeth with the other hand. If your mind is active, time will seem passing more quickly.

5 Academic Writing

Summary and Response

Brainstorm > Organize > Write > Edit

In this writing cycle (Units 28-32), you will write summary and response paragraphs for the prompt below. In this unit (28), you will learn how to analyze and summarize a text.

Write a summary paragraph of "Nontraditional Weddings." Then write a response paragraph giving your opinion about the changes in wedding traditions described in the article.

Exercise 5.1 Preparing to Read

Work with a partner. Ask and answer the questions about weddings in your culture.

1 How long do weddings usually last?
2 What time are guests expected to arrive before the ceremony? How long should they plan to stay?
3 How have wedding traditions changed in the past 50 years?
4 What is the most interesting wedding you have ever attended?

Exercise 5.2 Focusing on Vocabulary

Read the definitions. Complete the sentences with the correct form of the words in bold.

> **belief** (n) an idea that you are certain is true
> **ceremony** (n) a formal event (such as a wedding) with special traditions, activities, or words
> **couple** (n) two people who are married or in a relationship
> **engaged** (adj) having a formal agreement to get married
> **reception** (n) a formal party that is given to celebrate a special event
> **relative** (n) any member of your family
> **theme** (n) the main idea, subject, or topic of an event, book, musical piece, etc.

1 In many countries, the wedding ___________________ traditionally takes place in a church or other religious building.

2 A honeymoon is a time for a newly married ___________________ to relax after the wedding.

3 Children tend to have the same ___________________ as their parents, but their thinking often changes as they become adults.

4 My sister and her partner were ___________________ on New Year's Eve. They plan to get married next year.

5 Some people choose unusual ________________, like superheroes or Star Wars movies, for their weddings.

6 My best friend got married at city hall, and then had the ________________ at a fancy hotel.

7 I enjoy getting together with all my ________________, especially my cousins, during the holidays.

Nontraditional **Weddings**

Even if they have never attended a traditional American wedding in person, most people have probably seen such weddings in movies or on television. People enjoy seeing the beautiful bride in her white dress, the handsome groom, the **ceremony** in the church,
5 the romantic music—these customs are familiar to people all over the world. Though most American **couples** still choose to have this kind of traditional wedding, more and more couples these days are deciding to have unique weddings that reflect their **beliefs**, hobbies, and personal style. Three types of nontraditional weddings are
10 adventure weddings, destination weddings, and theme weddings.

Adventure weddings typically involve combining the marriage ceremony with a physical activity that has special meaning for the couple. Cathy and Frank Mason are enthusiastic scuba divers who enjoy diving all over the world. In 2012, they met on a shark-diving
15 adventure near Key West, Florida. A year later, they were **engaged** and started to plan their wedding. Cathy had always dreamed of a large, traditional wedding in a church, but from the start Frank had a different idea. He suggested combining their wedding with their love for each other and the activity they loved most—scuba diving. Cathy
20 finally agreed, and the couple were married underwater in May, 2015— surrounded by numerous friends and **relatives**, all in scuba gear. Other adventure-seeking couples have gotten married while surfing, skydiving, or riding in a hot-air balloon.

Most people are less adventurous than the Masons, but many
25 of them love to travel. It is becoming more and more common for such couples to get married in a distant location. An American couple, Arielle Cogan and Richard Thompson, met when both of them were spending a year studying history in Edinburgh, Scotland. They fell in love and became engaged, but neither of them wanted
30 to have an ordinary wedding. Instead, they were married in a small, 18th-century church in Edinburgh with just their families and a few close friends as guests. The bride wore a traditional white dress and the groom wore a kilt, which is a traditional Scottish skirt for men. Destination weddings like the Thompsons' allow couples to get
35 married in the place of their dreams. The main disadvantage is the cost: It can be expensive to have family and friends fly to an exotic location on the other side of the world.

Finally, a theme wedding allows couples to create a fun, nontraditional wedding that centers on a beloved book, song, story,
40 or historical period. A couple from Epping, New Hampshire, planned every detail of their wedding, from the wedding vows to the food at the **reception**, around the **theme** of the Harry Potter books by J.K. Rowling. Although it took a lot of planning, their guests will probably never forget attending the event. Other unique themes for weddings
45 have included pirates, superheroes like Superman, a Hawaiian luau, country music, Victorian England, the 1960s, a fairy tale like "Cinderella", and many, many more.

Unlike the past, when a traditional religious wedding was the only option available to marrying couples, couples these days are
50 free to choose almost any type of wedding they can imagine. The variety of wedding styles and locations is perhaps a reflection of the general trend toward individual choice and self-expression that has been growing stronger in the U.S. since the 1960s. Whether a couple chooses to have an old-fashioned church wedding or a ceremony
55 at the top of a mountain, the central purpose of a wedding—to celebrate the union of a couple in the presence of the people who love them—has not changed, and it probably never will.

Exercise 5.3 Comprehension Check

Read the text on page 371. Work with a partner. Ask and answer the questions.

1 Which is more common in the U.S., traditional or non-traditional weddings?
2 What are four examples of an adventure wedding mentioned in the text?
3 What is one reason a couple might not choose to have a destination wedding?
4 What is a theme wedding?

Exercise 5.4 Noticing the Grammar

1 Underline the gerunds and circle the infinitives in paragraph 1 of the text on page 371.
2 Look at the word *forget* in line 44. Is it followed by a gerund or an infinitive? Does changing the gerund or infinitive also change the meaning of the sentence? If so, how?

Analyzing a Text

To summarize and respond to an article, it is important for a writer to understand and analyze the original text carefully. Here are some steps to follow:

- Identify the main idea, or thesis, of the article. This is often in the first paragraph.
- Find the topic and main idea of each paragraph. Look for the topic sentences.
- Make notes about the most important details that support the main ideas. For example, look for key examples, advantages or disadvantages, and important reasons. Do not mark all examples or small details. Be sure to use your own words when you make notes so that you do not plagiarize in your summary.

These steps will help you write the summary paragraph.

Exercise 5.5 Applying the Skill

Work with a partner. Analyze "Non-traditional Weddings." Make notes in the chart on page 373.

1 What is the main idea of the reading? Write a short sentence in the chart.
2 Look at each paragraph of the reading. What was the topic? Which example(s) did the writer give? What advantage and /or disadvantage did the writer include? Write these details in the chart.
3 What was the writer's conclusion? Write it in your own words. Hint: The main idea and conclusion should be similar.

Paragraph 1	**Main idea/Thesis:**
Paragraph 2	**Topic:** adventure weddings **Example:** the Masons' underwater wedding **Key detail (reason):** to celebrate their love of diving
Paragraph 3	**Topic:** **Example:** **Key detail:**
Paragraph 4	**Topic:** **Example:** **Key detail:**
Paragraph 5	**Restatement of thesis:** **Final comment:**

My Writing

Exercise 5.6 Analyzing a Text

1 Review the article "Views of Time" on page 361. Make a chart like the one in Exercise 5.5. Use the chart to analyze the article.

2 Compare your chart with a partner's and revise it as necessary.

Summarizing a Text

A **summary paragraph** states the main ideas and important points of a longer text. You should always write a summary in your own words, but do not change the writer's ideas. This paragraph should not include your opinion.

A summary is always much shorter than the original text. Imagine if you were describing a movie to a friend. You would only include the essential parts of the story. In the same way, a written summary should only include the most important ideas and information. A good rule of thumb is to write about one sentence for each main idea in the original text.

Exercise 5.7 Applying the Skill

1 Use your chart in Exercise 5.6 to write a summary paragraph of "Views of Time." Remember to use your own words.

2 Compare your summary with a partner's. Give each other feedback. Pay special attention to your use of gerunds and infinitives.

Gerunds and Infinitives (2)

Civil Rights

1 Grammar in the Real World

ACADEMIC WRITING

Summary and response

A Are all people treated fairly in the United States today? Read the article about the civil rights movement. What types of discrimination have become illegal since the 1960s?

B Comprehension Check **Answer the questions.**

1 What kinds of discrimination were there in the United States in the past?
2 What are two examples of segregation?
3 What did civil rights workers want to change?
4 What other groups fought for civil rights after Congress passed the Civil Rights Act of 1964?

C Notice **Find the sentences in the reading and complete them.**

1 _____________________ the laws wasn't easy.

2 _____________________ against people because of their age or for other reasons was common in the United States in the past.

3 Now, because of this law, it is illegal _____________________ people.

4 Civil rights workers opposed this segregation and worked hard _____________________ attention to unfair laws.

Look at sentences 1 and 2. You learned that gerunds can come after certain verbs. Where else can gerunds occur in a sentence? Look at sentences 3 and 4. One infinitive shows a purpose or reason for the action. Which one?

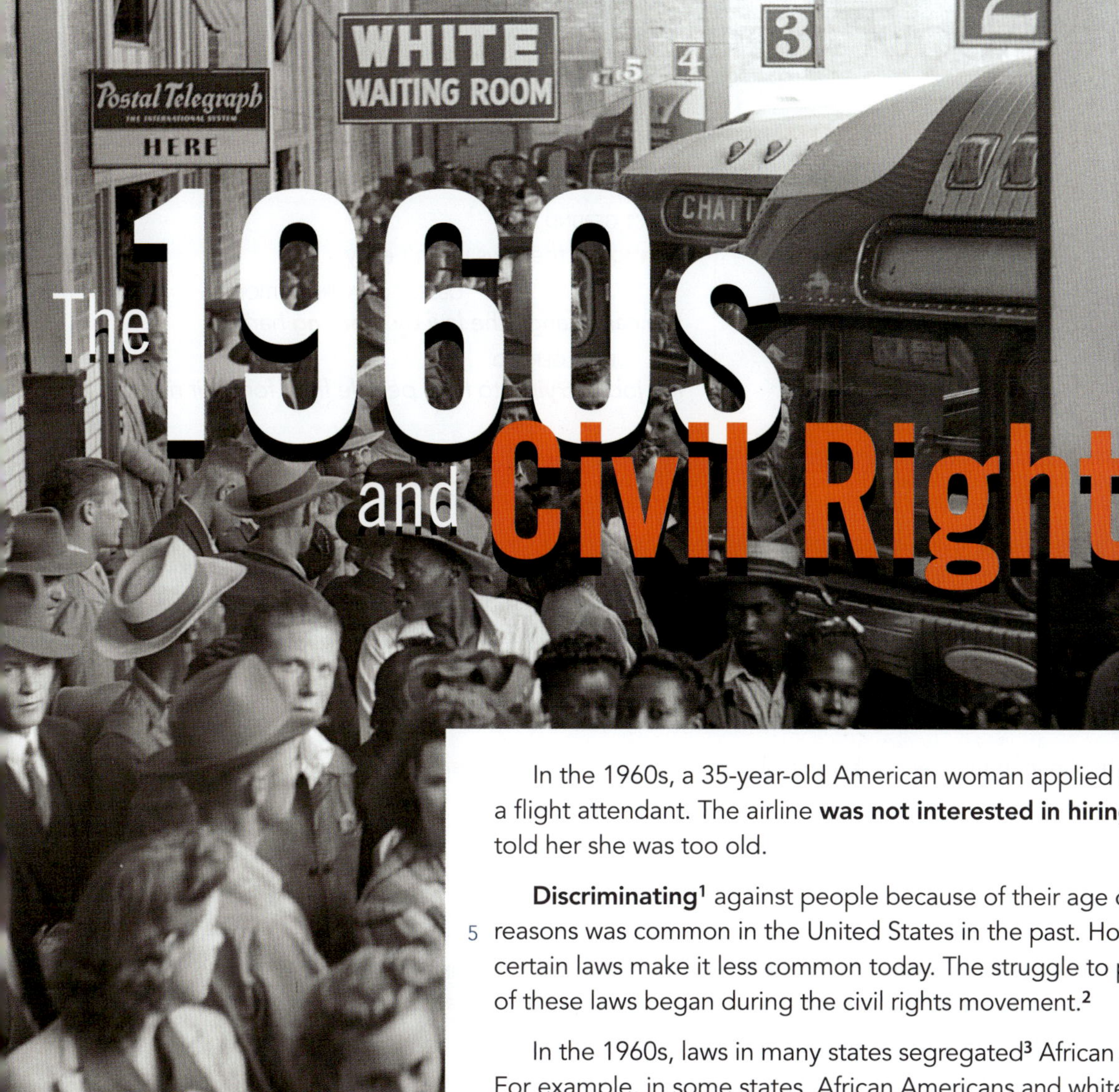

The 1960s and Civil Rights

In the 1960s, a 35-year-old American woman applied for a job as a flight attendant. The airline **was not interested in hiring** her. They told her she was too old.

Discriminating[1] against people because of their age or for other
5 reasons was common in the United States in the past. However, certain laws make it less common today. The struggle to pass many of these laws began during the civil rights movement.[2]

In the 1960s, laws in many states segregated[3] African Americans. For example, in some states, African Americans and whites went to
10 separate schools. In addition, African Americans couldn't buy houses in many "white" neighborhoods. Civil rights workers opposed this segregation and worked hard **to call** attention to unfair laws. **Changing** the laws wasn't easy. However, in 1964, the U.S. Congress passed the Civil Rights Act. Now, because of this law,
15 **it is illegal to segregate** people.

After the Civil Rights Act of 1964, other groups became **interested in fighting** for civil rights. These groups included women and people with disabilities.[4] This led to many new laws. Today, for example, **it is against the law to build** a school without access[5] for people in
20 wheelchairs. Not **hiring** people because of their age is also illegal.

Discrimination is still a problem in the United States today. Hopefully, however, people will **keep on working** for equal rights for all groups. **By working** hard, we can **succeed in passing** even more new laws to stop the spread of discrimination.

[1]**discriminate:** treat people differently, in an unfair way

[2]**the civil rights movement:** the struggle for equal rights for African Americans

[3]**segregate:** keep one group of people separate because of race, religion, etc.

[4]**disability:** a physical or mental challenge, such as difficulty walking or seeing

[5]**access:** easy ways to enter

 # More About Gerunds

Grammar Presentation

Gerunds can be the subjects of sentences and the objects of prepositions. They can also come after *be*.

SUBJECT GERUND
Changing the laws wasn't easy.

OBJECT OF A PREPOSITION
*We can change the law **by working** hard.*

BE + GERUND
*His job **is trying** to help people fight for their rights.*

2.1 Using Gerunds as Subjects, After Prepositions, and After *Be*

A Gerunds can be the subjects of sentences. A gerund subject is singular. It takes third-person singular verb forms.	***Discriminating*** *against people because of age is illegal.*
B Gerunds can be used after prepositions.	*We can succeed **in passing** more laws against discrimination.*
Note: An infinitive cannot be the object of a preposition.	*They weren't interested **in** ~~to hire~~ her.*
C Use *by* + gerund to express how something is done.	*You can change laws **by voting**.*
D Certain verb + preposition + gerund combinations are very common.	VERB PREP. GERUND *We **believe** **in** **fighting** for our rights.*
Certain adjective + preposition + gerund combinations are also very common, especially after the verb *be*.	ADJECTIVE PREP. GERUND *They weren't **interested** **in** **hiring** her.*
E Gerunds can also come after *be*.	VERB GERUND *The worst part of her job **was talking** to angry customers.*

🌐 DATA FROM THE REAL WORLD

Research shows that these are very common verb + preposition + gerund combinations:

believe in	forget about	succeed in	think about	worry about
disagree with	keep on (continue)	talk about	think of	

Research shows that these are very common adjective + preposition + gerund combinations:

afraid of	good at	important in	involved in	tired of
aware of	important for	interested in	sorry about	worried about

▸▸ Verb + Gerunds and Infinitives: See page A5.   ▸▸ Verb and Preposition Combinations: See page A5.

 # Grammar Application

A Complete the essay on Rosa Parks with the gerund form of the verbs in parentheses.

Rosa Parks is a hero in the American civil rights movement. Her work was important in

_____***ending***_____ (end) segregation in Montgomery, Alabama.
(1)
Parks's major contribution to civil rights was one very simple act. That act

was _______________ (refuse) to stand up and move to another seat
(2)
on a bus.

In Montgomery, Alabama, in the 1950s, African Americans had to stand

if a white person wanted a seat on a city bus. This was a law. Rosa Parks

did not agree with this law. She worked very long hours every day, and she

often had to stand up and give her seat to a white person, even though she

was exhausted and her feet hurt. Parks was tired of _______________ (do) this. She did not believe in
(3)
_______________ (give) her bus seat to a white person for no reason. In addition, she was not afraid
(4)
of _______________ (try) to stop something that was wrong. Therefore, one day, Parks refused to
(5)
stand up and move when the bus driver asked her to.

The police arrested Parks. Her arrest angered many African Americans in Alabama. In fact, many

people across the entire United States did not believe in _______________ (treat) African Americans
(6)
this way. They were interested in _______________ (support) civil rights. These people helped by
(7)
_______________ (send) money to the civil rights organizers in Alabama. This support succeeded in
(8)
_______________ (pressure) the state of Alabama. As a result, Alabama changed its laws.
(9)
Rosa Parks was involved in _______________ (get) an important civil right for African Americans.
(10)
Her one simple act also inspired other people around the country to keep on _______________ (work)
(11)
to end discrimination.

B Pair Work Ask and answer questions with a partner about Rosa Parks. Use a form of the words in the box and a gerund, or your own ideas.

be afraid of	be involved in	disagree with
be important in	believe in	keep on
be interested in	be tired of	succeed in

A *What was Rosa Parks tired of doing?*
B *She was tired of giving up her seat on the bus.*

A Complete the sentences in the civil rights time line with the words in parentheses. Use the gerund form, and add prepositions where needed. Note: All main verbs are in the present tense.

Civil Rights Time Line—The Early Days

1948 *Discriminating* (discriminate) against people in the military because
_(1)_
of race, religion, or national origin becomes illegal.

1954 After much debate and discussion, the U.S. Supreme Court
agrees to ending (agree/end) segregation in public schools.
_(2)_

1955 Martin Luther King Jr. _______________ (be involved/start) the
_(3)_
Montgomery bus boycott.

1957 Martin Luther King Jr. starts a civil rights organization, the Southern Christian
Leadership Conference. King and his organization have many ideas about
_______________ (fight) for civil rights peacefully.
_(4)_

1960 Four African-American students fight segregation by _______________ (sit)
_(5)_
at a lunch counter. No one serves them, but they _______________ (keep/sit)
_(6)_
at the counter. By _______________ (do) this, they start the idea of "sit-ins" —
_(7)_
peaceful demonstrations in the civil rights movement.

1962 James Meredith _______________ (succeed/become) the first
_(8)_
African-American student to enroll at the University of Mississippi.

1963 200,000 people _______________ (be involved/march) in
_(9)_
Washington, D.C. They do this to show their support for civil rights.

1967 _______________ (not allow) interracial marriage becomes illegal.
_(10)_
African Americans and whites can
now marry each other.

1968 More and more Americans
____
_(11)_
(be involved/work) for civil rights.

B Group Work **Discuss civil rights in a group. Answer the questions.**

1 Are there civil rights issues you are interested in supporting? If so, which ones?

2 Have you ever been involved in marching or protesting to support a civil right? If so, where and when?

3 More About Infinitives

Grammar Presentation

Infinitives can come after *be*. They are also often used with *in order* to show a purpose. *It* + infinitive sentences are also very common.	One idea was **to organize** farm workers. African-American children had to walk **(in order) to get** to school. ***It*** was difficult **to be** an African American in the 1960s.

3.1 Using Infinitives After *Be*, to Show Purpose, and in *It* + Infinitive Sentences

A Like gerunds, infinitives can follow *be*.	*Her job is **to help** other people.* *The purpose of the demonstration is **to get** people's attention.*
B *In order* + infinitive expresses a purpose. It answers a "*Why?*" question. You can use the infinitive alone when the meaning is clear.	*People are fighting **in order to change unfair laws**.* *People are fighting **to change** unfair laws.* *Why are people fighting? **To change** unfair laws.*
When *and* connects two infinitives of purpose, *(in order) to* is usually not repeated.	*They were working **(in order) to change laws and help** people.*
C *It* + infinitive sentences are very common. *It* + infinitive sentences often include the verbs *be*, *cost*, *seem*, and *take*.	***It*** *is important **to fight** against discrimination.* ***It*** *costs a lot of money **to run** for office.* ***It*** *seems difficult **to revise** immigration laws.* ***It*** *takes time **to change** people's minds.*
An *It* + infinitive sentence usually has the same meaning as a sentence with a gerund subject. The gerund subject is more formal.	***It*** *was her dream **to have equal rights for everyone**.* ***Having equal rights for everyone*** *was her dream.*

▶ Grammar Application

Exercise 3.1 Infinitives After *Be*, to Show Purpose, and with *It*

Listen to a podcast on an early hero in the women's rights movement. Complete the sentences with the words you hear.

It was difficult ___*to be*___ a woman in the United States in the early part of the
(1)
twentieth century. Women did not have many rights. For example, they were not
able to vote.

In 1917, Alice Paul organized a group of women _______________ for the right
(2)
to vote in national elections. The group demonstrated in front of the White House in
order _______________ the president's attention. This angered many people.
(3)
The police arrested many women _______________ the demonstrations. However,
(4)
this didn't work, so they arrested Paul and gave her a seven-month jail sentence in
order _______________ the other women. This was unfair, but Alice Paul was
(5)
strong. She stopped eating. She went on a hunger strike _______________
(6)
attention to the issue of women's rights.

Paul suffered in order _______________ the right to vote, but in the end, this
(7)
and other demonstrations worked. Congress finally gave women the vote in 1920.

Exercise 3.2 More Infinitives

A Complete the textbook passage about César Chávez. Use the correct form of the verbs in the boxes.

focus   ~~get~~   help   improve

César Chávez was a Mexican-American farm worker. He was also a civil rights worker. He fought _____*to get*_____ equal rights (1) for Mexican Americans and _____________ (2) the lives of farm workers.

Chávez was interested in workers' rights at an early age. He was born in Arizona in 1927. When he was growing up, he experienced discrimination. For example, it was against school rules to speak Spanish. If children spoke Spanish, the teacher punished them.

In the 1950s, Chávez joined a civil rights group _____________ (3) Mexican Americans register and vote in elections. He gave speeches _____________ (4) people's attention on workers' rights. Later, he started the National Farm Workers Association.

be   help   pay   stop   use

It was difficult _____________ (5) a farm worker in the 1950s. For example, it was common _____________ (6) farm workers very low wages. It was also common _____________ (7) dangerous pesticides (toxic chemicals) on farm crops.

It was Chávez's dream _____________ (8) these things. In the 1960s, he organized a strike _____________ (9) farm workers.

convince   get   help   show

The purpose of the strike was _____________ (10) higher pay for the workers. The strike succeeded, and finally, farm workers got higher wages. In the 1980s, Chávez used another strike _____________ (11) growers to stop the use of pesticides on grapes.

César Chávez worked all his life _____________ (12) Mexican Americans and farm workers. Today, his birthday is a state holiday in California and in seven other states. The purpose of César Chávez Day is _____________ (13) respect for his important work.

B Rewrite each **boldfaced** sentence from the reading. Use a gerund subject.

For example, it was against the rules to speak Spanish.

1 *For example, speaking Spanish was against the rules.*

2 ____

3 ____

4 ____

5 ____

C Pair Work Ask and answer the questions about César Chávez with a partner. Use infinitives.

1 What did César Chávez work for all his life?

   He worked to improve the lives of Mexican Americans and farm workers.

2 Why did Chávez join a civil rights group in the 1950s?

3 Why did Chávez give speeches in the 1950s?

4 Why was it difficult to be a farm worker?

5 Why did Chávez organize a strike in the 1960s? in the 1980s?

6 What is the purpose of César Chávez Day?

D Over to You Think about civil rights today. Are there still problems? What do we still need to work on? Complete the following sentences on a separate piece of paper. Then share your sentences with the class.

Today, it is still difficult to help women get the same pay as men.

It still seems hard for [group] to . . .

People are still fighting to . . .

We are still working to . . .

It is my dream to . . .

4 Avoid Common Mistakes ⚠

1 **Gerund subjects take singular verbs.**

*Changing laws ~~are~~ **is** a slow process.*

2 **Use the correct preposition in verb + preposition and adjective + preposition combinations.**

*They succeeded ~~on~~ **in** getting more rights.*

*Do not be afraid ~~for~~ **of** standing up for your rights.*

3 **Do not use an infinitive after a preposition.**

*They weren't interested in ~~to hire~~ **hiring** her.*

4 **Do not use *for* in infinitives of purpose.**

He worked hard ~~for~~ to help workers with disabilities.

5 **Don't forget *It* or *to* in *It* sentences.**

*~~Is~~ **It is** important ∧**to** attend the march this weekend.*

Editing Task

Find and correct 10 more mistakes in this paragraph.

It was more difficult **to** be disabled in the United States in the past.
It was hard do things like enter buildings or cross the street if you
were in a wheelchair. In many places, it was impossible bring a guide
dog into a restaurant. Many people were interested in to help the
5 disabled. They worked hard for to help people with disabilities.
They finally succeeded on passing an important law. It was the
Americans with Disabilities Act of 1990. Today, sight-impaired people
are not afraid for bringing their dogs into any building. Making streets
accessible to people with physical disabilities are another result of
10 the 1990 law. For example, adding gentle slopes to the edges of
sidewalks help the disabled. Now a person in a wheelchair doesn't
worry about to get from one side of the street to the other.
Making changes like these are a slow process, but an important one.

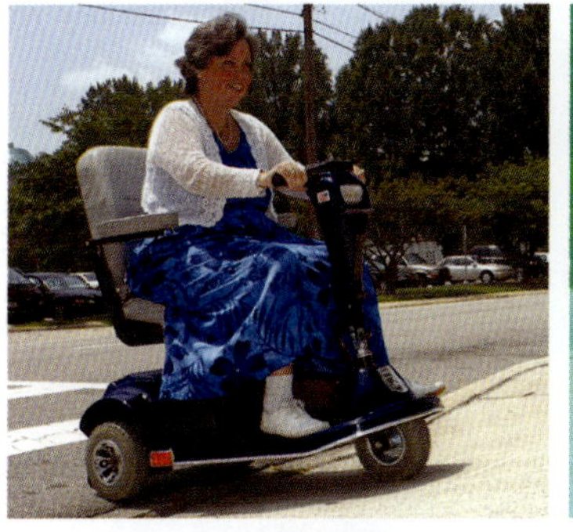

5 Academic Writing

Summary and Response

Brainstorm > Organize > Write > Edit

In Unit 28, you learned how to analyze and summarize a text. In this unit (29), you will learn how to paraphrase and respond to a writer's ideas in order to prepare for the prompt below.

Write a summary paragraph of "Nontraditional Weddings." Then write a response paragraph giving your opinion about the changes in wedding traditions described in the article.

Paraphrasing

Paraphrasing means rewriting someone else's ideas in your own words. A paraphrase is about the same length as the original text. It is used to restate short texts, such as a thesis statement, an important idea, or a good example.

Here are some tips for paraphrasing:

- Read the original sentence(s) carefully, then put away the text.
- Tell another person what you read.
- Write down the idea without looking at the original.
- Check the original sentence to make sure your paraphrase uses different words but does not change the meaning.

Here are some ways to change the language to paraphrase the sentence: "More and more couples these days are deciding to have unique weddings that reflect their beliefs, hobbies, and personal style."

- Replace key words or phrases with synonyms.

An **increasing number** of **modern** couples are **choosing** to have **unusual** weddings that **show** their **attitudes**, **interests**, and **individual tastes**.

- Change the order of some words or phrases.

Because weddings show a couple's attitudes, interests, and individual tastes, an increasing number of couples are now choosing to have unusual weddings.

- Break one long sentence into shorter sentences.

Weddings show a couple's attitudes, interests, and individual tastes. As a result, an increasing number of modern couples are choosing to have unusual weddings.

Exercise 5.1 Applying the Skill

Paraphrase the following sentences from "Nontraditional Weddings."

1 It is becoming more and more common for such couples to get married in a distant location.

2 Adventure weddings typically involve combining the marriage ceremony with a physical activity that has special meaning for the couple.

3 A theme wedding allows couples to create a fun, nontraditional wedding that centers on a beloved book, song, story, or historical period.

My Writing

Responding to a Writer's Ideas

When responding to a text you have read, you should respond to each of the writer's main ideas with your own point of view. Some common ways you could respond to a writer's ideas are to:

* Agree or disagree with the writer's points or ideas
* Give an example from your own experience or someone you know
* Connect the author's ideas to something you read or heard from another source
* Describe how an idea makes you feel or what it reminds you of

Exercise 5.2 Applying the Skill

1 Review the article "1960s and Civil Rights" on page 375. Discuss each topic with a partner.
* Paragraphs 1- 2: Discrimination in the U.S.
* Paragraph 3: Racial discrimination & segregation
* Paragraph 4: Other discrimination - gender & disabilities

2 Choose one of the writer's points or ideas and write a response paragraph. Paraphrase and respond to the writer's idea.

Using Gerunds and Infinitives in Academic Writing

Writers often use gerunds as subjects to focus on the importance of an action. They use infinitives to show a purpose when describing goals or reasons for doing something.

Marrying someone of another race was illegal in some states until 1967.

In 2011, New York changed its laws **(in order) to allow** same-sex couples to marry.

Exercise 5.3 Applying the Skill

Edit your response paragraph to use a gerund as subject and an infinitive of purpose.

Subject Relative Clauses (Adjective Clauses with Subject Relative Pronouns)

Sleep

1 Grammar in the Real World

A How many hours a night do you sleep? Read the article about scientific research on sleep. Why do some people need only a few hours of sleep?

B Comprehension Check Answer the questions.

1 What might control how much sleep we get?
2 What do scientists call people who do not need a lot of sleep?
3 Why did scientists study a mother and her daughter?
4 What did the experiment with mice show?

C Notice Find the sentences in the article and complete them.

1 There are many people ______________________ need eight or more hours of sleep a night.

2 Researchers recently found a gene mutation ______________________ might control our sleep.

3 The researchers then created mice ______________________ had the same hDEC2 gene mutation.

4 The mice ______________________ did not have the mutation needed extra sleep.

Look at the words you wrote. Circle the noun that each one refers to.

SLEEP & SCIENCE

Sleep is important. We need it to live, but not everyone gets the same amount of sleep each night. There are many people **who need eight or more hours of sleep a night**. However, there are also others **who are happy with only four or five hours**. Scientists call these
5 people "short sleepers." Is this simply a lifestyle choice? Not necessarily. Researchers recently found a gene mutation[1] **that might control our sleep**.

Recently, a research team studied a mother and her daughter **who are short sleepers**. They only sleep about six hours a night.
10 The researchers analyzed the DNA[2] of the entire family, and they found a gene mutation in both the mother and daughter. The team already knew about this gene, the hDEC2 gene. It controls sleep in animals. They made a guess: People **who have the mutation** might need less sleep than other people.

15 The researchers then created mice **that had the same hDEC2 gene mutation**. The mice **that had the gene mutation** slept less at night than mice **that didn't have the mutation**. After that, the researchers forced both kinds of mice to stay awake. The mice **that did not have the mutation needed extra sleep**. The mice **that had the mutation did not**.

20 These researchers think genetics might be more important for our sleeping patterns than lifestyle. If you only sleep four or five hours a night, your lifestyle might not be to blame. Perhaps it's just in your genes!

[1]**gene mutation:** a change in the structure of a gene, the pattern of cell structure that we get from our parents

[2]**DNA:** chemical in the cells of living things that controls the structure of each cell

2 Subject Relative Clauses

Grammar Presentation

Relative clauses define, describe, identify, or give more information about nouns. Like all clauses, relative clauses have both a subject and a verb.

RELATIVE CLAUSE

	SUBJECT	VERB	

The team studied people **who slept only four to six hours.** (**who** = *people*)

2.1 Subject Relative Clauses

	RELATIVE CLAUSE			
	Subject Relative Pronoun	Verb		
The scientists studied people	**who**	**slept**	**only four to six hours.**	
The mice	**that**	**had**	**the gene mutation**	slept less at night.
It is a gene	**which**	**controls**	**sleep in animals.**	

2.2 Using Subject Relative Clauses

A In a subject relative clause, the relative pronoun is the subject of the clause.

RELATIVE CLAUSE

RELATIVE PRONOUN

There are people **who** *only need about six hours of sleep.*

RELATIVE CLAUSE

RELATIVE PRONOUN

A mouse **that** *had a mutated gene needed less sleep.*

B The subject relative pronouns are *who*, *which*, and *that*.

Use *who* or *that* for people.

She's the researcher **who** / **that** *heads the sleep project.*

Use *which* or *that* for things and animals.

They created a mouse **which** / **that** *had the same gene.*

C Subject relative clauses combine two ideas.

The scientists studied <u>mice</u>. + <u>The mice</u> *had a gene mutation.*

The scientists studied <u>mice</u> **that** *had a gene mutation.*

2.2 Using Subject Relative Clauses *(continued)*

D The verb after the relative pronoun agrees with the noun or pronoun before the relative pronoun.

*People **who have** the hDEC2 gene need less sleep.*

*I know a **woman who sleeps** only four hours a night.*

E A subject relative clause usually comes right after the word it modifies. It can modify any noun or pronoun in a sentence.

SUBJECT
*Someone **who has the hDEC2 gene** sleeps less.*

*The scientists studied **mice who had a mutated gene**.*

*The women participated in a **study that ended last year**.*

Grammar Application

Exercise 2.1 Subject Relative Clauses

Read the student summary of a science article. Circle the relative pronouns and underline the relative clauses.

Many researchers have done studies (that) look at sleep. This article is about a study that compares the habits of good sleepers and bad sleepers. A group of scientists who specialize in sleep research did the study. First, the scientists studied people who sleep well. They
5   learned about the habits that might make these people good sleepers. Then the scientists studied people who do not sleep well. These short sleepers often have habits which are very different from the habits of good sleepers. From this study, the researchers have developed the following tips for people who cannot sleep. First, do not drink caffeinated
10   beverages like tea or coffee after noon. In addition, eat dinner at least three hours before going to bed, and, finally, get some exercise every day. These are three habits of good sleepers. If you are a person who does not sleep well at night, try to start doing these things. They could help you change your sleep patterns.

🌐 DATA FROM THE REAL WORLD

In conversation, people usually use **'s not** and **'re not** after pronouns.

A *Do you know the woman **who/that participated in the study**?*

B *Yes. She's my aunt.*

In formal writing, people use *who* to refer to people and *that* or *which* to refer to things. *Which* is more formal.

*Participants **who had the hDEC2 gene** slept less.*
*A report on the study **that/which showed a genetic basis for sleep patterns** appears in the journal Genetics Today.*

Complete the article about sleep with the correct **formal** relative pronouns. Circle the noun that each relative pronoun refers to.

A Good Night's Sleep

Everyone needs a good night's sleep. This is important for staying healthy. However, (people) _____**who**_____ have trouble sleeping often worry about their health. Troubled sleepers can get help
(1)
from recent studies. Researchers _____________ study sleep have good advice for people with sleep
(2)
problems. A study _____________ appeared recently showed some interesting results. Not everyone
(3)
needs the same amount of sleep. Most people need 8 to 8½ hours of sleep a night. However, some people
_____________ have a special gene need less sleep. People _____________ have this gene probably
(4)   (5)
cannot change their sleep habits. They should not worry about sleeping less. However, sleep researchers
have some advice for people _____________ do not have this gene.
(6)

People _____________ have trouble sleeping should avoid caffeine after noon. Some men and women
(7)
_____________ have trouble sleeping have found it helps to exercise. Even walking 20 minutes every
(8)
day can help. One idea _____________ has helped many people is for them to go to bed only when
(9)
they are tired. This might mean going to bed at 2:00 a.m. and waking up at 7:00 a.m. Another strategy
_____________ has helped people is moving bedtime back 15 minutes each night until it is 8 hours
(10)
before it is time to wake up.

A Complete the questions with a relative pronoun and the correct form of the verb.

1 Do you know someone _**who/that**_ _**has**_ (have) trouble sleeping? Who?

2 Do you know someone _____________ _____________ (sleep) nine
  hours most nights? Who?

3 Do you read websites or articles _____________ _____________ (give)
  tips on sleeping? Which websites or articles?

4 Do you have a friend _____________ _____________ (stay) up late? Who?

5 Do you have a relative _________________ _________________ (wake up)
   early most days? Who?

6 Do you have friends _________________ _________________ (take) naps? Who?

7 Do you have a favorite sleeping position _________________ _________________
   (help) you get to sleep? What position is it?

8 Do you have tips _________________ _________________ (help) you get to
   sleep? What are they?

B Group Work **Ask and answer the questions in A in a small group.
Compare answers.**

A *Do you have a favorite sleeping position that helps you get to sleep?*
B *Yes, I do.*
A *What position is it?*
B *I sleep on my back. What about you?*

Exercise 2.4 Sentence Combining

A **Complete the questions with a relative pronoun and the correct form of the verb.**

What's Your Position?

1 A study linked sleep positions with personality. The study looked at how people
   sleep.
   A study that looked at how people sleep linked sleep
   positions with personality.

2 In this study, a sleep expert studied people. The people sleep in several different
   positions.

   ____

3 The expert learned many things. These things surprised her.

   ____

4 People tend to be shy and sensitive. These people sleep in a fetal position.
   (*fetal position* = curled up on your side)

   ____

5 People are sociable and relaxed. The people sleep on their sides and have their
   arms at their sides.

   ____

6 People sleep on their backs and have their arms at their sides. The people are
   quiet and shy.

   ____

7 People are friendly and helpful. The people sleep on their backs and have their
   arms up near their pillows.

   ____

8 People sleep on their stomachs and hug their pillows. The people are easily upset.

   ____

B Underline the subject relative clauses in your new sentences. Circle the noun in the main clause that the relative pronoun refers to.

(A study) that looked at how people sleep linked sleep positions with personality.

C Group Work   Take a survey of sleeping positions in your group. What is everyone's usual sleeping position and personality? Talk about your group. Give examples. Use subject relative clauses.

I don't think all people who sleep on their backs are quiet. For example, Marcelo sleeps on his back, and he's outgoing and friendly.

3 More About Subject Relative Clauses

Grammar Presentation

Subject relative clauses can use a variety of verb forms. They can also show possession.	People **who have sleep problems** can join the study. People **who are having sleep problems** can join the study. People **who have had sleep problems** can join the study. Sally is a scientist **whose discoveries have helped many people**. (Sally's discoveries have helped many people.)

3.1 More About Subject Relative Clauses

A Verbs in subject relative clauses can take a variety of verb forms.	The woman **who <u>was participating</u> in the study** was my aunt. People **that <u>have participated</u> in the study** receive a payment.
B The possessive form of *who* is *whose*. *Whose* + a noun shows possession in a subject relative clause. A noun always follows *whose*.	NOUN WHOSE + NOUN SUBJECT The <u>scientist</u> **whose work** has helped many people won an award.
C *Whose* can combine two sentences. *Whose* replaces the possessive form in the second sentence.	**The woman** is my neighbor. + ~~**Her** daughter~~ was in a sleep study. <u>The woman</u> **whose daughter** was in a sleep study is my neighbor. They are **the scientists**. + ~~**Their** study~~ was on the news last night. They are <u>the scientists</u> **whose study** was on the news last night.

 # Grammar Application

Exercise 3.1 Verbs in Subject Relative Clauses

Listen to a student podcast about sleeping. Complete the sentences with the relative pronoun and the correct form of the verb you hear.

Why do we sleep? This is still a mystery. Scientists _**who study**_ (study) sleep are still not
(1)
completely sure of the reasons. They know some things about sleep, however. Here are some facts:

■ People ________________________ (be) asleep have active brains. Their brains are
(2)
   most active during the "rapid eye movement," or REM, phase of sleep.

■ Different animals sleep in different ways. For example, a dolphin
   ________________________ (sleep) may continue to swim.
   (3)

■ Humans and animals ________________________ (lose) sleep need to make it up later on.
(4)

■ A person ________________________ (need) less than eight hours of sleep should not worry about
(5)
   sleeping less than other people.

■ There are animals ________________________ (sleep) very little. For example, a horse only sleeps
(6)
   three hours a day. There are other animals ________________________ (sleep) a lot. For example, a
   (7)
   small animal called a ferret sleeps about 15 hours a day.

   Scientists ________________________ (study) sleep also have a few guesses about the
   (8)
reasons for sleep. There is a study ________________________ (show)
(9)
REM sleep helps learning and memory. However, there are other studies
________________________ (show) the opposite results. For example, certain drugs
(10)
shorten REM sleep. A group of people ________________________ (take) these drugs
(11)
showed no memory problems in a recent study.

   Most scientists agree on one thing. They need to do more research to solve the
mysteries of sleep.

A Combine the sentences to complete a web article about interpreting (giving meaning to) dreams. Make the second sentence a relative clause. Use *who*, *that*, or *whose*.

What Do Dreams Mean?

What do your dreams mean? Interpreting dreams is an important part of many cultures.

whose goal is to understand dreams

1 Some specialists study dream symbols. ~~Their goal is to understand dreams~~.

2 They believe dreams are about certain things. These things represent important ideas or feelings in our lives. Here are some examples of dream symbols and their meanings:

3 People dream about losing a tooth. They are worried about something.

4 People may have a special wish for freedom. Their dreams are about flying.

5 People dream about falling. They have a fear of losing control of something.

6 People sometimes dream about a frightening dog. They have trouble with friends.

7 A dream can represent extreme emotions. The dream focuses on fire.

8 Some other meanings seem obvious. For example, a person might also dream of fire. This person's room is too hot.

9 In any case, most people do not see symbols in a simple way. These people analyze dreams. Instead, they believe in looking at how the dreamer *feels* about the object in the dream.

B Group Work Discuss dream symbols in a group. Use the ones in A or your own ideas. Discuss possible interpretations for each symbol. Use subject relative pronouns. Present your ideas to the class. Use these questions to guide you.

- Which dream symbols are important in a culture you know well?
  Dream symbols that include animals are important in my culture.

- What are some interpretations of these symbols?

- Do you dream about any of these symbols? Which ones?

- What are some positive dream symbols?

- What are some negative dream symbols?

- Whose cultures have similar dream symbols?

- Do they have similar interpretations?

 Avoid Common Mistakes  

1 **Use *who* or *that* for people and *which* or *that* for things.**

              who/that

The scientists studied a woman ~~which~~ never sleeps.

        which/that

The research ~~who~~ proved the scientist's theory was interesting.

2 **Do not use a subject pronoun after a subject relative pronoun.**

Scientists study people who ~~they~~ sleep a short amount of time.

3 **The verb after the relative pronoun agrees with the noun before the relative pronoun.**

       have

People who ~~has~~ the hDEC2 gene need less sleep.

4 **Do not omit the relative pronoun in a subject relative clause.**

      who

Two women ʌwere "short sleepers" participated in a study.

5 **Remember to spell *whose* correctly.**

       whose

The scientist ~~who's/whoes~~ work has helped many people won an award.

Editing Task

Find and correct nine more mistakes in a web article about colors in dreams.

Dreaming in Color

Can dreams give us insights into our feelings? Some people who ~~they~~ analyze dreams believe this. There are dream analysts who's interest is the colors that they are in our dreams. In their opinion, these colors provide clues about our lives. For example, dreams about people which are wearing black represent sadness. Dreams who have a lot of gray, brown, or tan in them can represent happiness. A dream who's main color is orange can represent boldness. Many people who analyzes dreams think green represents life or new beginnings. On the other hand, there are some people do not dream in color. These people dream in black and white.

Do you remember the colors that was in your dreams last night? The next time you dream, try to remember the colors. Write down the colors appear in your dream, and think about how they made you feel.

Summary and Response

Brainstorm > Organize > **Write** > Edit

In Unit 29, you learned to paraphrase and respond to a writer. In this unit (30), you will study an example of a summary and personal response in order to prepare for the prompt below.

Write a summary paragraph of "Nontraditional Weddings." Then write a response paragraph giving your opinion about the changes in wedding traditions described in the article.

Exercise 5.1 Preparing to Write

Work with a partner. Ask and answer the questions.

1 Are sleep habits in your culture different from the United States? For example, is it common to take naps during the day?
2 What cultural tips would you give a visitor who is in your country for the first time?
3 How would you respond to a foreign visitor who made a cultural mistake in your country?

Customs around the World
— by Andy Schmidt

In recent decades foreign travel has become a multi-billion dollar industry. International travel has many benefits, but tourists or business people who are not prepared can run into trouble. That
5 is why it is very important for travelers to take the time to learn about the cultures they are visiting so that they know what to expect and how to avoid cultural misunderstandings. "Customs around the World" is a series that looks at three different
10 cultures every month to help people become well-informed travelers. This month's exciting destinations are Brazil, Japan, and India.

BRAZIL

In general, Brazilian culture is informal. Most
15 Brazilians are very friendly people, and it is important to say hello and goodbye to everyone. Women kiss men and each other on the cheek, but men usually just shake hands. Brazilians typically stand very close to each other and touch
20 each other's arms, elbows, and back regularly

while speaking, even in a business situation. You should not move away if this happens. However, if you go to a business meeting, you are not expected to take a gift. In fact, an expensive gift
25 can be seen as suspicious.

On the other hand, a person who is invited to someone's house should take a gift—for example, flowers or chocolate. For dinner invitations, it is important to arrive at least 30 minutes late, but
30 also to dress well because a person's appearance is very important in Brazil.

JAPAN

Japanese culture, which is often very formal, is quite different from Brazilian culture. For
35 example, the Japanese do not stand very close to one another. Similarly, kissing or touching other people in public is not common. When you meet Japanese people, they may shake your hand, although bowing without touching is a more
40 traditional greeting.

At business meetings, the Japanese often like to know your position in a company before they talk to you. This is one reason that business cards are important. In Japan, you should hand over
45 and receive a business card using both hands, and when you receive a business card, you should immediately read it carefully.

Being on time is also very important in Japan. In fact, you should arrive early and dress formally
50 for meetings or appointments. Gifts are often exchanged, but the recipient may refuse the gift at least once before accepting it. Remember to do the same if you receive a gift. When you present your gift, you should say that it is just a token of
55 your appreciation.

INDIA

People who visit India quickly discover that it is a huge country with many languages, cultures, and religions and that customs differ from region
60 to region. However, in general, hierarchy is important in India. Therefore, when you meet Indians, it is important to greet the oldest or the most senior person first. Men may shake hands with men, and women often shake hands

65 with women, but men and women tend not to shake hands.

Personal relationships are important in business in India, and the first meeting is usually spent getting to know everyone. In addition,
70 many Indians do not like to say "no," so it may be difficult to know what they are really thinking. Appointments are necessary and being on time is important. Business dress is formal, so men and women should wear dark suits.

75 Finally, if you are invited to an Indian home, arrive on time. You do not have to bring a gift, but gifts are not refused. However, do not bring white flowers because they are used in funerals.

Exercise 5.2 Comprehension Check

Read the article on pages 396-397. Work with a partner. Ask and answer the questions.

1 According to the writer, who often has trouble in foreign countries?
2 What is one business-related custom in Brazil?
3 How do Japanese people generally feel about time?
4 Who should you greet first in a home in India? Why?

Writing a personal response is an opportunity to evaluate and express opinions about a writer's ideas.

In a **response** paragraph, you should give your ideas about the points in your summary. Your response can include examples from your personal experience, additional facts, or knowledge from other sources. Language that you can use includes the following:

I agree/ disagree with the writer that ... because ...   In my opinion,...

In my experience,...   I think that...

Read a student's summary and response to the article. "Customs around the World."

[Summary] In the article "Customs around the World," author Andy Schmidt says that people who visit other countries should learn about national customs before they go in order to prevent cultural misunderstandings when they travel. Schmidt focuses on three countries—Brazil, Japan, and India—and describes some customs visitors should know about. According to the author, Brazilians are informal people. They touch a lot, and punctuality is not always expected on some occasions. Japanese culture is exactly the opposite. People do not touch in public, and there are rules for how to exchange business cards, how to dress, what kind of gifts to give, and when to arrive at a meeting or someone's home. Indian culture is also formal, and some of the rules are similar to those in Japan. For example, it is important to arrive on time for business meetings. The author stresses the importance of personal relationships and cautions that Indian people avoid saying "no" if possible.

[Response] In my opinion, the author's idea that it is easy to make a mistake if you do not know about other people's customs is an important one. To give an example from my own experience, I was traveling to India for a summer wedding near Delhi. It was my first Indian wedding, so I decided to read about their wedding traditions. Fortunately, I learned that a guest should never wear white to an Indian wedding because white is associated with death. In short, these examples remind us that all travelers, including me, must study the customs of a new country before visiting it.

Exercise 5.3 Analyzing the Summary

Work with a partner. Look at the article on pages 396-397 and the student's summary paragraph above. Ask and answer the questions.

1 What is the main idea in the introductory paragraph of the article? Highlight it.
2 Which sentence restates the main idea of the article in the summary paragraph? Highlight it.
3 Which paraphrasing strategies did the student use to restate the main idea of the article?
4 Put a check mark (✓) above each of the examples in the summary paragraph. Do you think there is too much, too little, or the right amount of detail? Explain your answer.
5 How many references to the original author are in the summary paragraph? Circle them.

Exercise 5.4 Analyzing the Response

Work with a partner. Look at the response paragraph on page 398. Ask and answer the questions.

1 Where is the student's opinion in the response paragraph? Underline it.

2 How does the writer support this opinion? Is it effective? Explain your answer.

3 How does the writer conclude the response paragraph? Find and highlight the transition. What other transitions could replace this one?

Using Subject Relative Clauses in Summary Writing

A subject relative clause is helpful in summary writing to describe which specific people or things you are referring to. It adds variety to your writing and can help you paraphrase without plagiarizing.

The author says that people **who visit other countries** should learn about national customs before they go.

In Brazil parties **that start late** are common.

Exercise 5.5 Applying the Skill

Write a subject relative clause to complete each sentence.

1 Tourists _________________________________ Brazil will find a friendly, informal culture.

2 In Brazil, gifts _________________________________ bring to business meetings may look like bribes.

3 In India, business clothes _________________________________ dark are normal in the office.

My Writing

Exercise 5.6 Writing a Response Paragraph

1 Review the article "Customs around the World."

2 Discuss the following questions with a partner.
- What are the most interesting main points of the article?
- Have you or someone you know ever made an embarrassing cultural mistake?
- Have you ever seen a foreign visitor make a cultural mistake?

3 Write a response paragraph to the article. Use a personal experience, additional facts, and/or knowledge from other sources to support your opinion about the writer's ideas.

Object Relative Clauses (Adjective Clauses with Object Relative Pronouns)

Viruses

1 Grammar in the Real World

A How do you feel when you get a cold or the flu? Read the article from a health website. Why is it so easy to get a virus?

B Comprehension Check Answer the questions.

1 What are two illnesses that viruses cause?

2 How do viruses spread?

3 How long can viruses live on a surface?

4 What are three things you should do to protect yourself and others against viral infection?

C Notice Look at the underlined words in these sentences from the article. Circle the nouns that the underlined words refer to.

1 The common cold and the flu are two well-known illnesses <u>that</u> viruses cause.

2 Infected people can pass viruses easily to others <u>who</u> they interact with.

VIRUSES

When was the last time you had a viral infection?[1] Almost everyone has at least one a year. If you are like most people **that viruses attack**, you feel
5 pretty miserable once they enter your body. In addition, it can take several days or even weeks to get better. Therefore, it is a good idea to avoid catching or spreading viruses.

10 Viruses are tiny disease-causing particles.[2] The common cold and the flu are two well-known illnesses **that viruses cause**. Infected people can pass viruses easily to others **who they**
15 **interact with**. This is because they blow small drops of liquid into the air when they cough or sneeze. These drops contain viruses. You can catch a virus from a person **that you touch** or even
20 from someone **that you stand near** if these drops enter your mouth or nose.

Viruses can also live on surfaces[3] from a few minutes to many hours. This means you can also catch viruses from things
25 **you touch**. This is especially true if you then touch your face before washing your hands.

There are ways to avoid spreading viruses. First, always wash items such
30 as dishes and towels **that an infected person has used**. Cover your mouth and nose when you cough or sneeze. Wash your hands frequently. Also, try to stay home if you get sick, so the people
35 **who you work with** can stay healthy.

Viruses are difficult to control. However, knowing more about them and following the tips above can help you slow the cycle of viral infection.

[1]**viral infection:** illness caused by a virus
[2]**particle:** a very small piece of something
[3]**surface:** the top or outside of something

2 Object Relative Clauses

Grammar Presentation

Object relative clauses describe, identify, or give more information about nouns. In an object relative clause, the relative pronoun is the object.

RELATIVE CLAUSE

| OBJECT | SUBJECT | VERB |

There are many diseases *that* *viruses* *cause*.

2.1 Object Relative Clauses

	RELATIVE CLAUSE			
	Object Relative Pronoun	Subject	Verb	
You can infect people	**that** **who / whom**	**you**	**meet.**	
The virus	**that** **which**	**the scientist**	**studied**	was a type of flu.

2.2 Using Object Relative Clauses

A In an object relative clause, the relative pronoun is the object of the clause.

RELATIVE CLAUSE

| OBJECT |

Cold and flu are illnesses *that* *viruses cause*.

B The object relative pronouns are *who*, *whom*, *which*, and *that*.

Use *that*, *who*, or *whom* for people.

RELATIVE CLAUSE

| OBJECT |

The professor *that* *I met yesterday* *has the flu*.

Use *that*, *who*, or *whom* for people.

RELATIVE CLAUSE

| OBJECT |

She has a virus *that* *young people often get*.

C Object relative clauses can combine two ideas.

That is the virus. + *Rob gave me the virus.*
*That is the virus **that** Rob gave me.*

D You can omit the relative pronoun in an object relative clause.

***The doctor (who) she spoke with** had a cold himself!*
*Wash **the things (that) you touch** if you are infected.*

E The object relative pronoun is followed by a subject and a verb.

SUBJECT   VERB

*I wash the towels **that** **she** **uses**.*

SUBJECT   VERB

*The flu vaccine **that** **they** **use** didn't work.*

2.2 Using Object Relative Clauses (*continued*)

F An object relative clause usually comes right after the word it modifies. It can modify any noun or pronoun in a sentence.

SUBJECT
*The <u>virus</u> **that she studied** was a type of flu.*

OBJECT
*She washed the <u>towels</u> **that she used**.*

PRONOUN
*He's the <u>one</u> **who I contacted on the phone**.*

2.3 Comparing Subject and Object Relative Clauses

	Subject Relative Clauses	Object Relative Clauses
In a relative clause, the relative pronoun is . . .	the subject.	the object.
In a sentence, the relative pronoun modifies . . .	any noun or pronoun.	
In a sentence, the relative pronoun usually comes . . .	right after the word it modifies.	
In a sentence, the relative clause has . . .	a new verb.	a new subject and verb.
The relative pronoun can be omitted.	no	yes, except for *whose*
The relative pronouns include . . .	*who, which, that, whose.*	*who, whom, which, that, whose.*

2.4 Using Subject and Object Relative Clauses

Subject relative clause	*The **doctor** who treated her had a cold.* SUBJECT *The **doctor** had a cold. + The **doctor** treated her.*
Object relative clause	*The **doctor** who she visited had a cold.* OBJECT *The **doctor** had a cold. + She visited the **doctor**.*

🌐 DATA FROM THE REAL WORLD

Which is common in academic writing. It is much less common in informal language.	*The virus copies the host cell **which** it has invaded*
In informal speaking and writing, *that* is more common in object relative clauses than *who* to refer to people. *Whom* is only used in rather formal situations.	**A** *Is she the scientist **that you met at the lab**?* **B** *Yes, she is.*

Exercise 2.1 Object Relative Clauses

A Read a passage from a history textbook about an epidemic (a disease that spreads quickly). Underline seven more relative clauses. Circle the relative pronouns. Three of the relative clauses do not have relative pronouns. Put a check (✓) above them.

In 1918 there was a global flu epidemic. It spread to almost every part of the world. The regions that the flu affected ranged from the Arctic to the South Pacific. In addition, the effects that it had were devastating. The number of people this flu actually

5 killed was between 50 and 100 million. However, the number of people that the virus infected was around 500 million. This was an epidemic scientists could not control. The virus spread very quickly, and it was very powerful. The people who viruses usually affect are very old or very young. However, the people who this

10 virus infected were healthy young adults. The 1918 flu was one of the worst natural disasters the world had ever seen.

B Pair Work Compare answers with a partner. Which relative clauses do not have a relative pronoun?

Exercise 2.2 Combining Sentences

Combine the sentences using object relative clauses with *who*, *that*, and *which*.

1 Another name for the flu epidemic was the "Spanish flu." The world experienced this flu epidemic in 1918.

   Another name for the flu epidemic _that the world experienced in_ 1918 was the "Spanish flu."

2 The people were mostly young adults. The flu killed them.

   The people ____________________________ were mostly young adults.

3 The people are typically elderly. The flu usually affects these people.

   The people ____________________________ are typically elderly.

4 The countries were very far apart. The flu affected countries.

   The countries ____________________________ were very far apart.

5 The 1918 flu was an unusual virus. Scientists could not control the virus.

   The 1918 flu was an unusual virus ____________________________ .

6 Strange flu viruses also occur today. Scientists do not understand these strange flu viruses.

   Strange flu viruses ____________________________ also occur today.

7 SARS, bird flu, and swine flu are recent examples of strange new viruses. Many people fear these viruses.

SARS, bird flu, and swine flu are recent examples of strange new viruses

____ .

8. Scientists are interested in people. These strange new viruses affect these people.

Scientists are interested in people _______________________________________ .

Exercise 2.3 Using Object Relative Clauses

A Over to You **Complete the sentences about getting sick. Use your own ideas. Write a correct relative pronoun, or Ø for no relative pronoun.**

1 The thing _*that /which/Ø*_ I usually do when I have a cold is _*drink hot lemon juice with honey*_ .

2 The thing _______________ I usually do when I have the flu is _______________ .

3 I like the doctor _______________ I go to when I get sick because he / she

_______________ .

4 The best cold medicine _______________ I know is

_______________ .

5 _______________

was the cold remedy _______________ my family used when I was a child.

6 _______________ is the flu remedy

_______________ my friend uses.

7 _______________ is something _______________ I avoid when I get sick.

B Pair Work **Compare the sentences in A with a partner. Then tell the class about some of the interesting home remedies you discussed.**

A *The thing that I usually do when I have a cold is drink hot lemon juice with honey. What about you?*

B *The thing that I usually do is . . .*

A Complete the article about swine flu. Use the correct relative pronoun and the correct form of the verb in parentheses. Use Ø for no relative pronoun. If more than one pronoun is possible, write them all in the blank.

A NEW FLU

The flu is one of the most common diseases ___*that/which/Ø*___ (1) viruses __*cause*__ (2) (cause). Sometimes the virus ___________ (3) ___________ (4) (cause) the flu isn't serious.

Other times, it is. The number of people ___________ (5) it ___________ (6) (attack) determines this. The number of places around the world ___________ (7) it ___________ (8) (affect) also decides this. A disease ___________ (9) ___________ (10) (attack) a large number of people and areas is an epidemic. For example, the 1918 flu was an epidemic. In 2009, another flu, swine flu, became an epidemic. Some people feel swine flu is still a serious threat. Regions ___________ (11) swine flu still ___________ (12) (affect) include Europe, Africa, North and South America, the Middle East, and Asia. A lot of people ___________ (13) ___________ (14) (have) swine flu have mild symptoms. Others ___________ (15) ___________ (16) (have) the disease have more serious symptoms. Swine flu became less serious after the 2009 outbreak, but it could return at any time.

B Pair Work Compare answers in A with your partner. Which sentences have subject relative pronouns?

3 More About Object Relative Clauses

Grammar Presentation

Object relative clauses can use a variety of verb forms.	He doesn't touch surfaces **that the patient touches**. He didn't touch the surfaces **that the patient touched**. He hasn't touched the surfaces **that the patient has touched**.
They can also show possession.	The student **whose towel she used** had the flu. (It was the student's towel.)

3.1 More About Object Relative Clauses

A *Whose* + a noun shows possession in an object relative clause.	WHOSE + NOUN The woman **whose husband** the doctor saw also needs an appointment.
A noun always follows *whose*.	WHOSE + NOUN The scientist **whose article** we read is giving a lecture.
Do not omit *whose*.	WHOSE The scientist˄article we read is giving a lecture.
B *Whose* can combine two sentences.	The woman is sick. + The doctor saw ~~her~~ **children**. The woman **whose children** the doctor saw is sick.
Whose replaces the possessive form in the second sentence.	That is the scientist. + We read ~~his~~ **article**. That is the scientist **whose article** we read.

▸ Grammar Application

Exercise 3.1 Verbs in Object Relative Clauses

A Listen to a podcast about the flu vaccine. Complete the sentences with the relative pronoun or Ø (for no relative pronoun) and the correct form of the verb.

A vaccine is a substance ______*that*______ (1) a health practitioner ______________ (2) (give) to help a person avoid getting a disease. There are two types of flu vaccines. One is a shot ______________ (3) a practitioner usually ______________ (4) (give) the patient in the arm. The other type is a nasal spray ______________ (5) the practitioner ______________ (6) (spray) directly into the patient's nose. Scientists develop new flu vaccines every year. They study flu viruses ______________ (7) people around the world ______________ (8) (had) the previous year. Then they choose three critical viruses and make vaccines for them. For example, in 2009, the viruses ______________ (9) they ______________ (10) (choose) were the most likely to continue to cause disease in 2010.

People often don't like to get their flu shots. However, the flu shot ______________ (11) scientists ______________ (12) (develop) for 2009 was in high demand in the United States. More people than usual received that shot. According to doctors, getting a flu shot each year is the most important thing ______________ (13) a person ______________ (14) (do) to prevent the flu. Maybe their message is now being heard.

B Listen again, and check your answers.

C Pair Work Compare answers with a partner.

Combine the sentences about Louis Pasteur. Use *that*, *which*, *who(m)*, Ø, or *whose*.

1 A biologist of the nineteenth century was Louis Pasteur. Doctors today still value his research.
A biologist of the nineteenth century *whose research doctors today still value*
was Louis Pasteur.

2 Pasteur was a scientist. We still use his vaccines.
Pasteur is a scientist ____ .

3 Pasteur developed vaccines to prevent diseases. Farm animals often get the diseases.
Pasteur developed vaccines to prevent the diseases

____ .

4 He also developed a vaccine to prevent a disease. People get the disease from dogs and other animals.
He also developed a vaccine to prevent a disease

____ .

5 This is a disease. People get it from animal bites. The name of the disease is rabies.
This is a disease ____ .
The name of the disease is rabies.

6 Pasteur first tried his rabies vaccine on a young boy.
A dog bit the boy.
Pasteur first tried his rabies vaccine on a young boy

____ .

7 The vaccine worked. He cured the boy. The boy became his friend.
The vaccine worked. The boy
____ became his friend.

8 Another disease is called anthrax. A lot of farm animals still get the disease.
Another disease ____ is called anthrax.

A Over to You **Answer the questions. Use object relative clauses.**

1 In your opinion, what is the best thing that you can do to prevent the flu? Why?
The best thing that you *can do to prevent the flu is get a flu shot. If you get a flu*
 shot, you won't get the flu, and you won't give it to other people .

2 What is the best thing that you can do to prevent the common cold? Why?
The best thing that you ____ .

3 When you get the flu or a cold, what is the remedy that you use? Why?
The remedy that I ____ .

4 What disease worries you the most? Why?
The disease that I ____ .

5 What is the thing you worry about the most when you get sick? Why?
When I get sick, the thing that I ____ .

B Pair Work Discuss your answers with a partner. What do you agree or disagree about?

4 Avoid Common Mistakes ⚠

1 Use *that* / *who* / *whom* / Ø to refer to people in object relative clauses; use *which* / *that* to refer to things.

    that / who / whom / Ø

The scientist ~~which~~ I remember reading about was Louis Pasteur.

2 Do not confuse *whose* with *who*. *Whose* is possessive.

    whose

A person ~~who~~ computer is infected with a virus can use software to solve the problem.

3 Use *whom* in object relative clauses only (and in rather formal situations).

    who

The man ~~whom~~ had the virus was very ill.

4 Do not use an object pronoun at the end of an object relative clause.

The articles that I read ~~them~~ are about Louis Pasteur.

Editing Task

Find and correct eight more mistakes in the web article about computer viruses.

A New Kind of Epidemic

Are computer viruses similar to human viruses? In some ways, they are. A virus that invades your computer sometimes behaves like a virus that infects your body.

        that / Ø

Computer viruses became a serious problem in the 1990s. One of the first types of virus ~~who~~ computer scientists created was a "worm." A worm is a computer virus that a computer receives it without

5 the user's knowledge. A user who computer is attacked by a worm may lose data or suffer damage to his or her computer system.

The people which we must blame for the very first worm developed it in 1979. Much like a human virus, the worm of 1979 gradually spread until it became an "epidemic." A virus who thousands of computers received very rapidly was the famous "Melissa" virus of 1999. Luckily, someone developed a

10 "vaccine" for this virus, and it is no longer the cause of a computer virus epidemic.

However, people continue to create viruses of different kinds. For example, one virus attacks people's electronic address lists and sends e-mails to everyone who name is on a list. The people who you know them may be surprised when they get an e-mail from you that is really an advertisement!

People who computers were infected with viruses needed protection, so companies began to

15 produce anti-virus software in the 1990s. Nowadays, a user whom has good anti-virus software doesn't need to worry about a sick computer. However, people create new viruses all the time. Viruses will continue to be a problem, and new computer virus "vaccines" will need to be developed to fight them.

Summary and Response

Brainstorm > Organize > **Write** > Edit

In Unit 30, you analyzed a student's summary and response and then wrote your own response paragraph. In this unit (31), you will plan and answer the prompt below.

Write a summary paragraph of "Nontraditional Weddings." Then write a response paragraph giving your opinion about the changes in wedding traditions described in the article.

Using Object Relative Clauses in a Personal Response

Using object relative clauses can make your writing smoother and more interesting. Use them in your response paragraphs to describe, indentify, or give more information about a noun.

Compare these two examples:

Some couples plan weddings in exotic places. They are usually expensive.

Weddings **that couples plan in exotic places** are usually quite expensive.

The second sentence is smoother and more interesting than the first example.

Exercise 5.1 Applying the Skill

Complete each sentence with an object relative clause. Then compare your sentences with a partner's.

1 These days, couples in my country want to have a wedding _________________________

____.

2 Most couples will choose food ____.

3 They will also choose a place ____.

4 Most importantly, they will include people ____________________________________.

My Writing

You first read "Nontraditional Weddings" in Unit 28. Re-read it, and do the exercises that follow.

Nontraditional **Weddings**

Even if they have never attended a traditional American wedding in person, most people have probably seen such weddings in movies or on television. People enjoy seeing the beautiful bride in her white dress, the handsome groom, the ceremony in the church, the romantic music—these customs are familiar to people all over the world. Though most American couples still choose to have this kind of traditional wedding, more and more couples these days are deciding to have unique weddings that reflect their beliefs, hobbies, and personal style. Three types of nontraditional weddings are adventure weddings, destination weddings, and theme weddings.

Adventure weddings typically involve combining the marriage ceremony with a physical activity that has special meaning for the couple. Cathy and Frank Mason are enthusiastic scuba divers who enjoy diving all over the world. In 2012, they met on a shark-diving adventure near Key West, Florida.

A year later, they were engaged and started to plan their wedding. Cathy had always dreamed of a large, traditional wedding in a church, but from the start Frank had a different idea. He suggested combining their wedding with their love for each other and the activity they loved most—scuba diving. Cathy finally agreed, and the couple were married underwater in May, 2015—surrounded by numerous friends and relatives, all in scuba gear. Other adventure-seeking couples have gotten married while surfing, skydiving, or riding in a hot-air balloon.

Most people are less adventurous than the Masons, but many of them love to travel. It is becoming more and more common for such couples to get married in a distant location. An American couple, Arielle Cogan and Richard Thompson, met when both of them were spending a year studying history in Edinburgh, Scotland. They fell in love and became engaged, but neither of them wanted to have an ordinary wedding. Instead, they were married in a small, 18th-century church in Edinburgh with just their families and a few close friends as guests. The bride wore a traditional white dress and the groom wore a kilt, which is a traditional Scottish skirt for men. Destination weddings like the Thompsons' allow couples to get married in the place of their dreams. The main disadvantage is the cost: It can be expensive to have family and friends fly to an exotic location on the other side of the world.

Finally, a theme wedding allows couples to create a fun, nontraditional wedding that centers on a beloved book, song, story, or historical period. A couple from Epping, New Hampshire, planned every detail of their wedding, from the wedding vows to the food at the reception, around the theme of the Harry Potter books by J.K. Rowling. Although it took a lot of planning, their guests will probably never forget attending the event. Other unique themes for weddings have included pirates, superheroes like Superman, a Hawaiian luau, country music, Victorian England, the 1960s, a fairy tale like "Cinderella", and many, many more.

Unlike the past, when a traditional religious wedding was the only option available to marrying couples, couples these days are free to choose almost any type of wedding they can imagine. The variety of wedding styles and locations is perhaps a reflection of the general trend toward individual choice and self-expression that has been growing stronger in the U.S. since the 1960s. Whether a couple chooses to have an old-fashioned church wedding or a ceremony at the top of a mountain, the central purpose of a wedding—to celebrate the union of a couple in the presence of the people who love them—has not changed, and it probably never will.

1 Work with a partner. Use the chart below to discuss and make notes about your responses to the main idea in each paragraph. You may want to review your summary chart in Unit 28.

Paragraph	Main Topic/Idea	My Response
1	today's couples plan unique weddings to match their beliefs, hobbies, & personal style	
2	adventure weddings	
3	destination weddings	
4	theme weddings	
5	weddings reflect modern trend of personal choice & self-expression	

2 Use the outline below to plan your summary and response paragraphs on your own.

<u>**Summary paragraph**</u>

Topic sentence (author's main idea):

Supporting detail 1:

Supporting detail 2:

Supporting detail 3:

<u>Response paragraph</u>

Topic sentence (my reaction to the author's main idea):

Supporting detail 1:

Supporting detail 2:

Supporting detail 3 (optional):

Concluding sentence (restates my opinion):

Exercise 5.3 Writing Your First Draft

Write a summary paragraph of "Nontraditional Weddings." Then write a response paragraph giving your opinion about the changes in wedding traditions described in the article.

1 Grammar in the Real World

A What holidays do you celebrate each year? Which are your favorite days? Read the magazine article about "Black Friday" (the day after Thanksgiving). What's good and bad about Black Friday?

B Comprehension Check **Answer the questions.**

1 Why is the holiday shopping season important?

2 Why do people want to shop on Black Friday?

3 What are the problems with shopping on Black Friday?

4 What are some ways to avoid the problems of Black Friday?

C Notice **Complete the sentences from the article. Circle the correct words.**

1 It is the start of the holiday shopping season, **but / so** it is an important day for retailers.

2 For instance, a store will advertise a big-screen TV at a very low price, **but / because** there may be only one in the store.

3 Shoppers occasionally get into arguments **and / so** even fistfights.

4 They shop on the weekend after, **since / or** they stay home and buy online.

Think about the meaning of each word you circled. In which sentence above does the word express these meanings?

a a result *1*   b an addition ____   c an alternative ____   d a contrast ____

Black FRIDAY

Black Friday is the Friday after Thanksgiving Day in the United States. It is the start of the holiday shopping season, so it is an important day for retailers.[1] It is called "Black Friday" **because**
5   it is the day when retailers go "into the black." That is, they make a profit. Retailers can make 18 percent to 40 percent of their yearly sales in the month between Thanksgiving and Christmas, **so** the holiday shopping season is crucial for them
10 **and** the U.S. economy in general.

Although Black Friday is not an official holiday, many workers have the day off and start their holiday shopping. Shopping on this day is popular **because** retailers offer very low prices on
15 items such as electronics.

There is a sense of excitement about Black Friday. Stores advertise their prices in advance and open their doors at 5:00 a.m. Shoppers often line up outside a store hours before it opens **so** they
20 can be the first ones in. Some people even camp in the parking lot the night before.

However, Black Friday shopping is not without its problems. **Even though** the deals sound fantastic, they are often not as good as they seem.
25 For instance, a store will advertise a big screen TV at a very low price, **but** there may be only one in the store. **Since** there are not enough low-priced items for everyone, sometimes people get stressed **and** angry. Shoppers occasionally get
30 into arguments **and** even fistfights. In addition, **since** people are excited and stores are crowded, there are sometimes accidents on Black Friday.

Some people avoid the problems of Black Friday. They shop on the weekend after, or they
35 stay home and buy online. Black Friday can mean crowds and bad deals, **and yet** it remains one of the busiest shopping days of the year.

---

[1]**retailer:** store owner

2 Conjunctions

Grammar Presentation

The conjunctions *and, or, but, so,* and *yet* can connect single words, phrases, or clauses.

WORD   WORD
Black Friday causes problems for <u>shoppers</u> **and** <u>stores</u>.

PHRASE   PHRASE
They shop <u>on weekends</u> **but** <u>not on weekdays</u>.

CLAUSE   CLAUSE
<u>He wanted to save money</u>, **so** <u>he shopped on Black Friday</u>.

2.1 Conjunctions

A You can use *and* to connect related information and add ideas.	The shoppers were tired **and** hungry. (words) People go out **and** spend money. (phrases) The store opened at 5:00 a.m., **and** shoppers were waiting outside. (clauses)
B You can use *or* to give alternatives or choices.	You can shop today **or** tomorrow. (words) They camp in the parking lot **or** in front of the store. (phrases) You can shop today, **or** you can wait until tomorrow. (clauses)
C You can use *but* (*not*) to connect contrasting ideas.	The store is small **but** successful. (words) They liked the clothes **but** not the high prices. (phrases) She has invited Jim for the holiday, **but** she has never invited us. (clauses)
D You can use *so* to connect causes and results.	The stores are crowded, **so** I'll stay home. (clauses)
You can use *and* before *so* to show a result.	Stores cut their prices, **and so** they make less money. (clauses)
It is not common to use *so* to connect words and phrases.	

2.2 Using Conjunctions

A Use a comma when you connect two long clauses. However, you do not need a comma when the clauses are short.	*This is an important day,* **and** *it is the busiest shopping day.* *Stores cut prices* **and** *people save money.*
B When you connect two clauses and the subject is the same, you do not need to repeat the subject.	*People go shopping* **and** *(people) buy holiday gifts on this day.* *They save money* **but** *(they) don't realize the items aren't new.*
If the verb is the same, you do not need to repeat it.	*People can shop online* **or** *(can shop) at the mall.* *Shoppers start arguments* **and** *even (start) fistfights.* *Stores are cutting prices* **and** *(are) hoping to sell more.*
In addition, you often do not need to repeat prepositions after conjunctions.	*People are not at work on Thursday* **and** *(on) Friday.*
C You can often use *but* + *not* to shorten contrasting clauses to words or phrases.	*They shop on Friday* **but not** *Thursday.* (= They shop on Friday, but they do not shop on Thursday.) *They liked the clothes* **but not** *the high prices.* (= They liked the clothes, but they did not like the high prices.)
Do not use *not* if the contrasting ideas are both affirmative.	*The store is small* **but** *successful.* (= The store is small, but it is successful.)

2.3 Yet, And Yet

A Yet is a formal word. It has a similar meaning to *but*. Yet connects strongly contrasting ideas or surprising information.	*It is often cold,* **yet** *shoppers still sleep in doorways.* *The deals are often not good,* **yet** *people still go shopping.*
B You can use *and* with *yet*.	*There is a downside,* **and yet** *it is a popular shopping day.*

Grammar Application

Exercise 2.1 *And, Or, But, So, and Yet*

Complete a news article about the holiday shopping season. Circle the correct words.

Holiday Shopping in Our City

The malls are decorated **and / but** (1) ready for the holiday shopping season. The stores are hoping to attract a lot of customers **yet / and** (2) make big profits this year.

The holidays are a time for giving gifts, **or / and** (3) the shopping season is important for stores.

Black Friday used to be the start of the shopping season, **but / or** (4) people are starting to shop earlier in November. We talked to some retailers **so / and** (5) analysts about their expectations for the holiday shopping season this year.

"This year, stores are busy, **but not / but** (6) as busy as last year," said one retailer. "People are tired of the crowds, **but / so** (7) they're shopping by telephone **but / or** (8) online," he added.

"Unemployment in the city has gone up this year, **so / and yet** (9) people are still spending." An analyst told us, "People are spending, **but / or** (10) they are spending more cautiously this year. The popular items are electronics **and / but** (11) toys."

She added, "Stores are offering discounts **but / or** (12) gifts with purchases. They are staying open later on Saturdays **and / yet** (13) Sundays."

Exercise 2.2 Repeated Subjects, Verbs, and Prepositions

Read an online interview with shoppers about Black Friday. If you do not need to repeat a subject or verb, cross it out.

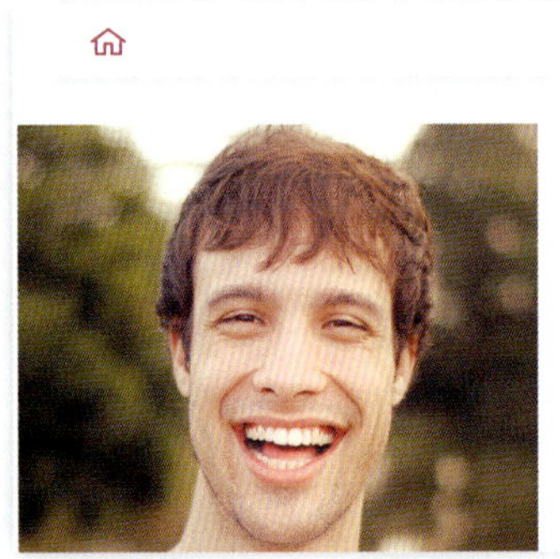

Alex B., Detroit: (1) Black Friday can be a good thing or ~~Black Friday can be~~ a bad thing. (2) There are good deals and there are special offers. (3) For example, at a lot of stores, I can choose free shipping or I can choose a gift with my purchase. (4) I love the deals but I hate the crowds.

Maria S., Chicago: (5) People become over-excited and people become aggressive on Black Friday. (6) People push and people fight to get to the deals. (7) I stay home and I shop online, or I order things over the phone.

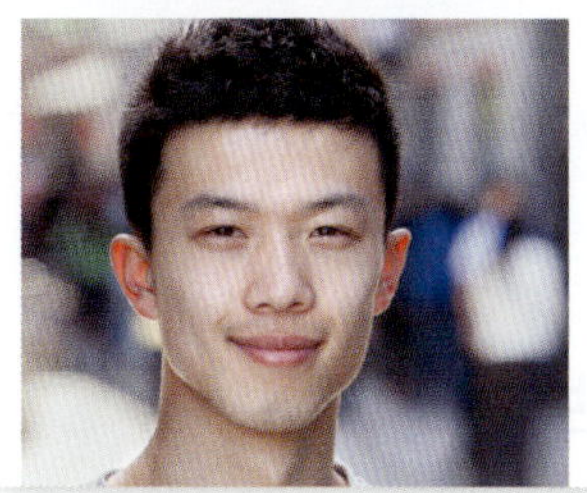

Wei P., San Francisco: (8) I can buy all of my gifts and I can save money, too. (9) We go shopping as a family and we enjoy our day out together.

Exercise 2.3 Using *And, Or, But,* and *So*

A Pair Work What do you know about Thanksgiving in the United States and Canada? When are the two holidays? How do people celebrate them? How did the holidays start? Make a list of facts with a partner.

B Listen to a radio show about Thanksgiving in the United States and Canada. Complete the chart below.

		Canada	The United States
1	What year was the first Thanksgiving Day?	*1578*	
2	Who started it (according to history books)?		
3	What month is it in?		
4	What day of the week is it on?		
5	What do people eat on Thanksgiving?		
6	What day of the week do they eat Thanksgiving dinner?		
7	What is the big shopping day?		

C Complete these sentences about Thanksgiving in the United States and Canada. Use the information in the chart to help you. Circle the correct conjunctions.

1 Thanksgiving is a holiday in _the United States_ **(and)/but** Canada.

2 Thanksgiving is in November in the United States, **but/so** the Canadian Thanksgiving is in ___________________ .

3 In the United States, Thanksgiving Day is always on a ___________________ , **or/but** in Canada, it's on a Monday.

4 In ___________________ , people get together with family **and/but** have a traditional Thanksgiving dinner.

5 People eat turkey **and/or** ___________________ .

6 In the United States, the meal is always on Thanksgiving Day, **but/so** in Canada, the meal can be on ___________________ .

7 Canadians can have Thanksgiving dinner on Saturday, Sunday, **or/but** ___________________ .

8 In the United States, Black Friday is the big shopping day, **but/and** in Canada, the big sales are on ___________________ .

Exercise 2.4 More Conjunctions

Group Work Make a list of favorite holidays and special days in your group. Talk about why the day exists, how people celebrate it, what they wear, what they eat or drink, where they go, and so on. Then discuss the similarities and differences among the days on your list. Use *and, but, or, so,* and *yet.*

3 Adverb Clauses

Grammar Presentation

Adverb clauses show how ideas are connected. They begin with conjunctions such as *because, since, although,* and *even though.*

MAIN CLAUSE	ADVERB CLAUSE
	CONJUNCTION

Many people have the day off work *even though it's not an official holiday*.

3.1 Adverb Clauses

Adverb Clause		Main Clause
Because Since	there is a big sale today,	the stores are crowded.
Although Even though	it is not a holiday,	a lot of people have the day off.

3.1 Adverb Clauses *(continued)*

Main Clause	Adverb Clause	
The stores are crowded	**because** **since**	there is a big sale today.
Many people have the day off	**although** **even though**	it isn't a holiday.

3.2 Using Adverb Clauses

A Like most other clauses, an adverb clause must have a subject and a verb.

ADVERB CLAUSE
 SUBJ.   VERB
 People shop on Black Friday **because prices are lower**.

B An adverb clause on its own is not a sentence. It is a fragment.

They have the day off work **although it's not a holiday**.
 They have the day off work. ~~Although it's not a holiday~~.

C An adverb clause can come before or after the main clause. Use a comma when the adverb clause comes first.

Black Friday is an important day for retailers **because it is the start of the holiday shopping season**.
 Because Black Friday is the start of the holiday shopping season, *it is an important day for retailers.*

D *Although, even though,* and *though* connect contrasting ideas.

Although it is not a holiday, *workers have the day off.*
 Even though some deals sound fantastic, *they are not.*
 Though prices are low, *the deals are often not good.*

E *Because* and *since* introduce reasons or causes and connect them with results.

RESULT   CAUSE
 It's a popular day **since stores offer special deals**.
 CAUSE   RESULT
 Because prices are low, *the stores are crowded.*
 REASON   RESULT
 Because stores are crowded, *many people stay home.*

You can use *since* when the reader or listener knows about the reason from general knowledge, or because you have explained it.

Most stores cut their prices on Black Friday. **Since** *prices are lower, it is a popular shopping day.*

F *So* introduces results.

The stores are crowded, **so** *many people stay home.*

So can also introduce a purpose or reason.

They camp in the parking lot **so** *they can be first in the store.*

Do not start a sentence with *so*.

Research shows that *since* is more common in formal writing than in speaking.

Writing
Speaking

Grammar Application

Complete the magazine article about "Cyber Monday" (the Monday after Thanksgiving in the United States). Circle the best conjunctions.

CYBER MONDAY

The holiday shopping season is important for the U.S. economy **since**/**although** a high percentage of retail sales
(1)
occur between Thanksgiving and Christmas. **Although/Because**
(2)
Black Friday is an important day for retailers, Cyber Monday has become equally important. Cyber Monday is the first Monday after Thanksgiving Day. It's called "Cyber Monday" **although/because** a
(3)
lot of retailers have online sales on that day.

There are a number of reasons why so many people shop on Cyber Monday, **even though/because** they cannot touch or
(4)
handle the items they are buying. For one thing, it's convenient. **Even though/Because** most companies have rules against online
(5)
shopping, millions of people still shop online on Cyber Monday while they're at work and sitting in front of computers. Also, Cyber Monday deals are sometimes even better than Black Friday deals. **Although/Because** Monday is often the last chance for retailers
(6)
to get rid of all the items they had for Black Friday, they often cut prices on Cyber Monday. In addition, some people prefer to buy online **because/although** shipping is usually free, and they don't
(7)
have to carry heavy items home.

Since/Although most people think of the Friday after Thanksgiving as the biggest shopping day in the United States, Cyber
(8)
Monday is now almost as important for retailers as Black Friday.

Exercise 3.2 Adverb Clauses

Combine the sentences to make one sentence. Use *because*, *since*, *so*, *although*, *even though*, or *though*. Sometimes there is more than one correct answer.

1   Researchers study the psychology of giving gifts. Gift giving is an important part of life.

Researchers study the psychology of giving gifts because / since gift giving is an important part of life.
Gift giving is an important part of life, so many experts study the psychology of giving gifts.

2   Stores are crowded during the holiday shopping period. Some people decide not to give gifts.

3   Holiday shopping can be unpleasant and expensive. Sometimes people feel like they can't avoid gift giving.

4   Gift giving in the right situations can make our relationships with people stronger. It can be a nice reminder of how we feel about other people.

5   Gift giving varies from culture to culture. It's a good idea to learn about cultural rules for gift giving.

6   In some cultures, you open a gift as soon as you get it. You wait until the giver has left in other cultures.

7   A certain color can mean bad luck in some cultures. People will avoid using the color as a gift wrap.

8   Both men and women enjoy gifts. Researchers say that gift giving is more important for females.

A Complete the questions about gift-giving habits with an appropriate conjunction.

1 Do you ever buy gifts for people _**because**_ you want to say "thank you"?

2 Do you ever feel you have to buy gifts ________________ you can't really afford them?

3 Have you ever given a gift to someone ________________ you felt you had to?

4 Have you ever taken a gift back to the store for a refund or exchange ________________ you didn't like it?

5 Have you bought a gift for someone ________________ you didn't like that person?

6 Have you bought a gift for someone ________________ you wanted to say "I'm sorry"?

7 Have you ever given someone a gift ________________ you had no reason?

8 Have you ever pretended to like a gift ________________ you didn't like it?

B Pair Work Ask and answer the questions in A with a partner. Do you have the same gift-giving habits?

A *Do you ever buy gifts for people because you want to say "thank you"?*
B *Yes, I sometimes buy a small gift for my neighbor when she waters my plants for me.*

4 Avoid Common Mistakes ⚠️

1 **Check the spelling of _although_.**
Although
~~Althought~~ *the stores are crowded, it's my favorite day to shop.*

2 **Do not link three or more clauses with _although_, _though_, or _even though_.**
I like Black Friday. Although it is very tiring, it's a lot of fun.
~~*I like Black Friday although it is very tiring it's a lot of fun.*~~

3 **Do not forget to use a comma after the adverb clause when the adverb clause is first.**
Although we think it is a modern celebration, it is an ancient tradition.

Editing Task

Find and correct seven more mistakes in these paragraphs.

Although
~~Allthough~~ Mother's Day is an old holiday it may surprise you to know that Father's Day is a modern holiday. Some people say the first modern Father's Day was in 1908, althought most people agree it started in 1910. Father's Day was born in Spokane, Washington, on June 19, 1910. Father's Day was partly the idea

5 of Mrs. Sonora Smart Dodd. Because her father was a single parent and raised six children, she wanted to honor him. Although she suggested her father's June 5 birthday she did not give the organizers enough time to make arrangements. The holiday moved from June 5 to the third Sunday in June. Father's Day is now a popular holiday. Althogh people laughed at the idea of Father's Day at first it gradually

10 became popular.

Because retailers saw an opportunity to increase sales in the 1930s, they started to advertise Father's Day gifts. People then felt that they had to buy gifts for their fathers even though they realized this was commercialization, they still bought them. Father's Day is an international holiday. Even though people celebrate it on different

15 dates it is an important day in many cultures.

5 Academic Writing

Summary and Response

Brainstorm > Organize > Write > **Edit**

In Unit 31, you answered the prompt below. In this unit (32), you will review, revise, and edit your paragraphs.

> *Write a summary paragraph of "Nontraditional Weddings." Then write a response paragraph giving your opinion about the changes in wedding traditions described in the article.*

Using Adverb Clauses to Connect Contrasting Ideas

You can use an adverb clause to show that two ideas are both true and contrasting. This structure is useful for expressing opinions in a response paragraph. If you disagree with a writer, using an adverb clause allows you to state the original idea and show how your opinion is different.

Although a traditional wedding is less expensive, a creative wedding would be more memorable.

Even though the parents may prefer a traditional wedding, the couple should choose the type of wedding they prefer.

Exercise 5.1 Applying the Skill

1 Match the two parts of the sentences.

_______ 1 Even though one couple would like to have their wedding on top of a mountain,

_______ 2 Although a theme wedding would be fun,

_______ 3 While a destination wedding can be beautiful,

_______ 4 Even though traditional weddings are not creative,

a   it is usually expensive for guests to attend.

b   they should consider their older guests, like their grandparents.

c   it would require a lot of planning.

d   the guests know what to expect and how to dress.

2 Edit your response paragraph in My Writing in Unit 31 to include at least one adverb clause.

My Writing

Exercise 5.2 Revising Your Ideas

1 Work with a partner. Use the questions to give feedback on your partner's paragraphs.
   - Which of your partner's ideas seem strongest to you?
   - Which of your partner's ideas need to be explained more clearly?
   - What could your partner add or remove to make the writing stronger and easier to understand?

2 Use the feedback from your partner to revise your paragraphs.

Exercise 5.3 Editing Your Writing

Use the checklist to review and edit your paragraphs.

Did you completely answer the prompt?	
Did you paraphrase the original author's main idea in the summary paragraph?	
Did you summarize the most important details for each type of wedding?	
Did you state your opinion in the response paragraph?	
Did you give examples or other supporting details for your opinion in the response paragraph?	
Did you restate your opinion in the concluding sentence?	

Exercise 5.4 Editing Your Grammar

Use the checklist to review and edit the grammar in your essay.

Did you use gerunds correctly?	
Did you use infinitives correctly?	
Did you use subject relative clauses to summarize ideas?	
Did you use object relative clauses to respond to ideas?	
Did you use adverb clauses correctly to connect contrasting ideas?	
Did you avoid the common mistakes in the charts on pages 369, 383, 395, 409, and 425?	

Exercise 5.5 Writing Your Final Draft

Apply the feedback and edits from Exercises 5.2 to 5.4 to write the final draft of your essay.

Appendices

1 Capitalization and Punctuation Rules

Capitalize	Examples
1. The first letter of the first word of a sentence	*Today is a great day.*
2. The pronoun *I*	*After class, I want to go to the movies.*
3. Names of people	*Simon Bolivar, Joseph Chung*
4. Names of buildings, streets, geographic locations, and organizations	*Taj Mahal, Main Street, Mt. Everest, United Nations*
5. Titles of people	*Dr., Mr., Mrs., Ms.*
6. Days, months, and holidays	*Tuesday, April, Valentine's Day*
7. Names of courses or classes	*Biology 101, English Composition II*
8. Titles of books, movies, and plays	*Crime and Punishment, Avatar, Hamlet*
9. States, countries, languages, and nationalities	*California, Mexico, Spanish, South Korean, Canadian*
10. Names of religions	*Hinduism, Catholicism, Islam, Judaism*

Punctuation	Examples
1. Use a period (.) at the end of a sentence.	*I think I can pass this class.*
2. Use a question mark (?) at the end of a question.	*Why do you want to buy a car?*
3. Use an exclamation point (!) to show strong emotion (e.g., surprise, anger, shock).	*Wait! I'm not ready yet.* *I can't believe it!*
4. Use an apostrophe (') for possessive nouns. Add 's for singular nouns. Add s' for plural nouns. Add ' or 's for nouns that end in -s. Add 's for irregular plural nouns. Use an apostrophe (') for contractions.	*That's Sue's umbrella.* *Those are the students' books.* *It is Wes' house. It is Wes's house.* *Bring me the children's shoes.* *I'll be back next week. He can't drive a car.*

1 Capitalization and Punctuation Rules (*Continued*)

Punctuation	Examples
5. Use a comma (,): between words in a series of three or more items. (Place *and* before the last item.) after a time clause when it begins a sentence. after a prepositional phrase when it begins a sentence. after an adverb clause when it begins a sentence. before *and, or, but,* and *so* to connect two or more main clauses.	*I like fish, chicken, turkey, **and** mashed potatoes.* ***Before** I play soccer, I do my stretching exercises.* ***Next to** my house, there's a beautiful little park.* ***Because** she got a job, she was able to get her own apartment.* *You can watch TV, **but** I have to study for a test.*

2 Stative (Non-Action) Verbs

Stative verbs do not describe actions. They describe states or situations. Stative verbs are not usually used in the present progressive, even if we are talking about right now. Some are occasionally used in the present progressive, but often with a different meaning.

Research shows that the 25 most common stative verbs in spoken and written English are:

agree	dislike	hope	love	see
believe	expect	hurt	need	seem
care (about)	hate	know	notice	think
cost	have	like	own	understand
disagree	hear	look like	prefer	want

Other stative verbs are:

be	feel	matter	recognize	sound
belong	forgive	mean	remember	taste
concern	look	owe	smell	weigh
deserve				

Using the present progressive of these verbs sometimes changes the meaning to an action.

*Can you **see** the red car?*   (= use your eyes to be aware of something)

*I'**m seeing** an old friend tomorrow.*   (= meeting someone)

*I **think** you're right.*   (= believe)

*Dina **is thinking** of taking a vacation soon.*   (= considering)

*I **have** two sisters.*   (= be related to)

*We'**re having** eggs for breakfast.*   (= eating)

3 Irregular Verbs

Base Form	Simple Past	Past Participle	Base Form	Simple Past	Past Participle
be	was / were	been	keep	kept	kept
become	became	become	know	knew	known
begin	began	begun	leave	left	left
bite	bit	bitten	lose	lost	lost
blow	blew	blown	make	made	made
break	broke	broken	meet	met	met
bring	brought	brought	pay	paid	paid
build	built	built	put	put	put
buy	bought	bought	read	read [red]*	read [red]*
catch	caught	caught	ride	rode	ridden
choose	chose	chosen	run	ran	run
come	came	come	say	said	said
cost	cost	cost	see	saw	seen
cut	cut	cut	sell	sold	sold
do	did	done	send	sent	sent
draw	drew	drawn	set	set	set
drink	drank	drunk	shake	shook	shaken
drive	drove	driven	show	showed	shown
eat	ate	eaten	shut	shut	shut
fall	fell	fallen	sing	sang	sung
feed	fed	fed	sit	sat	sat
feel	felt	felt	sleep	slept	slept
fight	fought	fought	speak	spoke	spoken
find	found	found	spend	spent	spent
fly	flew	flown	stand	stood	stood
forget	forgot	forgotten	steal	stole	stolen
forgive	forgave	forgiven	swim	swam	swum
get	got	gotten	take	took	taken
give	gave	given	teach	taught	taught
go	went	gone	tell	told	told
grow	grew	grown	think	thought	thought
have	had	had	throw	threw	thrown
hear	heard	heard	understand	understood	understood
hide	hid	hidden	wake	woke	woken
hit	hit	hit	wear	wore	worn
hold	held	held	win	won	won
hurt	hurt	hurt	write	wrote	written

*pronunciation

4 Spelling Rules for Verbs Ending in *-ing*

1. For verbs ending in a vowel-consonant combination, repeat the consonant before adding *-ing*.
    get → *getting*   *swim* → *swimming*

2. However, if the verb has more than one syllable, repeat the consonant only if the final syllable is stressed.
    beGIN → *beginning*   BUT   *HAPpen* → *happening (no doubling of consonant)*

3. For verbs ending in a silent *e*, drop the *e* before adding *-ing*.
    move → *moving*   *drive* → *driving*

    For *be* and *see*, don't <u>drop</u> the *e* because it is not silent.
    be → *being*   *see* → *seeing*

    For verbs ending in *-ie*, change *ie* to *y* before adding *-ing*.
    die → *dying*   *lie* → *lying*

Verbs that end in *-ing* are also called *gerunds* when they are used as nouns. The same spelling rules above apply to gerunds as well.

5 Spelling Rules for Regular Verbs in the Simple Past

1. To form the simple past of regular verbs, add *-ed* to the base form of the verb.
    work → *worked*   *wash* → *washed*

2. For regular verbs that end in *-e*, add *-d* only.
    live → *lived*   *like* → *liked*

3. For regular verbs ending in a consonant + *-y*, change *y* to *i* and add *-ed*.
    study → *studied*   *hurry* → *hurried*

4. For regular verbs that end in a vowel + *-y*, add *-ed*.
    stay → *stayed*   *enjoy* → *enjoyed*

5. For regular verbs that end in a vowel-consonant combination, repeat the consonant before adding *-ed*. Exception: Do not double the last consonant for verbs that end with *-w*, *-x*, or *-y*.
    stop → *stopped*   *plan* → *planned*   BUT   *fix* → *fixed*

6. However, if the verb has more than one syllable, repeat the consonant only if the final syllable is stressed.
    preFER → *preferred*   BUT   *Visit* → *visited (no doubling of consonant)*

6 Verbs + Gerunds and Infinitives

Verbs Followed by a Gerund Only

admit	keep (= *continue*)
avoid	mind (= *object to*)
consider	miss
delay	postpone
deny	practice
discuss	quit
enjoy	recall (= *remember*)
finish	risk
imagine	suggest
involve	understand

Verbs Followed by an Infinitive Only

afford	hope	pretend
agree	intend	promise
arrange	learn	refuse
attempt	manage	seem
decide	need	tend (= *be likely*)
deserve	offer	threaten
expect	plan	volunteer
fail	prepare	want
help		

Verbs Followed by a Gerund or an Infinitive

begin	like	start
continue	love	stop*
forget*	prefer	try*
hate	remember*	

*The meanings of these verbs are different when they are followed by a gerund or an infinitive. See Unit 28.

7 Verb and Preposition Combinations

Verb + **about**
 ask about
 complain about
 talk about
 think about
 worry about

Verb + **against**
 advise against
 decide against

Verb + **at**
 look at
 smile at

Verb + **for**
 apologize for
 ask for
 look for
 pay for
 wait for

Verb + **in**
 believe in
 succeed in

Verb + **of**
 approve of
 dream of
 think of

Verb + **on**
 count on
 decide on
 depend on
 insist on
 plan on
 rely on

Verb + **to**
 admit to
 belong to
 listen to
 look forward to
 talk to

Verb + **with**
 agree with
 argue with
 bother with
 deal with

8 Adjective and Preposition Combinations

Adjective + *of*
afraid of
ashamed of
aware of
careful of
full of
sick of
tired of

Adjective + *by*
amazed by
bored by
surprised by

Adjective + *at*
amazed at
angry at
bad at
good at
surprised at

Adjective + *from*
different from
separate from

Adjective + *with*
bored with
familiar with
satisfied with
wrong with

Adjective + *in*
interested in

Adjective + *for*
bad for
good for
responsible for

Adjective + *about*
concerned about
excited about
happy about
nervous about
pleased about
sad about
sorry about
surprised about
upset about
worried about

Adjective + *to*
similar to

9 Modal Verbs and Modal-like Expressions

Most modals have multiple meanings.

Function	Modal Verb or Modal-like Expression	Time	Example
Ability / Possibility	can	present, future	I **can** speak three languages. I **can** help you tomorrow.
	could	present, past	She **could** play an excellent game of tennis when she was young.
	be able to	past, present, future	I **won't be able to** help you tomorrow. I'm **not able to** help you today.
Permission less formal more formal	can could	present, future	Yes, you **can** watch TV now. You **could** give me your answer next week.
	may	present, future	You **may** leave now.
Requests less formal	can will	present, future	**Can** you stop that noise now? **Will** you please visit me tonight?
more formal	could would	present, future	**Could** you turn off your cell phone please? **Would** you please come for your interview this afternoon?
Offers	can could may will	present, future	I **can** help you paint your room. I **could** drive you to work next week. **May** I carry that for you? We'**ll** help you find your wallet.
Invitations	would you like	present, future	**Would you like** to come to my graduation tomorrow?
Advice less strong	ought to should	present, future	You really **ought to** save your money. She **shouldn't** go to school today.
stronger	had better	present, future	They **had better** be very careful in the park tomorrow.
Suggestions	could might want to	present, future	He **could** take a train instead of the bus. You **might want to** wait until next month.

Modal Verbs and Modal-like Expressions (*continued*)

Function	Modal Verb or Modal-like Expression	Time	Example
Preferences	would like would prefer would rather	present, future	I **would like** to take a trip next year. We **would prefer** to go on a cruise. They **would rather** eat at home than in a restaurant.
Necessity less formal	have / has to need to	past, present, future	We **had to** cancel our date at the last minute. She **needs to** quit her stressful job.
more formal	have / has got to must	past, present, future present, future	They**'ve got to** study harder if they want to pass. You **must** be more serious about your future.
Lack of Necessity	don't / doesn't have to don't / doesn't need to	past, present, future	I **didn't have to** renew my driver's license. You **don't need to** worry about your brother.
Prohibition	can't must not may not	present, future	You **can't** attend tonight without an invitation. You **must not** fish without a license. You **may not** board the plane before going through security.
Speculation / Probability	could may might should	present, future	He **could** be late because he missed his train. I **may** stay home. It **might** rain later because I see dark clouds. We **should** probably leave now.
	must	present only	She **must** be sick because she didn't come to work today.

10 Adjectives: Order Before Nouns

When you use two (or more) adjectives before a noun, use the order in the chart below.

Opinion	Size	Quality	Age	Shape	Color	Origin	Material	Nouns as Adjectives
beautiful	big	cold	ancient	rectangular	black	American	cotton	computer
comfortable	fat	free	new	round	blue	Canadian	glass	evening
delicious	huge	heavy	old	square	gold	Chinese	leather	rose
expensive	large	hot	young	triangular	green	European	metal	safety
interesting	long	safe			orange	Japanese	paper	software
nice	short				purple	Mexican	plastic	summer
pretty	small				red	Peruvian	stone	training
reasonable	tall				silver	Thai	wooden	
special	thin				yellow		woolen	
ugly	wide				white			

Examples:

I bought a beautiful, new, purple and gold Indian scarf.

There is a tall, young woman sitting next to that handsome man.

We're going to learn an interesting, new software program.

The museum has expensive glass jewelry.

11 Conditionals

The **factual conditional** describes general truths, habits, and things that happen routinely. The simple present is used in both clauses. You can use modals in the result clause, too.

IF CLAUSE   RESULT CLAUSE

If you use the highway, the drive is much faster.   (general truth)

If you enter before 11:00 a.m., you can get a discount.   (general truth)

Use the imperative in the result clause to give instructions or commands.

If you don't like the oranges, give them to me.   (command)

The **future conditional** describes things that will happen under certain conditions in the future. The simple present is used in the *if* clause and a future form is used in the result clause. You can use modals in the result clause, too.

IF CLAUSE   RESULT CLAUSE

If it rains tomorrow, they're going to cancel the game.

If I finish my homework early, I'll go to the movies.

If she works hard, she could get a promotion.

You can begin a conditional sentence with the *if* clause or the result clause. It doesn't change the meaning. Use a comma between the two clauses if you begin your sentence with the *if* clause.

RESULT CLAUSE   IF CLAUSE
They're going to cancel the game if it rains tomorrow.

IF CLAUSE   RESULT CLAUSE
If it rains tomorrow, they're going to cancel the game.

12 Phrasal Verbs: Transitive and Intransitive

Transitive (Separable) Phrasal Verbs

Phrasal Verb	Meaning	Phrasal Verb	Meaning
add up	add together, combine	*give up*	quit
blow up	explode	*hang up*	end a phone call
bring back	return something or someone	*help out*	assist someone
bring up	(1) raise a child, (2) introduce a topic	*lay off*	lose a job, end employment
build up	accumulate	*leave on*	keep on (a light, clothing, jewelry)
call back	return a phone call	*let in*	allow someone to enter
call off	cancel	*look over*	examine
cheer up	make someone happy	*look up*	find information
clear up	resolve a problem or situation, explain	*make up*	create or invent (a story, a lie)
do over	do again	*pass out*	distribute (paper, a test, material, homework)
figure out	find an answer, understand	*pay back*	repay money
fill in	write in blank spaces	*pay off*	repay completely
fill out	complete an application or form	*pick up*	(1) go get someone or something, (2) lift
find out	look for or seek information, learn	*point out*	call attention to something
give away	donate, give for free	*put away*	(1) save for the future, (2) put in the correct place
give back	return		

Transitive (Separable) Phrasal Verbs *(continued)*

Phrasal Verb	Meaning	Phrasal Verb	Meaning
put back	return something to its usual place	*talk over*	discuss
put off	delay, postpone	*think over*	consider
put out	(1) extinguish, stop the burning of a fire or cigarette, (2) place outside	*throw away / throw out*	get rid of something; discard
put together	assemble	*try on*	put on clothing to see if it fits
set up	(1) arrange, (2) plan, (3) build	*turn down*	(1) lower the volume, (2) reject
shut off / turn off	stop (a machine, a light, a TV)	*turn on*	start (a machine, a light, a TV)
sort out	(1) organize, (2) solve	*turn up*	increase the volume
straighten up	(1) make something look neat, (2) stand tall	*wake up*	stop sleeping
take back	return something	*work out*	(1) solve, (2) calculate
take out	(1) remove, (2) obtain something officially	*write down*	write on paper

Intransitive (Inseparable) Phrasal Verbs

Phrasal Verb	Meaning	Phrasal Verb	Meaning
break down	(1) stop working, (2) lose control	*fall down*	fall to the ground
break up	end a relationship, separate	*fool around*	act playfully
come back	return	*get ahead*	succeed, make progress
come from	originate	*get along*	have a good relationship
come on	(1) hurry, (2) start	*get over*	recover from an illness or a shock
dress up	put on nice or formal clothes	*get up*	arise from bed
drop in	visit without advance notice	*give up*	stop
drop out	quit (school, a race, a club)	*go ahead*	start or continue
eat out	eat in a restaurant	*go away*	leave; go to another place

Phrasal Verb	Meaning	Phrasal Verb	Meaning
go on	continue	*run out*	(1) leave, (2) be completely used
go out	not stay home	*set in*	begin and continue for a long time
go up	rise, go higher	*show up*	appear
grow up	become an adult	*sign up*	register for a class or event
hang on	(1) wait, (2) keep going	*sit down*	sit; take a seat
hold on	(1) wait, (2) persist	*slip up*	make a mistake
look into	investigate	*speak up*	talk louder
look out	be careful	*stand up*	stand; rise
make up	end a disagreement	*stay up*	remain awake
move in (to)	(1) take your things to a new home, (2) begin living somewhere	*take off*	(1) leave on an airplane, (2) grow; be successful
move out (of)	leave a place you live in	*watch out*	be careful
run into	meet someone by chance or unexpectedly	*work out*	(1) exercise, (2) go as planned

13 Adjectives and Adverbs: Comparative and Superlative Forms

		Adjective	Comparative	Superlative
1 **One-Syllable Adjectives**				
a Add *-er* and *-est* to one syllable adjectives.		cheap	cheaper	the cheapest
		high	higher	the highest
		large	larger	the largest
		long	longer	the longest
		new	newer	the newest
		old	older	the oldest
		small	smaller	the smallest
		strong	stronger	the strongest
		tall	taller	the tallest
b For one-syllable adjectives that end in a vowel + consonant, double the final consonant and add *-er* or *-est*.		big	bigger	the biggest
		hot	hotter	the hottest
		sad	sadder	the saddest
		thin	thinner	the thinnest
Do not double the consonant *w*.		low	lower	the lowest

			Adjective	Comparative	Superlative
2		**Two-Syllable Adjectives**			
	a	Add *more* or *most* to most adjectives.	boring famous handsome patient	more boring more famous more handsome more patient	the most boring the most famous the most handsome the most patient
	b	Some two-syllable adjectives have two forms.	friendly narrow simple strict quiet	friendlier more friendly narrower more narrow simpler more simple stricter more strict quieter more quiet	the friendliest the most friendly the narrowest the most narrow the simplest the most simple the strictest the most strict the quietest the most quiet
	c	Remove the -y and add -*ier* or -*iest* to two-syllable adjectives ending in -y.	angry easy friendly happy lucky pretty silly	angrier easier friendlier happier luckier prettier sillier	the angriest the easiest the friendliest the happiest the luckiest the prettiest the silliest
3		**Three or More Syllable Adjectives** Add *more* or *most* to adjectives with three or more syllables.	beautiful comfortable creative difficult enjoyable expensive important independent relaxing responsible serious	more beautiful more comfortable more creative more difficult more enjoyable more expensive more important more independent more relaxing more responsible more serious	the most beautiful the most comfortable the most creative the most difficult the most enjoyable the most expensive the most important the most independent the most relaxing the most responsible the most serious
4		**Irregular Adjectives** Some adjectives have irregular forms.	bad far good	worse farther / further better	the worst the farthest / the furthest the best

Adjectives and Adverbs: Comparative and Superlative Forms *(continued)*

		Adjective	Comparative	Superlative
5	**-*ly* Adverbs** Most adverbs end in -*ly*. Add *more* or *most*. People usually only use *the* with superlative adverbs in formal writing and speaking.	dangerously patiently quickly quietly slowly	more dangerously more patiently more quickly more quietly more slowly	(the) most dangerously (the) most patiently (the) most quickly (the) most quietly (the) most slowly
6	**One-Syllable Adverbs** A few adverbs do not end in -*ly*. Add -*er* and -*est* to these adverbs.	fast hard	faster harder	(the) fastest (the) hardest
7	**Irregular Adverbs** Some adverbs have irregular forms.	badly far well	worse farther / further better	(the) worst (the) farthest / furthest (the) best

Glossary of Grammar Terms

action verb a verb that describes an action.

*I **eat** breakfast every day.*

*They **ran** in the 5K race.*

adjective a word that describes or modifies a noun.

*That's a **beautiful** hat.*

adjective clause see **relative clause**.

adverb a word that describes or modifies a verb, another adverb, or an adjective. Adverbs often end in *-ly*.

*Please walk **faster** but **carefully**.*

adverb clause a clause that shows how ideas are connected. Adverb clauses begin with conjunctions such as *because*, *since*, *although*, and *even though*.

***Although it is not a holiday**, workers have the day off.*

adverb of degree an adverb that makes other adverbs or adjectives stronger or weaker.

*The test was **extremely** difficult.   They are **kind of** busy today.*

adverb of manner an adverb that describes how an action happens.

*He has **suddenly** left the room.*

adverb of time an adverb that describes when something happens.

*She'll get up **later**.*

article the words *a/an* and *the*. An article introduces or identifies a noun.

*I bought **a** new MP3 player. **The** price was reasonable.*

auxiliary verb (also called **helping verb**) a verb that is used before a main verb in a sentence. *Do, have,* and *be* can act as auxiliary verbs.

***Does** he want to go to the library later?   **Have** you received the package?*

base form of the verb the form of a verb without any endings (*-s* or *-ed*) or *to*.

come   go   take

clause a group of words that has a subject and a verb. There are two types of clauses: **main clauses** and **dependent clauses** (*see* dependent clause). A sentence can have more than one clause.

MAIN CLAUSE   DEPENDENT CLAUSE   MAIN CLAUSE

I woke up when I heard the noise. It was scary.

common noun a word for a person, place, or thing. A common noun is not capitalized.

mother   building   fruit

comparative the form of an adjective or adverb that shows how two people, places, or things are different.

*My daughter is **older than** my son.* (adjective)

*She does her work **more quickly** than he does.* (adverb)

conjunction a word such as *and, but, so, or,* and *yet* which connects single words, phrases, or clauses.

*We finished all our work, **so** we left early.*

consonant a sound represented in writing by these letters of the alphabet: ***b, c, d, f, g, h, j, k, l, m, n, p, q, r, s, t, v, w, x, y,*** and ***z.***

count noun refers to a person, place, or thing you can count. Count nouns have a plural form.

*There are three **banks** on Oak Street.*

definite article *the* is a definite article. Use *the* with a person, place, or thing that is familiar to you and your listener. Also, use *the* when the noun is unique – there is only one (*the sun, the moon, the Internet*).

The *movie we saw last week was very good.*

The *Earth is round.*

dependent clause a clause that cannot stand alone. Some kinds of dependent clauses are adverb clauses, relative clauses, and time clauses.

After we return from the trip, *I'm going to need to relax.*

determiner a word that comes before a noun to limit its meaning in some way. Some common determiners are *some, a little, a lot, a few, this, that, these, those, his, a, an, the, much,* and *many.*

These *computers have **a lot** of parts.*

*Please give me **my** book.*

direct object the person or thing that receives the action of the verb.

*The teacher gave the students **a test**.*

factual conditional describes something that is generally true in a certain situation. The *if* clause describes the condition and is in the simple present. The result clause is in the simple present as well.

If *it's late, I don't stay online for a long time.*

formal a style of writing or speech used when you don't know the other person very well or where it's not appropriate to show familiarity, such as in business, a job interview, speaking to a stranger, or speaking to an older person who you respect.

Good evening. I'd like to speak with Ms. Smith. Is she available?

future a verb form that describes a time that hasn't come yet. It is expressed in English by *will, be going to,* and present tense.

*I**'ll meet** you tomorrow.*

*I**'m going to visit** my uncle and aunt next weekend.*

future conditional describes something that will happen under certain conditions in the future. The *if* clause describes the condition and is in the simple present. The result clause uses a future form of the verb.

If *I do well on this final exam, I**'ll get** an A for the course.*

gerund the *-ing* form of a verb that is used as a noun. It can be the subject or object in a sentence or the object of a preposition.

*We suggested **waiting** and **going** another day.*

*Salsa **dancing** is a lot of fun.*

*I look forward to **meeting** you.*

habitual past a verb form that describes repeated past actions, habits, and conditions using *used to* or *would*.

*Before we had the Internet, we **used to** go to the library a lot.*

*Before there was refrigeration, people **would** use ice to keep food cool.*

helping verb *see* **auxiliary verb**.

imperative a type of clause that tells people to do something. It gives instructions, directions to a place, and advice. The verb is in the base form.

***Listen** to the conversation.*

***Don't open** your books.*

indefinite article *a/an* are the indefinite articles. Use *a/an* with a singular person, place, or thing when you and your listener are not familiar with it, or when the specific name of it is not important. Use *a* with consonant sounds. Use *an* with vowel sounds.

*She's going to see **a** doctor today.   I had **an** egg for breakfast.*

indirect object the person or thing that receives the direct object.

*The teacher gave **the students** a test.*

infinitive *to* + the base form of a verb.

*I need **to get** home early tonight.*

infinitive of purpose *in order* + infinitive expresses a purpose. It answers the question *why*. If the meaning is clear, it is not necessary to use *in order*.

*People are fighting **(in order) to change** unfair laws.*

informal a style of speaking or writing to friends, family, and children.

Hey, there. Nice to see you again.

information question (also called ***Wh-* question**) begins with a *wh-* word *(who, what, when, where, which, why, how, how much)*. To answer this type of question, you need to provide information rather than answer *yes* or *no*.

inseparable phrasal verb a phrasal verb that cannot be separated. The verb and its particle always stay together.

*My car **broke down** yesterday.*

intransitive verb a verb that does not need an object. It is often followed by an expression of time, place, or manner.

*The flight **arrived** at 5:30 p.m.*

irregular adjective an adjective that does not change its form in the usual way. For example, you do not make the comparative form by adding *-er*.

good ➞ *better*

irregular adverb an adverb that does not change its form in the usual way. For example, you do not make the comparative form by adding *-er*.

badly ➞ *worse*

irregular verb a verb that does not change its form in the usual way. For example, it does not form the simple past with *-d* or *-ed*. It has its own special form.

go ➝ *went*   *ride* ➝ *rode*   *hit* ➝ *hit*

main clause (also called **independent clause**) a clause that can be used alone as a complete sentence.

*After I get back from my trip, **I'm going to relax**.*

main verb a verb that functions alone in a clause and can have an auxiliary verb.

*They **had** a meeting last week.*

*They have **had** many meetings this month.*

measurement word a word or phrase that shows the amount of something. Measurement words can be singular or plural.

*I bought **a box** of cereal, and Sonia bought **five pounds** of apples.*

modal a verb such as *can, could, have to, may, might, must, should, will,* and *would*. It modifies the main verb to show such things as ability, permission, possibility, advice, obligation, necessity, or lack of necessity.

*It **might** rain later today.*

*You **should** study harder if you want to pass this course.*

non-action verb *see* **stative verb**.

noncount noun refers to ideas and things that you cannot count. Noncount nouns use a singular verb and do not have a plural form.

*Do you download **music**?*

noun a word for a person, place, or thing. There are common nouns and proper nouns (*see* **common noun, proper noun**).

<table>
<tr><td>COMMON NOUN</td><td>PROPER NOUN</td></tr>
<tr><td>I stayed in a hotel on my trip to New York.</td><td>I stayed in the Pennsylvania Hotel.</td></tr>
</table>

object pronoun replaces a noun in the object position.

*Sara loves exercise classes. She takes **them** three times a week.*

particle a small word like *down, in, off, on, out,* or *up*. These words (which can also be prepositions) are used with verbs to form **two-word verbs** or **phrasal verbs**. The meaning of a phrasal verb often has a different meaning from the meaning of the individual words in it.

past participle a verb form that can be regular (base form + *-ed*) or irregular. It is used to form the present perfect and the passive. It can also be an adjective.

*I've **studied** English for five years.*

past progressive a verb form that describes events or situations in progress at a time in the past. The emphasis is on the action.

*They **were watching** TV when I arrived.*

phrasal verb (also called a **two-word verb**) consists of a verb + a particle. There are two kinds of phrasal verbs: separable and inseparable (*see* **particle, inseparable phrasal verb, separable phrasal verb**).

VERB + PARTICLE

*They **came back** from vacation today.* (inseparable)

*Please **put** your cell phone **away**.* (separable)

plural noun a noun that refers to more than one person, place, or thing.

students   *women*   *roads*

possessive adjective *see* **possessive determiner.**

possessive determiner (also called **possessive adjective**) a determiner that shows possession (*my, your, his, her, its, our,* and *their*).

possessive pronoun replaces a possessive determiner + singular or plural noun. The possessive pronoun agrees with the noun that it replaces.

My exercise class is at night. **Hers** *is on the weekend.*   (hers = her exercise class)

preposition a word such as *to, at, for, with, below, in, on, next to,* or *above* that goes before a noun or pronoun to show location, time, direction, or a close relationship between two people or things. A preposition may go before a gerund as well.

I'm **in** *the supermarket* **next to** *our favorite restaurant.*

The idea **of** *love has inspired many poets.*

present perfect a verb form that describes past events or situations that are still important in the present, actions that happened once or repeatedly at an indefinite time before now, and to give the number of times something happened up to now.

Lately scientists **have discovered** *medicines in the Amazon.*

I've **been** *to the Amazon twice.*

present perfect progressive a verb form that describes something that started in the past, usually continues in the present, and may continue in the future.

He **hasn't been working** *since last May.*

present progressive a verb form that describes an action or situation that is in progress now or around the present time. It is also used to indicate a fixed arrangement in the near future.

What **are** *you* **doing** *right now?*

I'm **leaving** *for Spain next week.*

pronoun a word that replaces a noun or noun phrase. Some examples are *I, we, him, hers,* and *it* (see **object pronoun, subject pronoun, relative pronoun, possessive pronoun, reciprocal pronoun, reflexive pronoun**).

proper noun a noun that is the name of a particular person, place, idea, or thing. It is capitalized.

Central Park *is in* **New York City***.*

punctuation mark a symbol used in writing such as a period (.), a comma (,), a question mark (?), or an exclamation point (!).

quantifier Some quantifiers are *much, many, some, any, a lot, plenty,* and *enough.*

reciprocal pronoun a pronoun *(each other, one another)* that shows that two or more people give *and* receive the same action or have the same relationship.

Mari and I have the same challenges. We help **each other***.*   (I help Mari and Mari helps me.)

reflexive pronoun a pronoun *(myself, yourself, himself, herself, ourselves, yourselves, themselves)* which shows that the object of the sentence is the same as the subject.

I taught **myself** *to speak Japanese.*

regular verb a verb that changes its form in the usual way.

> live ➞ live**s**
>
> wash ➞ wash**ed**

relative clause (also known as **adjective clause**) defines, describes, identifies, or gives more information about a noun. It begins with a relative pronoun such as *who, that, which, whose,* or *whom*. Like all clauses, a relative clause has both a subject and a verb. It can describe the subject or the object of a sentence.

> *People **who have sleep problems** can join the study.*   (subject relative clause)
>
> *There are many diseases **that viruses cause**.*   (object relative clause)

relative pronoun a pronoun *(who, which, that, whose, whom)* that connects a noun phrase to a relative clause.

> *People **who** have sleep problems can join the study.*
>
> *There are many diseases **that** viruses cause.*

sentence a complete thought or idea that has a subject and a main verb. In writing, it begins with a capital letter and has a punctuation mark at the end (. ? !). In an imperative sentence, the subject (*you*) is not usually stated.

> ***This sentence is a complete thought.   Open your books.***

separable phrasal verb a phrasal verb that can be separated. This means that an object can go before or after the particle.

> ***Write down** your expenses.*
>
> ***Write** your expenses **down**.*

simple past a verb form that describes completed actions or events that happened at a definite time in the past.

> *They **grew up** in Washington, D.C.*
>
> *They **attended** Howard University and **graduated** in 2019.*

simple present a verb form that describes things that regularly happen, such as habits and routines (usual and regular activities). It also describes facts and general truths.

> *I **play** games online every night.* (routine)
>
> *The average person **spends** 13 hours a week online.* (fact)

singular noun a noun that refers to only one person, place, or thing.

> *He is my best **friend**.*

statement a sentence that gives information.

> *Today is Thursday.*

stative verb (also called **non-action verb**) describes a state or situation, not an action. It is usually in the simple form of the present or past.

> *I **remember** your friend.*

subject the person or thing that performs the action of a verb.

> ***People** use new words and expressions every day.*

subject pronoun replaces a noun in the subject position.

> *Sara and I are friends. **We** work at the same company.*

superlative the form of an adjective or adverb that compares one person, place, or thing to others in a group.

*This storm was **the most dangerous** one of the season.* (adjective)

*That group worked **most effectively** after the disaster.* (adverb)

syllable a group of letters that has one vowel sound and that you say as a single unit.
There is one syllable in the word lunch *and two syllables in the word* breakfast. (Break *is one syllable and* fast *is another syllable.*)

tense the form of a verb that shows past or present time.

*They **worked** yesterday.* (simple past)

*They **work** every day.* (simple present)

third-person singular refers to *he, she,* and *it* or a singular noun. In the simple present, the third-person singular form ends in *-s* or *-es.*

***It looks** warm and sunny today.*   ***He washes** the laundry on Saturdays.*

time clause a clause that shows the order of events and begins with a time word such as *before, after, when, while,* or *as soon as.*

***Before** there were freezers, people needed ice to make frozen desserts.*

time expression a phrase that functions as an adverb of time. It tells when something happens, happened, or will happen.

*I graduated **in 2010**.*   *She's going to visit her aunt and uncle **next summer**.*

transitive verb a verb that needs an object. The object completes the meaning of the verb.

*She **wears** perfume.*

two-word verb see **phrasal verb**.

verb a word that describes an action or a state.

*Alex **wears** jeans and a T-shirt to school. Alex **is** a student.*

vowel a sound represented in writing by these letters of the alphabet: ***a, e, i, o,*** and ***u.***

***Wh-* question** see **information question**.

***Yes / No* question** begins with a form of *be* or an auxiliary verb. You can answer such a question with *yes* or *no.*

*"**Are** they going to the movies?"*   *""**No**, they're not."*

*"**Can** you give me some help?"*   *"**Yes**, I can."*

Art Credits

Acknowledgements

The authors and publishers acknowledge the following sources of copyright material and are grateful for the permissions granted. While every effort has been made, it has not always been possible to identify the sources of all the material used, or to trace all copyright holders. If any omissions are brought to our notice, we will be happy to include the appropriate acknowledgements on reprinting and in the next update to the digital edition, as applicable.

Key: U = Unit.

Photography

All the photos are sourced from Getty Images.

U16: Istvan Kadar Photography/Moment Open; Paul Bradbury/The Image Bank; Juanmonino/ iStock/Getty Images Plus; Gary John Norman/The Image Bank; LauriPatterson/E+; **U17:** Westend61; Catherine MacBride/Moment; Baona/E+; Maria Taglienti-Molinari/Stockbyte; R_Type/iStock/ Getty Images Plus; Alan Bailey; Hero Images; **U18:** Monkeybusinessimages/iStock/Getty Images Plus; Jose Luis Pelaez Inc/DigitalVision; Bettmann; Wedwam/iStock/Getty Images Plus; Hero Images; **U19:** Robert Lachman; JIJI PRESS/AFP; PASIEKA/ Science Photo Library; fazon1/iStock/Getty Images Plus; **U20:** Saul Loeb/Afp; Tetra images; Aldo murillo/E+; Klaus Vedfelt/DigitalVision; Pavel Usachenko/EyeEm; **U21:** DaniloAndjus/E+; George Doyle/Stockbyte; Eva-Katalin/E+; Drbouz/E+; **U22:** EmirMemedovski/E+; Dong Wenjie/Moment; **U23:** Hero Images; Monkeybusinessimages/iStock/ Getty Images Plus; Ariel Skelley/DigitalVision; Chayakorn lotongkum/iStock/Getty Images Plus; **U24:** Sam Edwards/Caiaimage; Fuse/Corbis; Anchiy/E+; Moodboard Brand X Pictures; Scanrail/ iStock/Getty Images Plus; **U25:** KTSDESIGN/ Science Photo Library; David Arky; Shih Wei Wang/ EyeEm; **U26:** Thomas Barwick/Taxi; DragonImages/ iStock/Getty Images Plus; Robin Skjoldborg/ Cultura; PeopleImages/E+; AntonioGuillem/iStock/ Getty Images Plus; **U27:** ParkerDeen/iStock/Getty Images Plus; DEA/A. DAGLI ORTI/De Agostini Picture Library; Chicago History Museum/Archive Photos; Cameron Davidson/Photolibrary; Hero Images; **U28:** Westend61; Sue Barr/Image Source; Hill Street Studios/DigitalVision; VvoeVale/iStock/ Getty Images Plus; Andersen Ross Photography Inc/ DigitalVision; Comstock/Stockbyte; **U29:** Universal Images Group; Universal Images Group; Library of Congress Washington, D.C. 20540 USA; Bob Riha Jr; Fotosearch; Jim Craigmyle/Corbis; Santorines/iStock/ Getty Images Plus; **U30:** RomoloTavani/iStock/Getty Images Plus; Michael H/Photodisc; Moncherie/E+; Robert Decelis Ltd/Stockbyte; Jose Luis Pelaez Inc/ DigitalVision; FG Trade/E+; **U31:** Jose Luis Pelaez Inc/ DigitalVision; PhotoQuest/Archive Photos; Tim Hale/ Photographer's Choice; GARO/Canopy; Hero Images; Paul Nadar/Hulton Archive; Alex Tihonovs/EyeEm; **U32:** MANDEL NGAN/AFP; Lívia Fernandes - Brazil/Moment; Ajr_images/iStock/Getty Images Plus; Shannon Fagan/Taxi; JGI; Jose Luis Pelaez Inc/ DigitalVision; Thomas Lukassek/EyeEm.

The following photos are sourced from other library.
U19: Jeff Morgan 09/Alamy Stock Photo; **U22**: J.R. Bale/Alamy Stock Photo; **U27**: Cal Sport Media/Alamy Stock Photo; **U29**: Digital Image Library/Alamy Stock Photo.

Illustrations

Ben Hasler; Ed Fotheringham; Maria Rabinky; Monika Roe; Rob Schuster; Oxford Designers & Illustrators.

Audio

Audio production by John Marshall Media

Typeset

Q2A Media Services Pvt. Ltd